Gladys Gardner Jenkins
Associate Professorial Lecturer in Education
College of General Studies
George Washington University

Illustrated by Howard Mueller

HELPING

CHILDREN REACH

THEIR

POTENTIAL

Scott, Foresman and Company

Library of Congress Catalog Card No. 60–53109
Copyright © 1961 by Scott, Foresman and Company, Glenview, Illinois 60025
All rights reserved. Printed in the United States of America.
Regional offices of Scott, Foresman and Company are located in Atlanta,
Dallas, Glenview, Palo Alto, and Oakland, N.J.

FOREWORD

This book has grown out of discussions with teachers, as we have met together in courses and workshops on child growth and development. It has been built around the questions they have asked and the answers we have sought together. It is not a book of methods. It is rather an attempt to think together about children and about some of the attitudes and approaches toward them that will make it possible for them to reach their fullest potential.

The boys and girls in this book are real. Their names and their identities have been concealed, but these are children whom the teachers knew and talked about and tried to teach. The stories were written by teachers and contain the kind of information a teacher is able to secure in the limited time she has. For this reason, the studies are not complete, as a case worker would write them, but rather fragments caught here and there through the busy days of teaching. Yet these fragments give real insight and understanding into some of the ways in which boys and girls grow, think and feel, and respond or fail to respond.

To those teachers who have contributed so much to the material in this book, as it has grown from semester to semester and workshop to workshop, I give my thanks. Without their help this book could never have been written. I wish that it were possible to mention each one by name, but those who have sat and thought and talked with me over the years know that they are included here and share with me again by helping to make this book.

It is my hope that this book will be of use, not in presenting final answers, but rather in giving perspective to those things we will each do in our own way in our own classrooms, and that it will open the way to further thinking about the needs of the boys and girls we teach.

GLADYS GARDNER JENKINS

CONTENTS

PART ONE   FIVE BASIC NEEDS OF CHILDREN IN SCHOOL

Chapter 1   ACCEPTANCE AS A FRAMEWORK FOR LEARNING

Chapter 2   ACHIEVEMENT FOR EVERY CHILD

Chapter 3   PARTICIPATION PROMOTES LEARNING

Chapter 4   EXPRESSION OF FEELINGS FOR EMOTIONAL GROWTH

Chapter 5   SELF-DISCIPLINE IS THE REAL GOAL

PART TWO   BASIC UNDERSTANDINGS FOR TEACHERS

Chapter 6   QUESTIONS ABOUT GROWTH AND DEVELOPMENT

Chapter 7   QUESTIONS ABOUT HOME AND FAMILY

INTRODUCTION

KEEPING THE FOCUS ON THE CHILD

In every profession, there comes a time when it is important to stop and evaluate the progress that has been made and to determine the changes that will be necessary to meet new times and new demands. The world has moved swiftly into the age of space with its vast possibilities and unknown needs. The children who are in our classrooms today must be prepared to live in a kind of world unknown to us, their teachers. We are faced with the question of how best to prepare them to carry on their part in a new era in the experience of men.

Among the children in our classrooms are the creative ones who will forge ahead with new ideas, opening up ever increasing knowledge. There are those who will become our political and social leaders, using their knowledge for constructive or destructive purposes. And there will be those who, through their vote and the selection of their leaders, will help determine how the new knowledge will be applied to the practical life of our country. The time has come when we must reappraise our goals and ask ourselves whether these goals are adequate to meet circumstances that were unforeseen even a few short years ago.

In a period of change, many solutions are offered. We must expect that many of the things we are doing in our classrooms today will be examined and challenged by concerned individuals with many backgrounds. All of these people may have a genuine concern for the future of our country and the role the education of our children will play in it, but many of these people have little knowledge about children.

As new suggestions are offered for a modification of our educational system, we must appraise them thoughtfully and carefully to see that all children are considered and that individual differences are not overlooked in planning for those very gifted students of whom we have a spectacular need today. Otherwise we may crowd out of our schools the less intellectually capable and tend, perhaps, to put too many strains on some of the highly gifted youngsters. Every child in a democracy is of worth. Our task is to teach each child so that he may become as fine and as productive a citizen as possible. We can do this only if we continue to use our knowledge of children and how they learn. We must not lose the gains of the past as we work to fill the needs of the future.

In a democracy where the vote of every man and woman counts, it is necessary to give to boys and girls the education they will need to use their vote wisely and to contribute their best talents for the good of all. This cannot mean the same education for every boy and girl, for children differ in their capacity to learn. It does mean that every child should have the kind of education that will help him develop as far as he possibly can through growth in knowledge and in ability to see issues clearly, and through growth in self-confidence and self-respect, which makes it possible for him to think for himself. Equality of education does not mean similar education for all, but education that develops the best potentialities in each one. This is a unique goal and one we must not lose sight of.

The new pressures on boys and girls may be subtle ones. We may not become fully aware of them for many years. But in times like these, there is a temptation to look for the quick solution, to become overrigid, to talk in terms of selecting boys and girls of high intelligence and directing them into fields of study useful and necessary to us all, without sufficient consideration of the interests and drives of the individual child. There is a tendency to select children for more intensive training in the fields of science and mathematics before they are sufficiently mature to know whether this is the real direction of their potential strength. There is very real danger, also, that in trying to meet the immediate needs in the scientific fields we may make boys and girls feel that other areas of learning are not important and thus destroy the balance we need in our national life.

It is possible, too, that pressures will be put upon parents and children to conform to standards of education which are based on intelligence alone. In a desperate effort to make boys and girls live up to capacities indicated by their Intelligence Quotient (I.Q.), educators may be urged to pile on more and harder work by those persons who forget or do not know that motivation and readiness are as necessary as ability if learning is to take place. Quantity of subject matter, difficult assignments, or long hours of homework alone will not produce a creative thinker. The "set to learn" must be sustained by the rewards of success and satisfaction. Learning takes effort. It is difficult to sustain effort without success. Sometimes an adult, sustained through interest, will push through failure and discouragement, if he can still see the possibility of ultimate success. But such effort requires a maturity not usually evident in adults and certainly beyond the capacity of most children. Most grownups, as well as children, find it difficult to keep on trying if they reach the point of fatigue or discouragement at which it looks as if they cannot succeed. The teacher who understands children will not push a child beyond the point at which he can achieve a satisfying and positive learning experience.

Oppenheimer* in a talk to young scientists about some of the attitudes that will be useful in learning says: "One of them is to have a deep reverence—not, certainly, for the learned man or the stuffed shirt, but for learning, for knowledge, and skill; to hold tight to that reverence, not to be talked out of it by any superficial parody of what it is. This reverence is the kind of thing we learn in school when we learn to do and create and understand, and when we learn really to act with the knowledge we get."

Teachers in the elementary and the junior high schools have a particular contribution to make, for in these formative school years boys and girls learn the basic skills they must have as tools with which to attack and solve more difficult problems and to attain further knowledge. It is also during these years that children develop their basic attitudes about the values of learning. And finally, it is during these years that we are able to spot and seek to remove the effects of emotional experiences that have already resulted in strain and tension which can be blocks to learning. If we are to teach a child well, we must get to know him as an individual and know what he is capable of. We must not forget, and must help others not to forget, that he is still a child with the growth needs of a child.

*OPPENHEIMER, J. ROBERT. "A TALK TO YOUNG SCIENTISTS." SCIENCE PERSPECTIVES, VOL. 1, NO. 2 (MARCH 1958), PP. 6-7.

5

BASIC

NEEDS OF CHILDREN

IN SCHOOL

PART ONE

As teachers, we have a practical interest in the way in which the growth needs of the boys and girls who come into our classrooms have been and are being met. Children come to school from different kinds of homes. They bring into the classroom many emotional experiences and varied attitudes toward life. They have accomplished their past developmental tasks with different degrees of success. We cannot, as teachers, change the past but we can help meet the present growth needs of these youngsters during the hours of the day they are with us in school.

Among these needs, five seem to be of particular significance for us to consider if children are to have an environment that is stimulating for their personal growth and educational development.

Acceptance. All children need to feel that they are accepted in the classroom as genuine members of the group.

Achievement. All children must have an opportunity to move ahead in the learning process through a personal experience of success in tasks within the range of their own levels of ability, experience, and emotional readiness to learn.

Participation. All children must have an opportunity to participate in the learning process. Passive and unreceptive "sitting" in a classroom may fill the hours of the school day but can never lead to the active and creative participation so necessary to real learning.

Expressing feelings. All children have feelings; these must be recognized and accepted as part of the child who has come to school to be taught. We must provide ways for feelings to be expressed—the intense feelings as constructively as possible; the joyous or creative feelings as freely as possible.

Guidance toward self-discipline. All children need the kind of steady guidance that will help them achieve self-discipline. The child who is undisciplined and lacking in constructive values and self-control is rarely able to profit fully by his work in the classroom or to develop to his potential as fully as we would wish.

In the chapters ahead, these five growth needs will be discussed more fully. Their importance must not be underestimated, for if they are ignored in the classroom, the children will not be emotionally free to learn that which we wish to teach. It is essential for us to keep the focus on the child if the high standards of education we desire are to be achieved.

CHAPTER 1

ACCEPTANCE

I would like to get to know my pupils better—
their likes and dislikes, their hobbies, something
about their home backgrounds. But I don't
know how to go about getting this information
without spending more time than I have.

We know that a friendly welcome and a
cheery room are important to early
elementary school children. Are these
factors as important to older children?

What about the days I don't feel
"up to par"? Must I keep
smiling as though nothing were wrong?

How can I accept a child who
is a disturber day in and day out?

What can I do if I simply cannot learn
to like a particular child? How can I keep my
antagonism from getting the upper hand?

I'm always afraid to give
special help to a child who needs it—
afraid he'll be called "teacher's pet" and I will
be accused of showing favoritism.

AS A FRAMEWORK FOR

LEARNING

ACCEPTING "AS IS"

We hear a great deal about loving boys and girls, but we do not always stop to think why they need to feel that someone cares. It is this feeling that makes a child secure enough to take each new step in growing up. A child who does not feel loved and accepted becomes anxious, unhappy, and confused about himself. When he is tied up within himself by such feelings, he cannot be emotionally free enough to learn well the many things he must know—whether it is reading, manners, or good character—if he is to live adequately and happily.

All of us need to be accepted, whether we are grownups or children. If a child has not felt wanted first in the family circle, next in the neighborhood, and then in his class at school, he may go through life seeking for acceptance. He may be afraid to be friendly to people, timid about trying out new things, because there has been no one who cared enough to stand behind him and encourage him as he tried himself out. Or else he may become overly domineering and aggressive as he battles his way through life—pretending that he does not care whether he is liked or not. The young delinquent, the difficult child in the classroom, the child who upsets the family circle, is often the child who feels left out, the child who is not sure that he is really liked or really belongs.

Perhaps Miss Ladd found the clue we are looking for when she said of her own ex-periences in the classroom, and her philosophy in meeting problems there:

I, as a classroom teacher, am faced with the responsibility of accepting each child "as is" and working with that child from there. I feel that my biggest task is to help each child help himself. If he is to be able to do this, he must feel good about himself. It is a long process sometimes. Often I feel that I am accomplishing nothing. Then gradually I will begin to see signs of progress and feel that it is worth the many hours of thought.

Unfortunately, there are some children whom I cannot help. I believe that one does occasionally find the child who cannot be reached in the classroom. However, I also believe that many children who might have been thought "lost" could be helped by the teacher's understanding and acceptance. The acceptance "as is" is the starting point.

The nicest compliment that has ever been paid me during my career was that of a very small, retiring youngster with whom I had worked hard and long. He could not seem to participate at all; his overwhelming shyness always seemed to hold him back. The time was mid-January and Jackie had just participated for the first time in our "sharing time." Throwing all our standards aside he had begun to share his experience en route to the front of the room. He had completed his "telling" by the time he reached the appointed place. I, of course, was delighted to accept his great effort and praised him for it. This tiny boy looked at me with appreciative eyes and said, "Teacher, you make me feel great!"

WE CAN SHOW OUR INTEREST IN CHILDREN BY—

MAKING A GOOD START

The first day of school sets the "feeling tone" of the year for many boys and girls. "Is the teacher friendly? Will she like me?" These are important questions in the minds of children from kindergarten on through high school as they pour into their new classrooms. Each room has its own individuality, depending, in large part, on the personality of the teacher. Miss Hobbs is pretty and friendly; Mrs. Booth is quiet and strict, but the children feel she is fair; Mrs. Long is full of jokes—the children laugh and the tension is relaxed. But Miss Krasny is tense. She talks rapidly, punctuating her sentences, telling the children what she expects of them. They are restless; they are not sure. The personal equation is always there in the classroom between teacher and children, determining the kind of relationship that will exist throughout the year. Children of all ages are very quick to recognize the teacher who likes children and who is sensitive to their personal needs and feelings. Mrs. Webb put it this way:

From the first time I say, "Good morning, John," I begin to help the child build desirable personal relationships. I want him to know that I am *his friend*. This is the purpose of our well-organized induction program for first-grade children. The child will meet the teacher in a friendly way on "visiting day." There I strive to be at my best. The primary group and I plan together an interesting day for the visitors. It usually consists of a movie showing activities of a "Day in School," a "Show and Tell" period, an independent work period where children are allowed to choose the type of activity they want to do—and as an added attraction, we have ice cream and cake. This visiting day helps take away the fear of school that some children have.

In the preschool conferences, where the physical as well as the emotional needs are reviewed, I act as receptionist. There again I get to see the child in a friendly way.

In the fall, I arrange the room carefully and make it as gay and colorful as possible. Bright pictures showing children at work and play are hung as low as possible in our extremely old building. About the room are many objects for the children to pick up and handle. In the back of the room is a center of interest. As soon as each child enters school, he is given responsibilities, and standards are set up to see that these duties are carried out to the group's satisfaction.

In this way, children feel a part of school and take pride in our room. The child feels that he belongs here. The principal carries out a similar plan for the school. The children feel that they are wanted here. It is their school.

Miss Hobbs also realized the importance of the first day of school, whether it is for the first-grader or for a new child who finds himself once more in a strange and different situation. Miss Hobbs decribes for us what she did one year for the new pupils in her room:

The first day of school was for new pupils only. Nine of the thirty-two children in my fourth-grade class appeared on this first day. I spent about an hour with these new pupils, going around the room looking at the pictures on the bulletin boards, finding interesting things to do. Each child found his name plate on his desk; saw where to hang his hat and coat when it was cool enough to wear them; saw the shiny mirror, sink, and toilet in the lavatory; saw the sink and drinking fountain—all right in our own room! We went on a tour of our school, visiting the other fourth-grade rooms, the multipurpose room, the kitchen, the nurse's office and infirmary, the office, and the playground.

The children responded to the pictures, aquarium, seashell and rock collections. In our sharing time, we talked about where we last went to school, our former homes, and our new homes in this city.

The next morning when all the children arrived, I assigned some of last year's students to help the new children get acquainted with their classmates and get used to the new school.

Both these teachers knew that although school is eagerly anticipated by many children, there are always those who have had unhappy experiences at school, who come hesitatingly, fearing what may happen this year. There are others like the first-grader who, when her mother asked her how she liked her first day at school, could only say over and over in bewilderment, "There is too much. There is too much." There are older children who come to school unwillingly—"What's the good of it anyway? I'd rather work." Or the child who fails so often that he feels he can never measure up. Each year he is haunted with the thought, "Will I pass?" And then there are the boys and girls, thousands of them today, whose families must move so much that the first day of school is also a first day in a whole new school community. At all ages, in all grades, the importance of the first contact with the children we teach, the establishing of a friendly relationship right from the beginning, will determine in part how effectively we are able to teach these children.

The good teacher has a wholesome curiosity about each new class. She is as eager to meet the youngsters she will teach and as curious about them as they are about her. "What will they be like?" "Which ones will be alert and eager—the good learners?" "Who are the problems?" "John over there with his restless roving eyes, his dissatisfied unhappy mouth—will he be difficult or can I arouse his interest and gain his cooperation? Problem or not?" "That shy youngster—will I be able to draw him out? Is there really deep anxiety there?" As she glances over the children as they come in, welcoming each one, she is gaining first impressions of them—just as they are "sizing her up" and gaining a first impression of her. These first impressions are valuable—to be remembered and added to when possible by little notes and comments on the cumulative record of the youngster. Such impressions can be vivid and give quick insight—providing we are willing to challenge and question them and not accept them as valid until we have seen the youngster in many situations and tested our impression of him.

KNOWING FIRST NAMES

"Mummy, she knew my name. She remembered me." Such a small thing perhaps but it made all the difference to eight-year-old Kenny when he entered the third grade in another new school. Kenny had been to seven schools in the first grade. Last year, he had had the misfortune to have three teachers in the second grade. He had played truant from school at the end of the last year. "They don't like me there," he had said. His mother, wisely, had talked with his forthcoming third-grade teacher and had taken Kenny to meet her before school had closed in the spring and his teacher had remembered. To Kenny, this remembrance was a wonderful thing—it marked the turning point in his attitude toward school.

Mrs. Webb and Miss Hobbs realized, as did Kenny's teacher, the need to learn and use names as quickly as possible. "John, would you pass the paper for me?" said early in the term helps the child feel that you know him already, that he is a person to you, not just a member of a class. Miss Hobbs made her children feel that she knew them by the attractive, welcoming name plates each child found on his desk on the first day of school.

As a primary teacher, Mrs. Webb was fortunate in being able to meet the children before the first day of school in the preschool conference. Each child could see "teacher" as he was registered and could get to know her a little bit during the morning he spent with her in school, and Mrs. Webb was able to familiarize herself with the children's names and to get a little information about each child before she greeted him on the first day of school.

Even in the upper grades it is important that each teacher be as familiar as possible with the names of the youngsters she will teach and spend some time reading records and talking with other teachers about her incoming pupils. Some teachers feel that they want to make their own judgments before gathering information about their pupils. The fact that you have read records and have some knowledge of each child does not mean that you accept the judgment of other teachers without reservation.

You will still need to listen carefully, gather your own impressions and objective material, add it to the cumulative record, and use your judgment as your impressions of the youngster grow through your contact with him. But it is valuable in your first contacts with a child to know as much about him as you can so that he becomes an individual for you—not just a member of a class group.

REMEMBERING SPECIAL OCCASIONS

The first day of school is only the beginning. Mrs. Webb writes:

All through the year, the teacher must make the pupil feel that he is wanted and that the teacher is interested in him. Specific examples of how I have done this are: *First,* whenever a child is sick, I call him on the telephone to let him know that I miss him. When a child is out indefinitely, the class and I send flowers from our gardens or a box of small presents from which the child takes only one out each day. *Second,* on special occasions—a birthday or a new baby in the family—I send a card. *Third,* at Christmas, I write each child a little letter during the holidays. I make it a very personal note wishing him and his family a happy holiday season. *Fourth,* during the year, there are many occasions that I share with the children. I have numerous invitations to dance and piano recitals. I attend the performance whenever possible or send a little note if I cannot be there.

These little touches of personal interest, which this teacher takes the trouble to show her children, are perhaps more possible in the elementary grades than later on. It is more difficult to reach the boys and girls of junior and senior high school years in the same personal way. Each teacher must meet with so many students each term. But there are still opportunities for the personal comment—the word of praise or sympathy, the note when a boy or girl is out of school because of illness or family trouble, the telephone call if a child is ab-

sent for several days—that can help take away the impersonality of a teacher with a large number of students. Every child may not be reached, but the word passes among the children that here is someone who has a greater interest in her students than just the teaching of subject matter. Knowledge that "she cares what happens to you" spreads.

Mrs. Knight feels that the teacher often must play a major role in meeting a child's unfilled need for affection. She says:

The children feel the teacher's affection. They can sense it through the teacher's expression and voice. A smile or a cheery comment will show the child the affection the teacher feels.

Sometimes it is a child in the class rather than the class as a whole who needs a particular word of affection. One day, I said to unhappy, neglected Arthur, "Do you know how much I like you?" He looked up as if he had been shot and said, "Do you really?" I am trying to give him a feeling of being liked that he has failed to get before. I call him each time he misses school and write him a little note. This pleases him very much. Through my sincere love for children, I try to let each child feel my affection for him.

As children grow older, one may not be able to say, "Do you know how much I like you?" but through interest and support, one can convey to boys and girls a feeling that each one of them has a place in the classroom, that each one is a person who is important to the teacher, who is liked by her.

However, it is important to remember that a teacher is not a mother nor a mother substitute. She has a different role to play. She should not become too emotionally involved with any youngster in her room. She must be able to see each child objectively, focus on his needs, and be able to pass him on to another teacher at the end of the year. A mother cannot and should not be able to do this.

Witmer and Kotinsky (1)* felt that this was an important point to remember:

In school, as at home and elsewhere, the quality of human relations is preponderant among all factors in furthering healthy personality development, and this quality is directly related to emotional stability and warm feelings towards others. Without stability and warmth on the part of teachers, supervisors, and administrators, knowledge about, and machinery for, improving human relations rests on a shaky foundation.

While emphasizing the importance of warmth, outgoingness, and spontaneity in the teacher's relationship with his pupils, it is perhaps pertinent to call attention to what, from the mental hygiene point of view, is conceived to be his essential role. His is not primarily the role of mothering the child in an intimate, dependent relationship that gives large play to immediate gratification of impulse. Rather, he strengthens the child in his efforts to meet the social demands properly made upon him and helps him find socially acceptable outlets for his feelings. Important among these demands and outlets are his relationships with other children and adults. The teacher properly helps him to cope with others, their feelings toward him, and his toward them. Among the teacher's chief means toward this end are his own basic acceptance of the child and the help he extends to him in attaining status in his group.

FINDING FRIENDLY, PERSONAL THINGS TO SAY

Joseph was taking part in a panel discussion at a teachers' meeting. He was asked the question, "What do young people want from grownups?" His answer, almost poignant, was "A little personal recognition. You blame teen-agers for all the things we do that are not right—but seldom do you speak to us of the things we do well. This

*Full references are cited at the end of the chapter.

year, I wrote an essay on citizenship that won a prize and recognition in our town paper. But not one of my teachers said, 'That was a fine essay' or 'I am proud of you, Joseph.' It hurts when nobody seems to care."

A comment on a paper—"Good work! I knew you could do it" can make a child feel that we have a real interest in what he is doing. "I liked this. You make your story come alive," or "That's a good idea. Won't you bring it up in class?"

A personal, friendly word to a child that shows we have noticed something is worrying him, a word of commendation for a picture seen on a bulletin board, or a comment about a project we have noticed in another room—little things, but they convey to the youngster the fact that here is somebody who has an interest in him, somebody who cares what he does. The moment of listening when a high-school boy drapes himself over the desk after school and starts "Say, did you know—" is a priceless opportunity to show we care. Even if we are busy and hurried, it is the moment to stop and listen and enter in. Confidences, thoughts, and ideas are often shared at unexpected moments. Planned conferences are valuable, but in establishing a friendly relationship with boys and girls, it is the moments of listening and entering in spontaneously that count— "Here is someone I can talk to at the moment the thought comes into my mind." The wise teacher is rarely too busy to listen, to talk, or, if time is really pressing as another class is coming in, to carry the talk over to another, more appropriate, time. It takes time to help children feel we are their friends, but the help that can be given through confidences spontaneously shared is worth the time.

SHARING FUN AS WELL AS PROBLEMS

One can show acceptance, too, through enjoying some of the experiences shared in class—even the moment taken to enjoy a joke and laugh with the children. One shy little girl said in sharing time when the class was talking about what they liked about school: "I like to hear Teacher laugh. She sort of laughs all over!" An enthusiasm shared for a class project says to the children: "I like to do this with you. I like to be in this class with you." The first-grade teacher who danced the hokey-pokey with the children, the eighth-grade teacher who invited her home-economics class to a picnic in her backyard and let them help prepare all the food, the science teacher who took the trouble to make a contact with a scientist in the community who was willing to help a boy work out a problem in electronics were all showing their genuine interest in their children.

CONTRIBUTING TO CHILDREN'S SPECIAL INTERESTS

We need to find out something about the interests and special abilities our youngsters have, as well as the "holes" in their experiences and learning. We know that children learn best when they are motivated through interest and when the learning experience has meaning for them. Mrs. Webb was aware of this when she took the time to talk with each child to try to find out about some of the experiences her youngsters had outside of school.

A teacher can show her interest in a youngster, at any age, in the way in which she plans her program and thinks in terms of each child's particular need or interest: "Billy, I thought you might enjoy this book about rocks. There are some particularly good pictures in it." "John, you mentioned that you are interested in working with boys when you grow up. I came across this material in my files. Would you like to look it over?" "Martha, I enjoyed those poems you put on my desk. Have you ever read these?" To slow-thinking Mike, "Mike, I brought you some red loops. They are so gay, I thought you could make a pot-holder

out of them." These are the touches that show we have spotted the interests of a youngster and that we care enough to take the trouble to remember them.

Miss Norris was convinced that shy fourteen-year-old Booth had a great deal to contribute to the class if she could only help him overcome his fear of speaking out loud. He never took part voluntarily in class discussions, but she noticed the alert look in his eyes whenever she spoke about Indians. One day after school, she stopped him when he was leaving the classroom and said, "You know, Booth, whenever we talk about Indians, I see a gleam in your eyes that makes me think they are a pet interest of yours." For the first time, Booth really broke through his shyness and told her that he had lived as a little boy on a reservation where his father had been a government agent. He had collected Indian arrowheads. His face lit up as he talked enthusiastically about them. Later in the year, Miss Norris found a spot in a unit on American history in which she felt she could use Booth's knowledge. Together they worked out a question-answer talk about Indian weapons with a demonstration of arrowheads from Booth's collection. From this point, Miss Norris began to reach Booth. They had something in common—a shared experience—and Booth responded.

TAKING TIME TO GET REALLY ACQUAINTED

INSIGHT THROUGH OBSERVATION

Let us look at some of the youngsters in a first-grade class of thirty children as they are seen through the eyes of an experienced teacher who is able to see her class as a whole and yet remain keenly aware and accepting of each child. Miss Leslie taught in a typical school situation. Her building was old and drab, her equipment not nearly as adequate as she would have wished it to be. The small playground was near a busy street, the basement was crowded, and there was no assembly room or extra space into which one could overflow with a class of thirty active primary children. What Miss Leslie did had to be done within the four walls of a not-too-large classroom. In addition, she worked under the pressures that many teachers feel, for she says:

It was necessary to put children of many levels in the same classroom. The age range had too wide a spread. The levels of learning were too diverse. The group was too large. In addition, unusual emotional problems were present. All this presented a terrific problem of working under time pressure to meet the needs of all the various groups, as well as the individual children. As I got to know my thirty children, I found, as I had expected, many different kinds of youngsters in my classroom. Among them were:

Stanley

Stanley had just returned to America from Japan. It was necessary for his mother to return to America, while his father stayed in Japan. Emotionally, this may have affected Stanley slightly, but educationally, the experience of living in Japan had been wonderful for him. He attended nursery schools in America and kindergarten in Japan. He verbalized well. He told the children many interesting experiences and brought many things to exhibit in the "Show and Tell" period. He sang a song about the sun in Japanese. Stanley's family motivated the child into entering varied activities and bringing in extra items of interest. Stanley had excellent coordination and was well-adjusted socially. He was vivacious and eager to learn.

Marilee

Marilee had the most severe problem of the class. She had cerebral palsy and wore braces. She attempted all physical-education activities. In a conference with her parents, I was concerned with the danger of her hurting herself and they replied, "We would rather she be hurt physically than emotionally. Go ahead. Let her take part in anything she wants to attempt." One couldn't help admire her courage and the wisdom of her parents. She didn't ask for any special help. The class

accepted her and it was amazing the way they handled the situation. In races, her partner would "slow down" without letting Marilee know that he was doing it.

Mark

Mark had many real problems. He was hostile, aggressive, and insecure. On the surface, he looked like a very hard child to manage. Mark's father didn't want him around after he came home. Mark's mother gave him his dinner early and "got him out of the way." Mark annoyed his father. His mother said, "He drives me crazy. I can't do a thing with him." Mark was jealous of his younger sister, Ellen, who was two. Apparently he felt little security or love at home. The mother and father refused to come to school on visiting day. They told Mark and me they "didn't want the children to know that they were his parents."

Tony

Tony was a fine, well-built lad. He came from a highly intellectual home. Both of his parents were employed. He was a well-integrated boy. Tony was excellently prepared for his grade. He attended private kindergarten for one year. In addition to this, his parents took him on many trips and gave him a wide variety of experiences. He had been read to constantly since he was a small child. Tony came to school with all the eagerness to learn that any child could possess. He ranked highest in the room on the Metropolitan Reading Readiness Test. As judged by the teacher, he also ranked high. Tony was a natural leader and was very dependable. He exhibited this by taking important messages, by making an excellent host for the room, and taking charge of the game when the teacher was called out. Socially and emotionally, Tony was well-adjusted.

Nevill

Nevill was socially maladjusted. His performance was erratic. He did well whenever it suited him. Whenever he did not feel like it, he did not put the slightest effort into his task. He needed to have everything on his terms. It was as if he were saying, "I want my way and will fight for it. I do only what goes with what I want." The school psychologist who talked with Nevill thought that underneath his attempted dominance, he felt quite anxious about himself. Nevill's parents had moved many times all over the United States. While the family was traveling, his mother said that they had to give in to him over and over again. Nevill seemed to have found out that by making enough fuss, he could get what he wanted. Since he was an only child and had moved so constantly, he never had friends of his own age for any length of time.

Nora

Nora came to the first grade last year. She had a bright, happy face. The first time she tried to tell me something, I could not understand a word she was saying. She had a speech defect and spoke with a lisp. The children were unkind. Some of them even laughed when she tried to talk. She immediately closed up like a clam. She stopped talking. Her happy face turned into a very sad one. Nora was the oldest in the family and had two younger brothers, one five and one a new baby. In physical education, Nora scored a success. She threw and caught a ball very well. In games, children liked to have her on their side.

Paul

Paul lived in a land of make-believe. He had a good make-believe story to top any story of any kind that another child told. Paul was the younger of two children. He was seven and his brother was nine. From the first, his parents told me, Paul tried to measure up in all ways to his brother's standards. This was hard as he was not quite as intellectually capable. He thought he should read out of a "big" book the first day he came to school. In fact, he was ashamed that he couldn't.

In Miss Leslie's room, Nora and Marilee had obvious handicaps, which their teacher could see. But often there are children with physical difficulties that are less obvious. We might pass by the restless youngster who roves around the classroom until it is discovered that his eyes do not focus well, and the directions on the board are nothing but a blur to him. Or we might overlook the youngster who never seems to pay attention, who is considered dull and uncooperative until a routine hearing test indicates a gross hearing defect that accounts for the child's apparent inattention to and lack of interest in his work.

If there is no apparent and obvious cause why a child is not learning or is not adjusting well to school, it is always wise to ask for a physical checkup to rule out possible physical causes for the difficulty.

Miss Leslie knew that she must also look for, accept, and try to understand the abilities and limitations with which each child was born. She knew that some, like Tony and Stanley, would learn easily and quickly, absorbing ideas and mastering skills, whereas others, like little Peggy with her 35 per cent readiness for first-grade reading, might never have the same capacity to master reading, number concepts, or abstract ideas. She knew also that some of the children, because of their fine coordination, could be expected to cut and write and throw a ball better than some of the others. Some of the children would always turn in messy papers, poorly put together notebooks, hems with uneven stitches, and shop work in which the corners didn't fit. Yet their work might be the result of real effort in terms of their basic capacities. Miss Leslie knew that if she were to hold Marilee to the same kind of neat work she expected of Tony, with his well-knit, capable body, she would be pushing Marilee into an even greater feeling of inadequacy.

It is also important to know the kind of will power or drive a youngster may possess, which can be utilized to help him to overcome some of his difficulties. Little crippled Marilee possessed courage and a will to do, which carried her beyond what might have been expected of a child with her handicap. Mark had become so discouraged that his drive had been turned into a frustrated hostility toward those who had hurt him.

These are real children from a real class. Anyone of us might find a Tony or Paul or Marilee sitting in our classroom the first day of school. Each child is different, and, in order to teach effectively, we need to know all children as Miss Leslie tried to know them "with their own unique combination of experience, personality traits, and individual needs."

LETTERS AND QUESTIONNAIRES TO PARENTS

When we are faced with the problem of teaching thirty or thirty-five boys and girls, the task of trying to gather information about each child may seem too much of a burden. We may feel that we do not know where to begin or to what sources to turn.

Some teachers have found that sending letters and questionnaires to parents near the beginning of the school year yields invaluable background information about each child. The letter should be a friendly one—welcoming the child to the school, inviting the parents to visit the school often, and asking the parents to fill out an enclosed questionnaire, which, it is explained in the letter, will help the teacher and the school provide for the maximum growth and development of the child.

The questionnaire, usually mimeographed, asks for such information as: the child's full name and birth date, family history (mother's and father's names, names and ages of brothers and sisters), environmental factors (address, kind of home, etc.), previous school history, physical and health traits, general information about the child's nature, habits, and special interests. Teachers find such a questionnaire a very useful device for gaining insight into both the needs and backgrounds of their children. They often refer to it for added understanding as new questions come up during the year.

In many schools, such questionnaires are sent out routinely to all new students and are on file in the cumulative record. However, schools have many different policies about contacting parents, which make it necessary for the classroom teacher to "clear" the matter of sending questionnaires with her principal.

HOME VISITS

A teacher cannot be expected to know the intimate life history of each of her children, but she does need enough personal information to be able to see the child as an individual personality—to have some clues to his behavior. Home visits can give us some important insights into the child's personality and the background that has helped shape him.

There are many children who bring to school home experiences that have disturbed and hurt them. In every classroom, there are children who are tense from too much pressure at home, children overanxious at home because they feel success at school is the price for love. Such children, whatever their mental ability, are not emotionally free to learn. We may grow discouraged as we find ourselves failing to help unhappy children learn what we want so much to teach unless we realize that their behavior and lack of achievement spring from roots that were growing before they came to school.

Most parents will welcome a visit from the teacher, but there are some who are afraid that such a visit means that their child is in trouble. There are others who are not interested enough to be bothered. Still others may be embarrassed about their homes and unwilling for the teacher to call. Such parents can often be reached by a pleasant telephone call or a friendly note. Unfortunately, however, there will always be some whom we are unable to reach.

In some communities, home visits are difficult to make because both parents work, and it may be hard to find either one of them at home at a time when the teacher is able to call. In some industrial areas, or in communities in which many of the mothers work, visits must often be made in the evening. This puts a heavy burden upon the teacher unless such visits are allowed for in the planning of the teaching load.

It is especially difficult for the teacher in junior or senior high schools to make home visits. The number of boys and girls in each class and the wide areas from which they come may make home visits impractical. This is true even in small communities and rural areas in which pupils are often taken by bus long distances to a consolidated school. Yet home visits are especially valuable in the junior high school if they can be arranged. It is frequently possible for the home-room teacher to be the one who makes the home visit and then include her report of the visit in the child's school file. In this way, her appraisal of the home and the home influence on the youngster can be shared with the other teachers.

As with questionnaires, the matter of home visits must be cleared with the principal. In some communities, the home visit is made only by the visiting teachers; in others, each teacher is encouraged to visit as many homes as possible. Sometimes a distinction is made concerning the aim of a home visit. The regular teacher may go into the home so that she may gain better understanding of the background of her children, and the visiting teacher may have the responsibility of contacting parents when problems arise. Where no visiting teacher is available, the classroom teacher may have to function in both roles. This is a matter of school policy, which is an administrative decision.

CUMULATIVE RECORDS

Even though conditions may make it impossible for us to study each child as fully as we would like, it is encouraging to find how much information and insight we can gather about each child without taking an undue amount of time. A cumulative record is easy to keep once we develop the habit of putting items into it. It is the attitude of wanting to know—the habit of observation, of noting little things as well as big ones—

that will help us in getting to know all our children.

It is important to build on the cumulative record but we must also remember that children grow and change. The fact that a child does badly at the beginning of the first grade does not mean that he will do badly in second grade. Children mature and situations change. A child who has been unhappy at home may find the home situation much improved another year; a youngster who did poorly with one teacher may do well with another. A child who was dreamy and uncooperative according to the record of last year's teacher may be alert and interested in the next class. A child's health may improve, eyesight may have been corrected, or a change in pupil-teacher relationships may have worked a great change in the child's motivation and interest. Yet it is important to know how he reacted before—and why.

When we know that a child's record will be cumulative and go with him through the years, it becomes increasingly important to report as accurately as we can the actual actions of a child as well as our opinions about him. We must put down facts—things the child did and said, actions we observed —rather than only subjective statements such as "John was very lazy today" or "Betty is such a lovely child." Subjective comments about children may be added to the record but should be used to interpret one's own reactions to the child—what John did that made him seem lazy or what Betty does that makes us feel she is a lovely child. In this way, the observed event is distinguished from our feelings about a particular child.

BUILDING A MUTUAL SENSE OF

TRUST AND CONFIDENCE

Boys and girls feel the acceptance of their teacher through the general climate of trust present in a classroom. Children need to feel that their teacher is ready to listen, will hear their point of view, and will not immediately jump to conclusions. One youngster's teacher failed at this point when she was too ready to accuse the boy of cheating without really finding out. The feeling of trust—"I am all right. Teacher believes in me. I may make mistakes, but if I do, I can talk to my teacher about them"—is a stabilizing one. Some youngsters have never experienced this feeling of trust and confidence between themselves and another person. They may have been brought up in an atmosphere of suspicion, criticism and scoldings. But without trust, it is difficult to feel that one is accepted as a worth-while person.

Timothy came from a very disturbed home. He never knew when he got up in the morning whether his parents would be pleasant to him or whether it was better for him to make himself as inconspicuous as possible and duck out of the house to school. His father had an irascible temper and his mother, though fond enough of Timothy, retreated into nervous headaches. When her husband was on the rampage, she just pulled down the shades and stayed in bed. This added to Timothy's uncertain feeling about himself—for he often felt that his one support had failed him. In school, he showed his anxiety by "taking things." Often these were things he didn't really need—a pencil when he had three of his own, rubber bands from the teacher's desk, a piece of chalk slipped in his pocket when he passed the board, a pencil sharpener from his neighbor's desk. His teacher knew what was happening and one day, she drew him to her as he slipped some paper clips into his pocket and quietly said, "You know, Timothy, you did not need to do that. I would have shared with you. Next time, when you want something, come to me and ask for it. You are my friend, you know, and friends share." Timothy looked at her and said nothing.

But he did come to her later, trying her out, and asked for things. His teacher shared—pieces of chalk, pencils, a cookie from her lunch. A little later, when the second-grade class was writing sentences about "My Teacher," Timothy carefully wrote in his bold manuscript writing:

> My Teacher
> I like my teacher.
> She is good to me.
> She shares with me.

Underneath, he drew a picture of "My Teacher" with her arms outstretched and beneath it, he drew a heart in which he wrote *I Love You.*

We can also help a child feel our belief in him when we give him an opportunity to do things for us.

Little Billy had been a difficult youngster during his first year in school. He was really too young for school. He had come from a home in which he was the youngest child. He had been babied by the older children in his family; he had no responsibilities because everyone expected him to be the baby. Billy's teacher had been understanding of his immaturity and had helped him grow. Billy had had temper tantrums in the classroom; it had been necessary many times to take him out of the classroom, but Billy knew his teacher was right there believing in him and he loved her. One day he came to school with his eyes shining, carefully clutching in his two grimy hands an egg carton. Inside were six brown eggs. "For you," he said, "because you love me. I bought them from Jimmy with my own money. He has a hen, you know. They are very fresh."

A real tribute to a teacher who cared.

Affection is a two-way thing. Billy's teacher, in being able to accept the eggs from Billy, accepted his affection, too. A child wants to be free to give in return. If healthy affection is to exist in the classroom, each child must be helped to feel secure enough within himself so that he can feel a bond with his teacher and give back to her again. For this reason, affection asks as well as gives.

Miss Drew was right when she said, "Ned, I've given you lots of time today for you have disturbed us all. Can you stay and help me fix up this room?" Ned stayed, worked well, and felt his teacher liked him after all, or she wouldn't have asked him to stay and make amends like that. Unless a child can experience something of success so that he can develop pride in himself and can like himself, he will not be able to accept the thought that there is anything in him which someone might honestly think was worth while. Miss Drew, in giving Ned the feeling that she wanted him to help because he could do a good job, was also helping him regain self-confidence and self-respect, which she hoped would ultimately make it possible for him to show better classroom behavior.

Mrs. Northrup taught a special class of thirteen boys of low I.Q. She said:

I know I am on the right track with most of these boys (9-14) when even the ones with the least improvement say, "We ought to do something for Mrs. Northrup. She is always doing something for us." And they all have something they can do whether it is being able to sing a song for us, bringing in something they have made, or just not getting bored quickly by menial tasks.

Mrs. Northrup, too, knew the value of showing confidence in her boys when she saw the pride that two of her slowest youngsters showed when she sent them into the woods to get dirt for flower pots and they came proudly back with dirt that was rich with humus because "That's the kind she likes."

AVOIDING FAVORITISM

We are sometimes afraid to show warmth and interest in a particular child for fear that other children will misunderstand or be jealous. We fear that the child who is singled out for special help or attention may be labeled "teacher's pet." But if we have established a friendly, comfortable relationship between ourselves and all of the children in our room, we do not need to fear this reaction. Then our attention to one child, because he needs it, is usually accepted by the other children.

If we are honest in our relationships with children, they will usually respond with equal honesty to us. Children have a feeling for motives. If attention is given out of a genuine need for help—if it is child-directed —most of the children will be able to accept it. "Mary has been ill. I must help her catch up." "You know, John has moved a lot. He needs the help of all of us." The attitude of the teacher is quickly communicated to the class. The youngsters who cannot accept it will be those who have an equal need at the moment—who themselves have such a deep need for affection that they cannot bear to share their teacher with any other child.

Sometimes a teacher does single out a child for special attention because she is particularly drawn to the youngster and is satisfying a need within herself rather than a need within the child. Mrs. Janke was drawn closely to Lisa, a charming fourth-grader. Lisa seemed to her to be everything a child should be. In addition, she was a friendly child and responded to the teacher's demonstrations of affection— bringing her flowers and gifts. One day Mrs. Janke drew Lisa to her in front of some classmates and another teacher and said, "This is my Pet." Such a demonstration of affection naturally boomeranged on the child, who became the butt of much teasing and unfriendliness on the part of the other children. Such favoritism did not serve a useful purpose in the development of this child.

Most teachers would not be as open in their expression of favoritism, but it is easy to single out constantly the child who handles situations well and give him the major role in an assembly program or a conspicuous place when an audience is expected. The child serves as security to the teacher that "He will be a credit to her" in the eyes of the supervisor or visiting parents.

In the same way, teachers will often select certain children for special classroom jobs or outstanding positions—so that the same children are chosen many times when others are more in need of experiences of responsibility or leadership, even if they do not perform so well. Special attention to the few who do well at the expense of the others is neither good for the group nor for the "chosen" youngster.

SOME PROBLEMS THAT MAKE ACCEPTANCE DIFFICULT

CONCEPTS OF CHILDREN AS "GOOD" OR "BAD"

Sometimes we let our ideas about children get in the way of real acceptance. It is natural that over the years we should have accumulated attitudes about children and ideas about the ways in which they should behave. But our understanding of children may be seriously hampered by some of these ideas if they are not based upon what is really known about boys and girls and why they behave as they do. One concept that sometimes gets in the way is: children are "good" or "bad." "Mary is such a good child. It's a joy to have her in my class." "Jerry is so bad, I can't do anything with him. I'll be glad when you get him next year —and sorry for you, too." Most of us talk that way at some time or other. Concepts of goodness and badness are often based on whether the actions of the child are comfortable for the adults around him. In the classroom, the good children all too often are those who are a credit to the teacher when the supervisor or the principal opens the door or those who sit quietly in their seats and cause no disturbance or special problem. If we are to accept children, we must constantly remind ourselves that a child does not do certain things because he is innately good or bad, but because of certain patterns of behavior he has developed in response to the situations he has met in his growing up or because of certain needs and drives within himself.

A child may be a "good" child in his relationship with one person and a so-called "bad" child in his relationship with another. A third-grade teacher was surprised one day when a concerned mother came to school to talk over the troubles she was having with her small boy. "Dan acts like a demon possessed when he is at home," said the mother. Yet at school Dan had never been in difficulty and had seemed very happy. Neither mother nor teacher could understand the difference in the boy's behavior. But there was a new baby sister at home and, in later talks, the mother admitted, "Why, of course, we do love the baby best. She is so happy and cuddly, never mean like Dan." At school, Dan had found the warmth and support from his teacher that he did not get at home. He was happy during the hours he was at school. He was mean during the tension-ridden hours at home.

Then there was Joan who did not do well in school one day. Usually, she was a child who got along well, but on this day, she had been disturbing and difficult. On her way out of the classroom, the teacher put her arm around Joan and said, "What was the matter today, Joan?" Joan burst out crying and through her tears sobbed, "I hit Jimmy and Mother was so mad, she tore up my coloring book. I didn't mean to be bad."

Neither child was "bad." Each had a problem with which he needed help. If a child does not feel loved—even for a day— he can be very difficult.

In the same way, we sometimes label a child "bad" or "lazy" or "stubborn" because he is restless and difficult in school and does not study as he should. Again we need to remind ourselves of the effect that the inability to learn as rapidly as others may have upon a child. A child who cannot keep up, who constantly finds himself behind, who rarely if ever experiences success, may develop behavior patterns that make further learning much harder. His constant failure and feelings of inferiority may make him give up trying to learn and turn to other ways of attracting attention or proving to himself that he is all right. In the same way, we must not forget that the very bright child who is bored may become labeled "bad" because he has lost interest in the activities of his group and has become restless and a class disturber.

Our attitude also influences the attitude of the children to one another. One fifth-grader's teacher felt him to be lazy and a "no-good." She made sarcastic remarks that were picked up by the children. They teased and taunted him, "Go away, you lazy no-good! You can't play with us—we don't want you!" The youngster retaliated by throwing stones at the children on his way home from school, and the teacher thought he was not only lazy but mean.

The teacher who really wants to accept children develops the habit of always saying to herself, "Why does this child act this way?" She avoids labeling a child as either good or bad, accepting or rejecting him with the label as an excuse.

NEGATIVE FEELINGS TOWARD CHILDREN

There are some children who cannot be reached by the friendly word—who resent the kindly pat or even the friendly voice. Perhaps they have never experienced these things in their homes. Perhaps they have been hurt so much that they cannot respond easily to other people. Such children have a greater need than others for some reassurance that their teacher cares about them. The child who comes to school from a family who has rejected him and has shown him little affection will need repeated evidence that his teacher likes him. Until he finds roots of affection in the classroom, which he did not find at home, he will continue to show the same hostile, rebellious attitude at school that he brought with him from home. Sometimes it takes much patience on the part of a teacher before she can really reach such a child and help him feel that she cares about him and is his friend.

There are times, too, when we find it very difficult to accept the child who does not conform to the routines of the classroom or does not fit into the prescribed curriculum. We like children who do their work well, turn in neat papers, and attend to their business. We can also accept and understand the slow child; we realize that he cannot achieve, and our sympathy is drawn toward him. But we often find it very difficult to accept the child who has ability but does not conform, does not fit, is full of questions, daydreams, and does not perform as we feel a capable child should.

Sometimes we find it hard to like a child because his standards of cleanliness and good manners are not the same as ours. Perhaps he comes from a racial group we do not understand or from an area in which standards are different from those we are used to. He may have irritating personal characteristics. Or we may have had a brother or sister in a previous class who has proved to be a problem—and so we may say, "Another of those Jones children!" without giving the youngster a chance to prove himself. Sometimes we may even carry over our irritation with a parent and let it affect our feelings for a child.

Any one of us may have negative feelings toward an individual child. This is only human. There are some qualities that draw us toward other people, others that seem to push us away. But we have a responsibility not to let our feelings push us into situations of conflict with a child, which can destroy our relationship with the youngster and push him away from us. Our job is to teach *every* child.

Thomas Cohen was an unusually intelligent sixth-grader. He came from a home full of books. His parents answered his questions and encouraged his hobbies. He was eager and curious—his mind full of "whys." He had always been a friendly, out-going boy. He liked people although his own interests were so far beyond those of the other boys of his age that he did not have many close friends. In school, he was cooperative and helpful in projects and took part in assembly programs and plans. As the year in sixth grade progressed, his parents began to notice that he had developed a nervous tic, had become irritable, and did not go to school with his usual enthusiasm. Nevertheless, he worked hard on a relief map of South America, making it of papier-mâché—carefully measured to scale. It was a fine job, but when he took it to school, his teacher gave it a casual glance, and without a word of commendation put it on top of the piano instead of on display with the work of the other children. That night, he exploded and everything came out in tears—his teacher did not like him—she never called on him—she did not give him a part in the Christmas program although some other children had three—and now she ignored his map. He had worked hard on it; he knew it was good, but his teacher had said nothing. Mrs. Cohen discussed the matter with the principal—who in turn talked to the teacher. The teacher's feelings came out with equal vehemence—"I'm sorry, I cannot take that child! He asks me too many questions. I don't know the answers. Why should I know them? He pushes me to the wall with his questions. He is so much better than the other children. I didn't give him a part because I was afraid he would do so well that the others would get jealous. His map was perfect. It made the work of the other children look poor. I never taught a child like this before. He makes me feel stupid!"

Here was a real problem between teacher and child. But the teacher had let it run away with her. She had seriously hurt a child because of her intense feelings of frustration and dislike. If she had faced her feelings for this youngster earlier in the year, if she had talked over the situation honestly with her principal or her supervisor, she might have found the roots of her tension toward the boy much earlier. She could then have found more constructive ways of helping him use his questing mind. It is not necessarily a sign of failure if a teacher does not have all the answers to the questions a keen-minded child can ask.

It is not the feelings we have but what we do about them that is the significant difference between being a teacher who can help children or one who hurts them emotionally.

The first step in handling our negative feelings toward a youngster is to face them honestly, to take thought as to why we have these feelings. "What is it about this child that keeps me from accepting him?" "Is it some experience I have had that he reawakens?" "Why do I feel this way about him?" *In the second place, we have a responsibility to take care not to let our negative feelings—our irritation with him— make us unfair in our actions toward the child.* If a child has been a troublemaker, we sometimes make a snap judgment when something goes wrong in the classroom and quickly blame a child without really finding out if, this time, it really is his fault. We must be careful not to turn on such a youngster with sarcasm or abruptness of manner, which says plainly to the youngster, "I don't like you." *In the third place, we must make an effort to build a constructive working relationship—even if we cannot achieve a liking for the child.* We can find the child's interests and encourage them; we can ask the youngster to help us do something. We can try to understand what is behind the child's behavior or his personality difficulties—and in such understanding find the real child rather than the surface one.

If we have too many negative feelings toward the children we teach, or if our feelings are as intense as those of Thomas' teacher, so that we are harming a child, we may need to turn to our supervisor or principal or even seek some personal counseling to help us work through our feelings. We cannot teach well if our personal feelings destroy our relationships with the children we teach.

Mrs. Knight recognized this when she said: "I am constantly aware of how deeply my own personality and my own anxieties can affect the children under my care. I know I bring to the classroom not only my knowledge but my personality as well."

PERSONAL PROBLEMS OF OUR OWN

Sometimes we destroy the friendly atmosphere of our classroom by bringing into it too many of our personal problems. True, teachers have as many problems as other people. We may come to school tired, with a headache or other physical complaint, with anxieties and worries we have brought from home. We would not be normal people if we did not have some troubles and worries. But again it is what we do about them that is important.

Sometimes it is best to be frank with the children. "I am afraid I have a headache today, so I may be cross and irritable." And at the end of the day, "Thanks for helping me out today." Children can be considerate when the feeling between teacher and child is warm and friendly, and if the need for such understanding does not arise too frequently.

Sometimes, though, we take out our personal feelings in an unhealthy way with our children. One teacher had had a real family problem, which had ended in divorce. She talked to the children in her classroom about it, appealing to them to love her; she needed so much love because she had been hurt. She drew on the sympathies of the youngsters. If the class was difficult, she would say, "You make me feel so unhappy today—and you must give me love because I need it." A teacher's personal problems do not belong in the classroom. We must learn to handle our own anxieties and tensions without letting them disrupt the atmosphere of our room. When they begin to do so, we again have an obligation to ourselves and to the children we teach to seek intelligent help.

Far too often our own personal affairs crowd in in another way. Perhaps we find it hard to get up in the morning and do not arrive early enough in the classroom to be able to start the day with calmness and a feeling of being ready for work. The teacher who breathlessly dashes in a minute before her students is not ready to help them make the transition from confusion to a working atmosphere. Far too often they, too, have come from homes that were rushed and confused at breakfast time— with Father leaving the house at one hour, the children at another, while Mother tried to feed everybody and pay attention to smaller brothers and sisters who were demanding and fussy because they were hungry and wanted their breakfast.

The teacher who is sufficiently relaxed to greet the youngsters with a friendly, pleasant tone of voice and is comfortable enough to give them a smile rather than an irritated frown will be able to develop a feeling of well-being in her classroom. The children feel safe with her.

ACCEPTANCE DOES NOT MEAN LACK OF DISCIPLINE

A feeling of warm and kindly friendliness does not mean that there is never criticism or irritation or even a well-deserved scolding in the classroom. Affection for children can show itself in many ways. It does mean that when the limits must be set

—when children must be corrected or brought back into a reasonable kind of conduct—it is done with the same spirit of liking for children, of understanding and acceptance which exists when things are going well. The child does not feel that his integrity as a person is threatened; he can still trust his teacher, and he knows that she still has a warm interest in him. If trust does not exist in the classroom, then the child may feel that his teacher's correction is overwhelming, and its effect is lost in the tension and fear produced by an experience that to the child means once again—"There is no love here for me."

When this is the case, the boy or girl who feels "They don't like me here" may not run away physically; he may instead withdraw into himself, remain timidly apart from the group, daydream, or hit out in anger against a situation that seems unfriendly and unkind. If this happens, effective teaching usually ceases. The child may seem to learn but too often does not make what he learns a real part of himself. Instead he pushes it aside as soon as he can, because the experience is too laden with the discomfort of anxiety.

It is not easy for us, as teachers, to decide how much time we can fairly take from the group for special work with a youngster who is a disturber. There is no rule that can be given for deciding when such a youngster is taking up too great a proportion of time and attention—so that other children in the room are beginning to feel he is getting more than his share. Each teacher must decide for herself when her tolerance for difficult behavior is exhausted and when the problem of the child is reacting badly on the group as a whole. Mrs. Knight distinguished between behavior that was disturbing and behavior that could not be tolerated, such as serious fighting. In speaking of one of the children, she said:

Most of his poor behavior is of the type that is not particularly bad in itself but which must be modified and controlled in group living. Examples are: talking out, always wanting to be first, wanting to be chosen for popular jobs, not paying attention to school routines, wandering around the room, playing with small articles, not doing assigned work, annoying other children, and poor building behavior such as running through the building and up and down the stairs. Behavior that cannot be tolerated or overlooked is losing his temper and fighting with such fury that he could easily injure someone seriously.

Children do not have confidence in the teacher who is always smiling and pleasant but cannot keep order or see that her assignments are carried out. Sometimes the first real contact made with a difficult or disturbing youngster comes when the limits are set with firmness, and the child knows that you have not rejected him—that you still accept him, talk with him pleasantly at other times, continue to show an interest in him and in his work—but that beyond a certain point, he may not go.

A child who is permitted to go too far may feel that we do not care what he does. Sometimes a youngster will use this as a testing device to see whether anyone bothers about him.

A child is not always right, and the wise teacher knows that although acceptance, kindliness, and warmth are necessities in the development of children, they also need the security which comes from knowing that both parents and teachers are behind them and in control of the situation. Children want grownups to be kind but firm when it is necessary. Most boys and girls do not want to be allowed to "get away with everything." It frightens them. When things are out of control, the child is uncertain, often scared, and frequently guilty because things happen that he does not know how to handle or stop.

Love can be both constructive and destructive: Constructive love sustains and supports the child in the classroom so that he knows that through your interest in him, you will help him grow up to the point where he can master his schoolwork and control himself. Destructive love "smothers" the child and prevents him from growing into responsibility for his own actions.

Sheviakov and Redl (2) warn us against the kind of destructive atmosphere that comes from an outward expression of "love" which does not represent the real feelings of the teacher but is constantly used as a subtle means of control. It is what they label the "emotional blackmail climate." The teacher says she "loves" all children "and says so at the rate of three times a minute." In such a schoolroom, you may not get punished if you do wrong but you "feel like a heel" because the teacher keeps saying how much she has been hurt by your behavior. Such a teacher produces emotional dependence upon herself—an attitude that can be destructive to the best development of boys and girls.

REFERENCES

(1) Witmer, Helen L., and Kotinsky, Ruth. *Personality in the Making.* New York: Harper & Brothers, 1952, p. 263.

(2) Sheviakov, George V., and Redl, Fritz. *Discipline for Today's Children and Youth.* New Rev. Washington, D.C.: Association for Supervision and Curriculum Development, National Education Association, 1956, p. 50.

CHAPTER 2

ACHIEVEMENT

We hear so much about flexible groupings
in the classroom. Beyond the usual reading groups,
what other groups can we set up?

Most of the slow learners I have taught
were well aware that they were slower than
the others. I just don't see how I can
help these children to a sense of achievement.

We are often told that it is harmful to use
pressure to make a child work hard. Are we
expected to let mediocrity take over?

So much is being said about the
faults of I.Q. tests. I'm beginning to wonder
if they are any good at all.

Children have to learn to live in a
competitive world. Shouldn't we then stress
competition in our classrooms in order to
prepare them for living in the adult world?

I have several exceptionally gifted youngsters
in my class. More of the same work keeps them quiet
but not happy. I just don't know what
to do to help them work to their capacities.

FOR EVERY CHILD

ACHIEVEMENT DEPENDS ON THE CHILD'S IMAGE OF HIMSELF

Important as acceptance is, it is not enough. It is the basic need, but as teachers we have the responsibility to see that each child has the opportunity to grow and develop according to his own pattern. We must see that he is not forced into a mold he does not fit and that he is not subjected to pressures to achieve what he is not ready to achieve or cannot ever achieve. We are sometimes tempted to set standards to which we feel all children should conform at a certain age, forgetting that maturity, ability, and emotional readiness are much better criteria of what a child is able to do than age or grade placement. When we expect the slow child to compete with the fast child, the immature one with the mature one, we are retarding growth rather than aiding it.

If children are to be able to pass successfully through the stages of growth leading to maturity, they must have experiences as they are growing up that help them build a picture of themselves they can like and respect. Kanner (1) * stresses the point that every child "craves the friendly acknowledgment of himself as an individual who has a right to fulfill his destiny, to have his identity kept intact, and to be allowed a fair modicum of self-esteem." One cannot forget the story he tells of twelve-year-old Billy. Billy had a congenital malformation of the heart that made it inadvisable for him to go to school, kept him from normal play with other children, and curtailed his activities in many other ways. His father was away on business much of the time and his mother "had become a slave to Billy's heart condition" and, in her genuine concern, "a tyrannical watchdog over Billy himself." Billy knew of himself essentially as a "sick heart." But when given a chance to talk to an understanding psychologist, he

*Full references are cited at the end of the chapter.

unburdened himself and revealed his passionate desire to do things for himself by saying over and over, "I am a person! I *am* a person!"

The image of the self is something that gradually develops through the experiences a child has with other people. A little child who is loved by his parents sees himself first as a likeable person. Gradually as he grows up and learns to know other people—aunts, uncles, grandparents, teachers, neighbors, and other children—he either is encouraged in this feeling or begins to modify his feelings about himself. Perhaps he sees that the other children do things better than he does and he begins to criticize himself—"I'm stupid" or "I'm clumsy" or "Everyone does things better than I do. It's no good trying." Or if he finds himself quicker at learning and more skilled than others, he may see himself as better than others—"I'm the big shot." If he finds himself unsure of the affection and acceptance of his mother and father, he may seek the attention he wants so badly by undesirable behavior, which causes him to get scolded and punished. Then he may think even more, "Nobody likes me. I'm bad." Sometimes simply because he is unhappy, a cycle of behavior starts that makes the youngster really earn the label of "difficult child," and he continues to see himself as such.

The idea of self that children are building through their school years is important and significant in their ability to learn. A child who is exposed to experiences of continual failure may build a pretty sad and discouraged picture of himself. This may not be a true picture at all. In other circumstances, given tasks suited to the level of his developmental needs, he might have had a picture of himself as one who could succeed.

Kanner goes on to say that sometimes in our absorption with management, guidance, and education, we do not hear that cry—*I am a person!* Yet we cannot teach adequately unless we help each child become a person who can like and respect himself. We must test our methods of teaching, our approach to the children in our classroom, by asking ourselves whether we are helping each child gain confidence and self-respect so that he is *able to learn.* Erikson (2) feels it is during the years in the classroom that a child can be helped to attain sufficient confidence to have the initiative to go ahead and learn the skills and acquire the knowledge that will enable him to meet the needs of life in a complex world. If a child is not helped to achieve a feeling of self-confidence, he may develop feelings of inferiority and a sense of incompetence and failure that will hamper him throughout his life.

Phil Landers was a boy whose image of himself had been warped so that he thought of himself as dull. His personal problems were not recognized until he was a senior in high school, although they had prevented him from the achievement that his desires and ability would have made possible for him. At nineteen, he felt he was a failure. But nobody had ever stopped to ask, "What is the matter with Phil?" Miss Phelps, the teacher who finally helped him, tells us about Phil in this way:

Phil has been an enigma to me this entire school year. I have wondered how a boy could be so continuously present in body and so rarely present in mind. How could this boy be so intelligent in private conferences and appear so unintelligent in the group situation? What has caused this impassive resistance to learning, which is characteristic of his attitude in all of his classes? More specifically, as it relates to me, why is it that this boy can express himself so satisfactorily in a conference with me but is unable to do so in a group or on paper?

Phil has been no discipline problem; on the contrary, his behavioral record is excellent. He is always very polite and, when I see him in the halls or have a conversation with him before or after class, there is a very engaging cheerfulness, responsiveness, and dignity about him. During the class period, however, it is almost as if he were not there. For the entire first semester, he did not utter a word in class except "yes" or "no." Whenever discussions became especially lively and the group leader tried to draw him in, I always hoped that Phil would have some contribution to make; but each time he avoided saying anything. In fact, Phil was so unresponsive that it became embarrassing even to attempt to include him in the group. It was this realization that inspired me to search for the cause of this boy's absolute unresponsiveness in a group situation, for it seemed that this might be the key to his notable lack of success in school.

Phil is the son of middle-class parents who live in a modest but attractively furnished and well-cared-for apartment in a middle-west city. Phil is the second of four children. An older sister is studying to be a teacher, a younger sister is in junior high, and a brother is in the sixth grade.

Two very strong influences seem to be evident in Phil's home—religion and an abnormal concentration on work. The family are all devout members of a neighborhood church. Phil has mentioned many prohibitions that his religion has placed on him, though not in a critical manner. He is apparently active in the young people's groups of his church and has been considered a model of youth by his clergyman. Recently, he told me about an unfortunate experience in which he was involved.

It seems that a member of the young people's group had a party one Sunday afternoon where the guests, including Phil, danced. This is not permitted by the church and Phil, the "model boy," was severely criticized and condemned by both the clergyman and his father. Phil expressed intense feelings of guilt when he recounted this incident to me.

The work obsession I am unable to understand. Every member of this family has two jobs. Phil has two jobs, in addition to attending school. He works as a delivery boy for a drugstore after school and in the evenings, and as a stock boy for a hardware store on Saturdays. One of his employers told me that he was a very conscientious and reliable employee. I could understand this obsession if there were any evidence of a worship of material possessions. There seems to be no evidence of this, however. There is virtually no relaxation or recreation in the home.

Phil has superior intellectual ability, though he has never scored high on group tests. When he was in ninth grade, he gained an I.Q. of 88 on the California Mental Maturity Test and at the beginning of his senior year, 92. After working with Phil and talking to him in private conferences, it seemed obvious to me that he had more intellectual powers than the group test scores were indicating. I asked that he be given the Stanford-Binet Scale, and on this individual test, his I.Q. was found to be 132. He showed a high degree of verbal ability and an above-average store of information. His perception was good and his concrete reasoning ability above average. He seemed to possess less abstract reasoning power, however. His visual memory seemed stronger than his auditory memory. He is an intelligent young man in the very superior range. Because of the great difference in the scores between the group tests and the individual Stanford-Binet Scale, the psychologist also gave him the Wechsler-Bellevue on which he achieved an I.Q. of 133. This substantiated the fact that Phil has superior mental ability and through the years should have performed more successfully in school.

During his high-school years, Phil's achievement has been very low. The only classes in which he has made average marks are physical education.

Phil is a retarded reader. During the eighth grade, he scored 5.8 on the Iowa Silent Reading Test. In his senior year, on the Gates Reading Survey, which is a group test, he scored 7.6 in vocabulary, 8.5 in comprehension, and 6.5 in reading speed. This was a group test and certainly does not reflect his true reading ability. On the Gray Oral, he scored 10.5. This is an individual test. On both the Stanford-Binet and Wechsler-Bellevue, he scored very high in comprehension. He refuses to read orally before the group but reads quite satisfactorily in private conferences.

During the past four years, his home-room teachers have made the following comments in the anecdotal records: "Phil has average intelligence but does not apply himself; he is lazy." "He has difficulty with all academic subjects." "He is inclined to blame outside circumstances for his poor marks, which are caused by lack of application." "He feels he is not as smart as other people."

An analysis of Phil's emotional growth is not easy. On the surface, he seems to be very mature emotionally. Teachers for four years have rated him in the superior range in emotional control on the permanent record. On the California Personality Test, on the other hand, taken in the tenth grade, he rated below the 10th percentile in self-reliance, sense of personal worth, feeling of belonging, withdrawing tendencies, and nervous symptoms. The only area under self-adjustment in which he rated as high as average was sense of personal freedom.

I am not enough of a psychologist to analyze this area of Phil's growth in social development. He has no friends in school and is alone most of the time. His classmates pay no attention to him. I mentioned earlier that his presence in class is not noted by the other students, that it is almost as if he were not in the class.

My study of this young man has not led to a clear-cut solution. The image of personal failure that Phil has nurtured seems to be one of the salient factors. To understand how a boy with his intellectual potential has nurtured this image requires the knowledge and skills of the psychologist. That his failure is derived from his inability to adjust to society and that maximum use of his potential cannot be attained until this adjustment has been made seems very clear, however, even to the layman. Psychological help is needed for Phil to make the proper adjustment. Perhaps such help might not have been needed if Phil's problem had been spotted earlier and help had been given him before his senior year.

Perhaps the most significant thing that has come out of my study is showing Phil that he has the native ability to succeed. I was able to interpret to him his strengths, which were demonstrated on the Stanford-Binet and the Wechsler. This, I think, has somewhat increased his confidence in himself. He has volunteered for the first time to contribute to class discussions. His bookkeeping teacher tells me that he is beginning to volunteer in that class, too. His classmates were very surprised at first when he knew the right answers, and they are beginning to develop genuine respect for him.

Phil had the outstanding ability to achieve, but environmental and emotional factors had overshadowed that ability and prevented it from developing. As his teacher released him from the shadows of the past, he was able to move ahead and to begin to find his real self and use his long-buried abilities. His teacher encouraged him to go to night school, even though he was holding down a job, and today Phil is in college, working toward a career commensurate with his ability.

SOLID ACHIEVEMENT VS. BEING "BEST"

There are many ways of achieving besides the more conspicuous ones we usually equate with success—the A on the report card, the school honor roll, the lead in the senior play, the athletic letter on the sweater, the picture on display, the recital at assembly. The emphasis on being the "best" is a hard one to get away from because it is stressed throughout the society in which we live. A child may do an excellent piece of work but feels he has failed because someone else has done better still. So often we say to children, "Let's choose the best picture," "Mary has done the best writing," "Jim is the best speller." This is discouraging to the children who have put real effort into their work but can never seem to reach a place where what they have done is recognized.

Sixth-grade Susan, through hard work and great effort, did two years of reading in one and brought her reading achievement level from third- to fifth-grade standard. But she was crushed and discouraged, and her pleasure in her achievement was destroyed when she received a D in reading on her report card. She still had not achieved her grade level and was marked competitively with the other children. In great discouragement, she turned to her teacher and said, "Can't I ever get an A like the others—no matter how hard I work?"

Yet here was a child who had shown qualities of persistence, good work habits, concentrated effort, and great courage in the face of a big task. Evaluated in terms of her own growth, this experience could have increased her self-confidence and self-respect and provided her with initiative and motivation to go ahead to the limits of her capacity. As a result of the sense of achievement which could have been given to her, she would then have been better able to evaluate gradually her strengths and weaknesses and find the areas in which she could go ahead and those in which she would have to accept certain limitations.

In one classroom in which to be "the best" had become highly important, a new child, Cynthia, was slapped in the face by Annette. Annette's teacher kept a chart on the fifth-grade board on which she put the arithmetic scores for the day, and Annette's name had led all the rest until Cynthia arrived. "I just hate that smarty-cat new girl," Annette was heard to say on the playground.

It would be well for us to remember that children come to school *to learn,* not to compete with their classmates for high grades. The emphasis should be on personal growth —on each child's achievements in competition with his own record and past performance.

THERE ARE DIFFERENCES IN POTENTIAL

When we are working with large groups of children, it is necessary for us to have some objective way of evaluating children's educational needs as compared with their classmates and boys and girls of their age across the country. For this purpose, we use the results of psychological tests, which are devices for gauging an individual's relative standing in traits such as intelligence, aptitude, achievement, and interest. With such objective material to add to the information we gather about a child from his parents, from other teachers, and from our own experience, we are better equipped to know what is the best next step for each child.

WHAT TESTS CAN TELL US

Although we know that tests are not infallible, they remain one of the best tools available to us. Krugman (3) describes psychological tests and discusses their strengths and weaknesses in the following terms:

TESTS MEASURE ACADEMIC LEARNING

In the first place, they can give us a measure of an individual's learning capacity in academic fields, which is usually, although erroneously, called "intelligence." ... Actually the I.Q. measures only a part of the intelligence. It measures the ability to learn abstract and verbal subject matter in school. It does not measure practical or mechanical ability, or the ability to deal with people, or musical ability, art ability, or any of a host of other types of functions that require intelligence of other sorts.

*The skillful chemist can isolate a single element or compound and study it apart from others. Psychology has not as yet developed a method of analysis that can segregate human traits in this way, for human traits simply do not exist alone. Intelligent behavior is colored considerably by emo-*tions, by drives, by the physical condition of the subject, by environmental circumstances, and by many other factors. When we measure intelligence, we must allow for this. Failure to do so, coupled with naïve faith in an I.Q. score as an absolute measure of intelligence, leads us into trouble and is the basis of much of the current misunderstanding on the subject.*

TESTS MEASURE PRACTICAL ABILITY

In the second place, psychological tests can give us a measure of practical ability—another type of intelligence we often forget about. Many children and adults who lack a high degree of abstract intelligence may possess a high degree of concrete or practical intelligence. On the other hand, there is no warrant for assuming that a low abstract capacity is necessarily accompanied by a high practical capacity, as some people do. In fact, good ability in both often go together. For any individual child we must use various tests to find out.

TESTS MEASURE PAST LEARNINGS

A third use of psychological tests is to measure the extent to which an individual has benefited from school instruction and has learned what has been taught him, particularly in such educational fundamentals as reading, spelling, and arithmetic. These achievement tests do not, however, stop with the three R's, but can measure achievement in any field of learning, whether history, geography, higher mathematics, languages, music, or painting.

TESTS MEASURE SPECIAL APTITUDES

Fourth, psychological tests can give us some measure of special aptitudes, such as mechanical, clerical, musical, artistic, engineering, scientific, and many other types of ability. In these fields, however, psychological tests are not yet as highly developed as in some of the others, and we must use them with caution. For example, if a boy has demonstrated great interest and skill in working with tools over a period of years, such a fact would constitute a better measure of mechanical aptitude than a score on any presently known test of mechanical aptitude. The same is true of demonstrated musical ability, particularly when judged by a talented musician. The point is that aptitude tests aim to predict what a child probably will accomplish after he has had training. If the accomplishment has been demonstrated in the life situation, then the further test of ability loses much of its point.

TESTS MEASURE PERSONALITY FACTORS

Psychological tests have been developed in still another field, but with mixed success. In attempting to measure personality and emotional factors, psychologists and others have constructed instruments, a few of which have been successful, notably the Thematic Apperception and Rorschach Tests. Other tests have tried to imitate, by various devices, the techniques of the psychiatrist, and although they appeared logical, most of them have so far failed to produce the intended results. Somehow the essence of the personality eluded the testers. In spite of this such tests are widely used, and some of them are doing much harm. . . .

THE RELATIVE MERITS OF GROUP VS.
INDIVIDUAL TESTS

In view of the earlier statement concerning the limitations of psychological tests, it may seem contradictory to claim that tests are extremely valuable. . . . [But] we should distinguish between individual tests and group tests, as well as between individual tests administered by trained psychologists and those given by others.

Group intelligence and achievement tests —that is, those that can be administered to an entire class at once, or even to larger groups under certain circumstances—have become so much a part of modern school administration that most educators would not do without them today. But, like so many other useful instruments, they can be harmful as well as beneficial, depending upon the way they are used. No educator who understands his business would, for example, rely solely upon an I.Q. score obtained from one such test. He would obtain scores on at least two standard tests and, in addition, use achievement-test scores, teachers' judgments, and other available evidence before coming to a conclusion about a child's ability to do schoolwork. Used in this way group tests serve the double purpose of supplying objective support for more or less subjective judgment, or of indicating that further individual study of the situation is needed.

Even if used in the best possible way, however, the group test does not yield a measure of intelligence. It yields a score that in most cases correlates closely with academic achievement, provided interfering factors are not present. If a child is ill, or emotionally disturbed, or hard of hearing, his school achievement or his test score may not fairly represent his capacity. One can readily see how important it is to investigate significant disagreements between test scores and schoolwork. . . . Group intelligence tests could be more properly called academic aptitude tests. . . .

Individual intelligence tests are another matter. These highly specialized instruments are designed for use only by trained clinical psychologists. . . . The I.Q. is the least important of the results of adequate psychological testing. It is only a convenient rough approximation of a composite estimate of many types of abilities. Two individuals with identical I.Q. scores are not identical in their "intelligence"; they may not even be remotely similar. The many abilities that go to make up the blanket score known as the I.Q. must be analyzed and interpreted. To assess an individual's intelligence, an intensive clinical study of the particular child is required; and in a clinical situation the I.Q. test is almost never used alone. A great many procedures are employed to supplement it, and much supporting evidence is obtained for the final interpretation. . . .

THE DANGERS OF AN "I.Q. LABEL"

Kuhlen (4) writes about the "damage that may be done a person by parents or school authorities who shape his educational program or otherwise react to him in terms of an IQ label." He points out that:

TEMPORARY HANDICAPS MAY AFFECT THE IQ SCORE

One source of differences in IQ is to be found in variations with time in the same individual. A child may be shy and blocked on one occasion, and expansive and coöperative on another. Or a temporary environmental handicap may be later removed, or some basic skill deficiency later corrected. A reading disability, for example, may limit a child on one occasion and handicap him in the test; several years later the reading handicap may have been overcome and his test performance (especially on a verbal group test) greatly improved. Special limitations of opportunity may result in lower performance on one occasion, with improved performance following some years after these limitations have been removed.

ENVIRONMENT AND BACKGROUND MAY ALSO AFFECT THE SCORE

. . . a basic assumption in intelligence testing is that the individuals tested must have had equal opportunity to learn in the course of their daily lives the kinds of things intelligence-test questions call for. Although slight variations in background are not crucial, standard intelligence tests may be quite inappropriate for use with a child of extremely meager background, or with one of foreign background who has not yet adequately mastered the English language.

Some current effort in test construction is being directed toward the development of a "culture-free" intelligence test. But the cultural influence is so subtle and all-pervasive that it will be extremely difficult to do more than reduce somewhat, rather than completely eliminate, the role it plays in test performance.

A SINGLE TEST SCORE DOES NOT TELL THE WHOLE STORY

. . . growth patterns in measured intelligence for individuals are highly variable. Those who make practical use of test scores should take special note of these findings. Judgments of intelligence in schools, mental-hygiene clinics, and courts are frequently made on the basis of a single test score and that often (in schools at least) several years old. The planning of programs for individuals on such bases is obviously extremely dangerous. The importance of basing judgments on cumulative records, not only of measured ability, but of achievement and general adjustment is self-evident. . . .

ERROR EXISTS IN ALL TYPES OF MEASUREMENT

Error exists in all types of measurements. IQ's have been found to vary over five points in one third of the cases on short term retests (Stanford-Binet); and over the developmental period, from two to eighteen years, differences as great as fifty IQ points have been reported, with differences of over thirty IQ points occurring in 10 per cent of the cases. Users of tests obviously cannot make the assumption that a particular IQ represents a stable index of ability.

Kuhlen goes on to say:

Tagging a child with an IQ label may do him damage even though he, himself, does not know how he rates. A teacher, for example, may neglect a child who has earned a low IQ, considering his low performance in school work to be an inevitable result of *his low ability and thus effort expended in helping him as simply wasted effort. . . . But even a correct low IQ is hardly a justifiable basis for ignoring a child educationally; actually such an individual is perhaps more in need of attention, though efforts might be of a different kind and pointed in different directions than would be true of the average child. Bad also is the situation where the parent is aware of an offspring's*

high IQ (perhaps 140) and then sets out to groom him for genius! Constant pressures to succeed, constant reminding the child of his high ability, may result in unfortunate overspecialization at a young age, or frustration because of expectations that are too high, or may result in the development of socially obnoxious behavior patterns in a child overly conscious of his high IQ.

WE CAN FOSTER A SENSE OF ACHIEVEMENT BY—

RECOGNIZING THAT THERE ARE MANY KINDS OF EXCELLENCE

We know comparatively little about those children we call "nonverbal"—the boys and girls who have a hard time learning to read or who find it difficult to express themselves fluently with words. These youngsters often develop a feeling of failure because they find themselves inadequate in the classroom situation in which the use of words determines to such a large degree one's feelings of success or failure. But these boys and girls and those who, for a variety of reasons, are less able to do well academically in the classroom may have other potential avenues of success.

Some boys and girls, regardless of I.Q. level, have warm, friendly personalities that draw other youngsters to them. These children can be helped to learn the art of leadership and can get recognition for the way in which they lead or help others. We tend to underestimate the value of skill with the hands—one child may do excellent work in sewing, another in shop, a third in cooking. Still another youngster may be able to use his hands efficiently in cleaning up—in stacking books and papers neatly—and can find success in performing necessary housekeeping tasks well. A boy who

lags behind in his schoolwork may do wonders with the insides of a car or a broken piece of machinery. Many a boy who feels inadequate in his schoolwork has contributed by his competence in running the projector when films are shown in the classroom. One little girl gained recognition by bringing her camera to school and taking and developing wonderful pictures. Still another child grew beautiful flowers around the school building.

There are boys and girls who are not high on the honor roll who have stability, carefulness, and common sense in practical situations—qualities that can make them excellent patrol members or bus monitors. There are limitless ways of achieving, and we can help each child to have pride and respect for something he has done if our own horizons are wide enough to put value on a job well done and if we can learn to admit that excellence is possible in many ways.

Miss Hanson tried to help the children in her classroom understand that there are many ways of learning and of making a contribution. "Some of us learn to read rapidly and easily; others may learn more slowly. Each has his own way." She did not put the value on who did it "best"—but on those who tried hard, who made steady progress, who had good work habits. She did not put on display only the work that was "best," but found something each child could contribute to a project, to a mural, or to an exhibit. In order to do this, she searched for the interest of each child, for she felt that every child had something to contribute. She says, "A sense of personal achievement has been built through providing 'interest spots' to which children can go, when required work is completed, and work at something of absorbing interest to them personally. Giving children special recognition when they have legitimately done a good piece of work pays dividends. A good picture, a fine finger painting, clever construction with the big blocks or the Tinker Toys always brings special recognition in our class. So does good care of the aquarium or the plants, or help in straightening up the books, or doing a good job of cleaning the chalkboard."

We give honors in our high schools to those who are academically talented and are at the top of the group in grades. Why not honors in Vocational courses? Why not honors in Commercial studies? Why not honors in the General Course or in Home Economics? Excellence is possible for many children in these areas. But because we are verbal and because we hang on to the old tradition of the academic high-school diploma, we often value only ability of the academic kind. We say in essence to the other children, "No matter how hard you work, you'll never get anywhere." How can we hope that these other boys and girls will have pride in themselves and do "excellently" what they *can* do? We often downgrade the child who has lived up to his fullest potential, and we raise to high honors the child who may not be working anywhere near his capacity. This is not to say that honors should not be given to those who are academically gifted. The objection here is the failure to recognize other kinds of excellence in those whose academic gifts are not so high.

GROUPING SO THAT ALL CHILDREN CAN ACHIEVE

In most elementary schools and some of our junior and senior high schools, thoughtful attention is given to the grouping of children within the classroom, so that each child may have a chance to learn at his own rate and within the area of his own readiness and ability. Yet in spite of this wise planning, children are constantly exposed to pressures and failures that sap their confidence and prevent them from performing up to their ability.

Our attitude toward grouping is important, whether we are grouping the children within our classroom or are teaching youngsters in homogeneous classes. Sometimes we do not show the same concern and interest in all of our groups. One teacher who did excellent work with the first two groups in her class remarked after a conference with her supervisor, "This is the first time I have realized that it is worth bothering with the students who are slow learners. I never stopped before to think how they feel about it." Sometimes by our attitude and the remarks we make, we put the emphasis on being in the "top" group without realizing what we are doing.

A child cannot be helped to respect himself if he is constantly made to feel that the group in which he has been placed, because of the level of his ability or achievement, is inferior. Another teacher used groupings as an incentive to do better. She would say to a child in the lowest group, "If you work hard, you'll be able to get up with the good readers." Naturally, the youngster felt that his position in the lowest group was an unfortunate one—one to be escaped from, if possible. But what if it is not possible? What if the youngster is a child whose capacity will never permit him to go beyond the lowest reading group? Is he to be made to feel that he is a failure in the eyes of his teacher and in the eyes of his classmates—"a dumb kid"—because he can never pass into the next group? A teacher who wants to help each child live up to his capacity will avoid putting a stigma upon membership in any group within the classroom.

Jersild (5) was asked by the American Psychiatric Association to set down the current thinking about class grouping in elementary schools, since psychiatrists are often consulted about the type of groups most conducive to healthy child growth:

GROUPING OF SOME KIND IS NECESSARY

The problem of grouping is a perennial one at school. For convenience and economy some kind of grouping usually is necessary even in teaching things that might best be learned through individual instruction. Parents and teachers have assumed for many generations that there at least should be grouping according to our conventional grade levels. Most people take such grouping for granted as though it belonged in the nature of things. In addition, many school people have assumed that it is good to have sub-groups within grades on the theory that children learn better in homogeneous groups than in heterogeneous groups.

Actually, homogeneous grouping is impossible unless we conceive of education in narrow terms or look at children from a very fractional point of view. . . .

COMPLETELY HOMOGENEOUS GROUPING IS IMPOSSIBLE

Children who are homogeneous according to one criterion are likely, of course, to be quite heterogeneous in other respects. In a sampling of one hundred randomly selected children of the same chronological age there may be differences of six or seven years or more in mental age. If we select children who are similar both in chronological and mental age, there still will be wide differences in skeletal age, and if the group consists of high school children, there may be differences of as much as six or seven years in the ages at which the fastest and slowest maturing child has reached or will reach sexual maturity. If children are se-

lected to be similar not only in chronological and mental age but also in skeletal age and sexual maturity, there would still be a vast amount of heterogeneity in emotional or social maturity, practical information, common sense, self-understanding, moral judgment, ability to carry responsibility, and in numerous special talents and aptitudes. The more we see the child at school as an all-around person the more hopeless it becomes to achieve a fixed form of homogeneous grouping.

GROUPING ONLY IN TERMS OF BRIGHTNESS CAN DO GREAT HARM

. . . Now we cannot blink at the fact that some children are by nature much brighter than others as measured by intelligence tests or various forms of verbal achievement. But we go beyond a realistic recognition of this when we label the pupil's personality as a whole on the basis of a limited criterion of mental ability and consign him to a "gifted" or "average" or "slow-learning" group. Many of the "average" or "slow-learning" children may equal or surpass many of the so-called "gifted" children in a variety of other important qualities and aptitudes.

GROUPING SHOULD NOT BE USED AS PUNISHMENT

Also, the practical problem of grouping cannot be solved if it is colored by moral condemnation such as is the case when we hold a pupil back in the same grade for a second year because we want to punish him. We can even hear teachers or neighbors say of a child that "it serves him right" to be kept back. This tendency to think of grouping in moral terms is very widespread although it is not always recognized. Goodness is often confused with brightness and badness with stupidity. Teachers who are frustrated in their attempts to teach a child something are often tempted to view failure to learn as a moral wrong and to blame the child for being so stupid, as though he were deliberate about it. Sometimes, of course, failure to learn might be a form of moral weakness as when a child shirks or tries to get by through cheating. But even such a troubled child probably won't profit from moral condemnation, nor do children of this type justify a kind of grouping which directly or by implication gives large numbers of children who are doing their best the idea that they have failed or belong to an inferior group and should feel guilty about it.

Grouping should not be used as a means of punishment but as a means of helping each child to achieve optimum conditions for learning in a manner that is most convenient to all concerned, including the learner himself. A review of the literature by Adolph Sandin points out that the time-honored practice of nonpromotion generally does not achieve the avowed purpose of helping the nonpromoted child to "catch up" in his academic work. Nonpromoted children are likely to continue to be backward in their academic work and they probably will create as much trouble for other pupils in the younger class they are assigned to as they would create if they moved along with their own age-mates.

GROUPING SHOULD BE FLEXIBLE

The more grouping is designed as far as possible to achieve optimum conditions for learning for all children, the more likely it is that within a school of any size there will be considerable flexibility and variety. To help the child to gain in academic skill may require one kind of grouping, to help him to cultivate a talent for music or mechanics or woodcraft or nature lore may require other groupings. Within a class of thirty children there may actually be a dozen or more variously overlapping "groups" even when the children are continually together. Youngsters who need little or no instruction in reading may be busy on separate individual or group projects while other pupils read, but these children may in another grouping at another time get a great deal of instruction in music or in the graphic arts or social skills.

Grouping so designed will also permit, as far as is practicable, a certain amount of migration within the school and within the community as when a pupil plays in the orchestra, participates in outside nature study, or leaves his class to spend time with a science club or a hobby group.

Moreover, some groupings may even be formed for the sake of increasing heterogeneity. A recent study by A. W. Foshay of an "interage" class consisting of children from grades four, five and six indicated that such a grouping might have many values that need to be further explored. In the meantime, in most schools (other than small rural schools) grouping according to chronological age is probably the fairest and most wholesome solution. Such a policy can still allow leeway for some flexibility and variety. It will permit children with varying patterns and amounts of ability to find a place for themselves without being officially labelled and segregated as superior or inferior persons on the basis of a very one-sided appraisal of their worth.

In other words, flexibility of grouping and curriculum are essential if each child is to have a sense of achievement. One cannot use the same curriculum for all the children in the same grade, even if slow and fast learners are grouped homogeneously. Neither can one teach successfully if the ability and achievement span are too wide.

As Jersild has pointed out, there are many ways in which we can group boys and girls effectively for different purposes, either in the classroom or across classroom groups. Much consideration is being given today to the "teachable" group in which there would be enough differences within a classroom in ability, interests, and background experiences to make for a lively and stimulating interplay between the children without a wide spread in basic ability. Such a "teachable" group might contain children with an I.Q. spread of approximately 30 I.Q. points, instead of the wide spread of as many as 100 I.Q. points between the slowest and the most academically gifted youngster that is now found in many classes. If we keep a flexible attitude toward grouping, there are many variations we can work out to the benefit of the children in any given classroom or total school situation.

USING COMPETITION WISELY

It is often said that competition is necessary in the classroom because children will live in a competitive world. Such a statement does not take into consideration two points: (1) children must experience success before they can take competition, and (2) adults compete in many areas, with many standards.

CHILDREN MUST EXPERIENCE SUCCESS BEFORE THEY CAN TAKE COMPETITION

If the child is helped to have sufficient experience with success as he is growing up and is helped toward a self-evaluation that keeps his self-confidence and self-respect intact, he will be prepared to meet and evaluate the competition of the adult world. Competition too soon and too frequent, in which the child is consistently "the one who loses out," destroys his self-confidence and prevents him from meeting adult competition in a mature way. Competition too soon, competition that is destructive to the picture a child has of himself, is poor preparation for life in a competitive world.

If we use competitive methods in our classroom, we must consider the age of the children we are teaching. The ability to take competition increases with age. A little child of two or three is not really conscious of competition in relation to another person. He may feel unhappy or jealous if his mother shows affection to another child. He is focused on what he wants, not on the other person involved. He wants his moth-er's full attention or he wants Billy's wagon, which is prettier than his, so he pulls it away from Billy, but he has no real feelings about Billy in the matter. He does not say to himself, "Billy is better than I am—he has a better wagon." "I want this" is all he realizes and he takes the most direct way of getting it.

By the time a child is four or five, he begins to measure himself against other children. He notices and comments on the fact that his picture isn't as pretty as Mary's— "This old picture isn't any good. Mary's man looks like a man!" and he may tear his up or scribble all over it. Comparisons between the self and other people begin to be more prevalent between four and six years of age. The young child, when asked whose picture is the prettiest, usually says "mine." The older child begins to evaluate his own work and is also able to see beauty in that of another child.

The ability to take real competition comes slowly. Six-, seven-, and even eight-year-olds are still so centered on themselves, so engrossed in learning how to get along with other children and finding their place in the larger school world, that they have little emotional leeway left for competition or criticism that seems to lessen their opinion of themselves. The drive to "win," to be "first," is so great and seems such an integral part of the development of a picture of themselves they can like that many of these primary-age children will be easily pushed into cheating, using alibis, or failing to observe rules of the game if this is the only way they can win or come out on top. *Young children must have many experiences with success before they are able to live comfortably with failure.*

The Gesell Institute (6) discusses competition in this way:

The average competitive, egocentric six-year-old has not yet acquired or developed either the ability to lose at competitive games or a full, practical realization of the wrongness of cheating. Put him in a competitive situation and more often than not, if he is losing, he will cheat to win. The response is almost automatic. He needs to be flexible in a game, to change the rules in midstream, if necessary. But he must win, or he crumbles all to pieces or strikes out with ferocity. . . . He'll learn to lose in time, but by slow stages.

Cheating is actually a matter of great interest to the six-year-old, but most children at that age have come only far enough to be concerned about the cheating of others. They are quick to complain about their playmates, "Lila's cheating!" but they themselves, alas, are equally quick to cheat if they need to do so in order to win.

Things improve by slow degrees in the years which follow. By eight or nine the average child, if not pitted against opponents too greatly skilled, can usually play games without cheating. Eventually, even by nine years of age, he may begin to learn that "the game's the thing" (though he loses this insight in a few years and then later regains it again).

Cheating of another sort in lessons or examinations in school is usually not, in ordinary cases, a severe problem in the first ten years—due largely to lack of skill on the part of the cheater before the pre-teen years.

In one school cheating rose in a class of children of varying levels of ability as the significance of examination results were stressed. The child who knows he can pass an exam does not have the same incentive to cheat as the child who is less competent and knows that if he fails, he may not be promoted or may get a severe scolding at home. In such cases, the competition is unfair and unequal. The expectations of the adults are not reasonable.

One teacher who was very skillful in handling both competitive feelings and the use of competition in her sixth-grade classroom put her experiences with the use of competition into these words:

Competition used wisely between equals—individuals or balanced groups—may be a temporary incentive. When it is overemphasized or used as the primary incentive or to try to force a child to learn, it is rarely effective. If it is effective, the by-products of tension, sense of lack of achievement, perfectionism may destroy the results. To get an A, to be "the best," then becomes the primary objective rather than the acquiring of knowledge. The motivation and interest is often less. The goal —to find out for a purpose—is overlooked in the competitive struggle. "This is the thing to do" is pushed aside for "This will make me win."

In fair competition, whether in the classroom or on the playground, a youngster should have at least a sporting chance to win. A good tennis game, an old-fashioned spelling bee, a boxing match, a swimming contest, or a race can be fine sport and fun between near equals. Competition can be used on the playground in games and team sports, but if being chosen for the team becomes the major goal of the competition, then it can rob children of the fun and good sport they should have in games. If teams are always chosen "to win" so that being "best" or "good enough" is always at a high premium, the child who cannot run fast or throw a ball well feels left out and unwanted. Even more serious, he may become the object of angry taunts for having "lost the race" or having "kept the side from winning the game." He may hear far too often the whispered or even outspoken comment—"We don't want him on our side." It is going to become very difficult for such a child not to develop serious feelings of inferiority, which may stay with him all through his life.

It is a tough experience to be left standing while everyone else is chosen until you alone are picked last every time. A child who has this experience may be the very one who is most in need of team sports and some fun in games with other children, yet he is likely to turn away to more solitary pursuits rather than be humiliated time and again. There is a place for choosing sides, but this method should not be used in all games to the detriment of those children who are "chosen" unwillingly.

In the same way, an emphasis upon a winning team for the school can destroy the value of physical activities for the very children who need them.

Paul was a loyal member of the baseball team in the after school recreational program of his community. Every afternoon and on Saturday mornings, he was out there working hard and rooting for his side. When the teams were chosen to play neighboring schools, skill and winning were emphasized. You had to be good to play on the first team. Paul made the second. Still he went out, hoping against hope that he would have a chance to play, but he sat on the sidelines game after game. Other boys from the second team were allowed to substitute, but not Paul. Game after game, he came listlessly home, disappointed. "I guess I'm no good," he told his mother. Finally, the big play-off game came. The team from Paul's school was to play at the big Saturday field day. Paul gulped down his breakfast, picked up his mitt, and could hardly wait to get to school. The second team was to go along as substitutes, and Paul in his heart still hoped. Half an hour later, a dejected little boy came home. The bus wasn't big enough to take everyone, so the teacher had sent five small boys home with a "Sorry, boys, but we've got to take the good ones this time."

Competitive sports with an emphasis on the "best" team do not belong in the elementary school. Competition can be fun, but teams should be mixed so that every child feels that he is part of the program and has a chance to play. This is pointed up by Reichert (7) in an article in *The Journal of the American Medical Association:*

Opinions differ as to the intensity of competition that should be allowed to develop in athletics for children under the age of 13. A child induced to participate in highly competitive sports that imitate adult patterns is subjected to severe physical and emotional strains, and these sometimes profoundly affect his subsequent physical growth and social development. Especially in interscholastic and intercommunity championship games, with uniforms, parades, prizes, and publicity, and with the possibility of vicarious glorification of parent and school, the psychological responses of all concerned can be abnormal in many ways. . . . Competition must be recognized as normal and desirable in growing children, but it must be kept within bounds.

Similarly, if there is to be an emphasis on the "best" in high school, there should also be an intra-school program that brings in all the children, not just those who are capable of making the "varsity" team.

ADULTS COMPETE IN MANY AREAS, WITH MANY STANDARDS

In the adult world, we do not ask the unskilled person to compete with the highly skilled. For instance, when civil service examinations are given, they are given within areas dependent upon a special skill. The man who will operate an elevator is not given the same examination as the man who will work in a scientific laboratory. But in the classroom, we too often take the child who will become the elevator operator and set the same standards of achievement for him as we do for the boy who will become the scientist—and give the grade of D or failure to the "elevator operator" while we give an A to the scientist-to-be. A child cannot develop the sense of achievement that leads to self-confidence if he is exposed year in and year out to unfair competition in the classroom.

Competition that results in verbal comparisons between children involves the personal element and often results in feelings of rivalry and jealousy. "She likes

Johnnie's work better than mine" comes to mean too often to the child, "She likes Johnnie better than me." The exhortation to a class to "do as neat work as Ted does" overlooks the fact that many of the children in the classroom can never do as neat work as Ted because their coordination is not as good. But they can improve their own work and receive credit for such improvement. Ted's father was a draftsman and had taught Ted, who did have excellent coordination, to make careful line drawings. Miss North was impressed with these drawings and showed them to the class, saying, "Ted does such beautifully neat and careful drawings. I wish you could all draw like this." Her obvious preference for the kind of work Ted could do set a standard that was impossible for the others to achieve. As a result, Sandy, who had loved to paint in sweeping colorful lines stopped painting altogether in the classroom and looked at his own work as "just that junk." Miss North could have given credit to Ted's drawings without disparaging the others. She could have chosen one child's picture because of its color, another because of a creative idea, another for the feeling the child had put across, and Ted's to show another kind of drawing, which a draftsman needs. She could have talked about using different ways of expressing what we want to show.

We are also beginning to find that when a school system has more than the usual proportion of academically talented children in the school group, there is a tendency for the total school program to be so accelerated that the average child is penalized. Unfortunately, in some areas, children of average intelligence seem to be falling into disrepute—neither their parents nor their teachers are satisfied with them. Because the teachers are working with a large number of especially gifted children, the work of the average youngster often seems poor in comparison, and D's and E's begin to appear on a report card that would have borne C's and some B's in a more normal school situation. Because of the emphasis on the gifted learner, many fine, average boys and girls—*and this group constitutes two thirds of our children*—are being crippled in their progress through school and made to feel inadequate and of less worth than the gifted learner. This is a serious situation and warrants a careful scrutiny of the curriculum, examinations, and grading policies of any school in which the median I.Q. is warped in the direction of the academically gifted.

When a school system speaks with pride that the boys and girls are achieving at a year above the national average, care must be taken to see that the boy or girl who should have a sense of real achievement if he accomplishes the normal work of the grade is not made to feel that he is a laggard and a nonachiever. The average child should have the satisfaction and recognition on his report card and in the eyes of his parents and friends that he is doing good work when he does the work of his grade; he should not be made to feel that his work is poor because he is not keeping up with those who can work a year ahead. This is a false emphasis and a dangerous one if our schools are to be concerned with the welfare and development of the potential in every child. It is our task to see that every child is given the opportunity to respect himself and to develop a picture of himself as one who can do well—not as one who fails because someone else is more adequately endowed and can do better.

BEING VERY CAREFUL IN THE WAYS WE EVALUATE ACHIEVEMENT

Reporting to students and parents is one of the most important tasks of a teacher, for it is through reporting that the student and the parent get either a realistic picture of the youngster's achievement or a warped one. A report can discourage, overinflate, or be really helpful to a child. There are many kinds of reports used in different school systems in the country. The classroom teacher usually has little choice as to the kind of report she can make, but she *can* confer with parents and children to interpret the report to them in such a way that it will be a help rather than a hindrance to the child's progress.

THE REPORT CARD

The traditional method of reporting student progress, still used widely in many school systems, is based on the standing of children in relation to their classmates. It does not sufficiently take into account what we know about the individual differences between children. It places the child who learns rapidly and easily in an advantageous position and the average youngster or the child who is slower and less well-endowed intellectually in an undesirable one. The competition is not fair, and it is no wonder that after a while the average or slow learner may give up the race, accept the inferior position that has been handed to him, and fail to develop the potentialities he has.

One of the first steps toward truancy from school and sometimes subsequent delinquent behavior is the feeling of frustration and failure a child has met with in school. To the child, there seems to be nothing in it for him. Why should he go to school, day after day, to be made to feel dumb and stupid? Outside of school, he can often prove his worth as a real guy by pulling off stunts for the gang and showing he isn't "chicken." A child must compensate somehow. Or sometimes a youngster will become discouraged with the constant failure and simply say, as one sixth-grader did, "I can't do it. I can't read sixth-grade books like the others. I just can't."

Teachers often say that the parents demand competitive evaluation. This is certainly true in many situations. But it is most frequently true when parents have not been helped to understand the needs of children, the differences between them, and what a report card can be expected to do.

PARENT–TEACHER CONFERENCES AND DESCRIPTIVE REPORTS

The school systems that have taken the time to help parents understand what a real report from the school to the home can do have usually found that the majority of the parents, particularly in the elementary school, come to look with very real favor on parent conferences and descriptive reports, which give them an opportunity for greater understanding of their child and his progress, as well as his standing in the class.

The fact that a school system uses parent conferences and reports that evaluate each child as an individual does not mean that a parent or a child does not know where the child is in comparison with the other children of his age. This information can be put into words in a conference or in a written report, but the way it is presented and interpreted will determine its value in the growth of the child. Children quickly evaluate their position in the class. Whether groups are labeled one-two-three or A-B-C or Bluebirds, Larks, and Chick-a-dees, a youngster knows whether he is a good reader or a poor one. These facts cannot be kept from children—nor is it wise to try to cover them up. It is rather the attitude of the teacher and the parents toward such facts that is important. When they are accepted in a matter-of-fact way, as part of a realistic situation, and evaluated as something that must be taken into account in planning for the child, then a child can be helped to go ahead.

CHILDREN CAN EVALUATE THEIR OWN STRENGTHS AND WEAKNESSES

Conferences with children, whether little first-graders or high-school youngsters, in which they try to evaluate their own work objectively and talk over with us their doubts and problems as well as their strengths, are valuable, too. Such conferences help children see what they are doing in the present and are often the beginning of a wholesome attitude of self-appraisal that can be carried forward into other life situations.

Phil's teacher helped him evaluate himself in her conferences with him. These conferences, based on his answers to the tests that had been given to him, marked a turning point in Phil's understanding of himself. He began to see himself for the first time as a person who had potentialities. At the same time, he realistically acknowledged the fact that he had a severe handicap in his lack of mastery of certain important skills that he needed if he was to go ahead with the work he wanted to do.

Success in such conferences is possible, however, only if the child approaches them without tensions or anxiety. If a child has had experiences with us that make him trust us as a counselor, if we have shown appreciation for his efforts, if we have given encouragement and discovered strengths, we can usually help him recognize weaknesses.

An honest self-evaluation must also be based on an examination of *personal growth,* not on a comparison with others in the classroom. Such comparisons not only harm the child whose capacity is limited but can also be destructive to the child who is always rated as "best." A child who achieves an A without real effort on his part often develops a false self-evaluation; he fails to develop good work habits and rarely experiences the satisfaction of achieving through effort. Conversely, it is hard to help a child to an honest self-evaluation if he has been so constantly exposed to competitive situations in which he could not succeed that he doubts his capacity ever to achieve.

Children of elementary-school age are often afraid that they will not be able to live up to the standards set by their parents and teachers, that they will be found wanting and unworthy. They are in conflict about themselves as they begin to measure and compare themselves against other boys and girls and set standards for their own achievement. If we understand the way

children feel about these things and the comparisons they themselves are making, we will try to plan so that every child in our classroom has experiences of success. In this way, we will be able to help him accept failure better when it comes his way, as come it will to every child. Each child, even a very slow-learning child, should be helped to see that he has both strengths and limitations.

As we help a child evaluate his own growth, we help him assume some responsibility for the direction in which he grows. Allen (8) says that as he grows the child, too, has a part to play in building himself. He "must become a living participant in achieving a feeling of his own worth."

AVOIDING UNWISE PRESSURE

Many children fail to achieve because they are under too much pressure from their parents or from their teacher or from anxieties and concerns that are keeping their minds from focusing on their work. Rita Del Cello was a youngster who could have been helped to learn to read if her teacher had been willing to give her time to adjust to school, get used to a new situation, and grow up a bit. But her teacher was in a hurry and Rita suffered.

I saw Rita for the first time three summers ago, when her parents moved into the apartment next to mine. Rita was then almost five. She was leading her little sister, who was three years old, across the street protectively. Rita and her sister wandered off to join a group of children who were playing together in the little park across the street from the apartment house. Both children entered immediately into the activities of the group. I watched them and I observed that they were able to communicate with this group of children as though they had all been good friends. This is the real essence of Rita's personality—her sociable and generous nature. She looked like a cherub, with such full, rosy cheeks. She was a healthy and happy child, delighted with any suggestion of doing things.

When Rita entered first grade for the first time, she had much enthusiasm for this new experience and anticipated having a continual session of fun and play. Her reading readiness test showed that she was an average youngster—ready for first-grade reading experiences. But she was not sufficiently prepared for school. Her parents were wonderfully warm, generous, happy, fun-loving human beings, who, in addition to the necessities of life, provided for their children an abundance of social activities that included a variety of parties, weddings, and even funerals. They could be found present at any gathering of a social nature, and so Rita found herself continually thrust into a social situation of one kind or another. Rita and her family spent much of the week socializing, with no regular time for meals or rest. For them, life was very gay, and the social aspects of life were the most important of all. The father was warm, kindly, and easygoing. His discipline was practically nonexistent, or rather, it vacillated between occasional stern discipline and sublime indifference. Language was used in the home only for conversation. The parents read no books, neither did they read to the children. The vocabulary of the family was limited and the speech was full of colloquialisms and bad grammar. Rita had never learned to apply herself to a given task at a given time because such behavior was not expected of her at home. Her experiences had not enabled her to be ready for the learning process and the self-discipline involved in a classroom situation.

A year later, Rita was still in the first grade, a repeater because of her inability to learn to read. She had become a behavior problem, disturbing and interrupting other children and her teacher at school, while at home her unhappiness showed in unwarranted attacks on the little sister whom she used to take care of so protectingly. She disregarded her parents' wishes, and her former cheeriness and good nature disappeared.

This change began when Rita's first first-grade teacher sent home a critical note, with the suggestion that Rita needed sterner discipline and she believed that the child's reading difficulties would be resolved if her mother and father spent more time reading with her. She sent some books home for added practice. She said in her note that the class had read from a new book that day, and she had found that Rita had memorized her previous book, so that it appeared that she could read, but that she was unable to recognize the same words in another book. This meant that she was really far behind the other children.

The parents were deeply upset. Until this time, they had not realized that Rita was having any trouble at school. They had been proud of her when she brought home her primer and had rattled quickly through it as if she could read every word. They had realized that she was anxious about something but had passed it by as nothing. She had cried one day and asked, "Do you think I'll pass this year?" They had reassured her that she was a "real smart little girl"—and then this note had come.

Rita's parents are not educated people and have great respect for the school and education. Neither had attended school beyond the elementary-school level. Both, on occasions, have expressed regret for their own academic shortcomings but have indicated great expectations for their children. So when the note came from school, they accepted it without question and tried to follow the teacher's suggestions. They decided sterner discipline was needed and that this was Daddy's responsibility. They decided that immediately after supper, Rita was to read for an hour with her mother, while Daddy's persuasive shadow remained over the situation just in case of faltering.

This new regime changed nothing. The pressures that were put upon the child resulted in friction and hostility between parents and child, where before, there had been fun and enjoyment. It must have seemed to Rita that she was being punished for her inability to read and so she thrashed out against the world.

No one seemed to understand that Rita was asking for help. Now almost two years later, the real problem of teaching Rita to read remains to be worked out. At present, she is still not reading up to grade level. She cries frequently and will hurl her book in anger across the room. "I hate to read" she will sob and run from the room and angrily bang the door. She still has not gone beyond the book she was reading at the time her first teacher sent home the note. She is still struggling with the beginnings. This year, her new teacher is more understanding, and Rita's difficult behavior in school is much less frequent. She is beginning to like school a bit better again—but the reading block still remains.

Rita's first teacher was right. The youngster did need more help in learning to apply herself and conform to some of the school requirements. She was right that the youngster needed someone to read to her and to listen to her as she tried to read. But what went wrong? Her request to the parents boomeranged, for she did not understand the family at all, and Rita felt hurt and rejected when her gay, kindly parents, in their anxiety, became suddenly severe and punishing. She did not learn better; instead, her ability to learn was greatly lessened.

There are all kinds of ways of meeting pressures. Some children, like Rita, show anxiety and strain by building a block against learning. And there are some like Nels Swanson, who adjust to demands by going their own way and refusing to respond to the pressure. Mr. Nixon, his homeroom teacher, tells us about Nels:

Nels is a boy with a lot of vitality for living—but not for learning. He is a junior in high school now, but in spite of an I.Q. of 150, he has had only two grades above C since the eighth grade.

He has a very pleasant disposition, nice mannerisms, and is very polite in class. He ambles down the hall without visible signs of study or work materials. He wears a big grin and recognizes his friends and teachers with a nod and a wave. He seems to enjoy being in school and has a better-than-average attendance record. He is usually one of the last to enter the classroom because he enjoys talking to others so much. In classes that have activities, he is always with others; he seems to crave and enjoy attention, someone to be with. He places companionship and social adjustment above his studies.

In class he is polite and cooperative and is not a discipline problem. But I recall plans for many projects in biology that Nels never put into action. Numerous projects were started and never completed; he preferred to help others and to talk. If asked to do something specific for someone else or for me, he would work very well and show real ability. At other times, he would just fool around, seemingly enjoying himself and just having fun. He would frequently offer to give oral reports. But when the day came to give them, he was either absent or he would say, "Oh! I forgot— honest I did, Mr. Nixon, but I will do it yet." He never came through—never gave the reports. He could have been a good student, capable of doing A work. He seemed interested in biology, but was just lazy. He would forget his books, pencil, paper —usually he was never prepared to work.

Yet, from his conversation, I knew he was not living up to his capacity. Then on looking up his record, I found out that he had the intelligence but wasn't using it.

The comments from some of his other teachers show the way they felt about him.

"Lazy. Prefers to sleep, even though he says he must pass English to graduate."

"Nels has a noncommittal attitude in math. Should do straight A work. Likes to talk."

"Could be an A student but is just lazy."

"Pleasant, cooperative, mentally lazy. May I suggest re-testing for this fellow. Also, he needs good guidance urgently."

"Either his I.Q. is incorrect or something is wrong!"

"Has improved in his Spanish, but could do much more. He is still lazy and does not exert himself. He only does what he has to do to pass the subject. He failed it last year."

Nels' mother came to see me because I had sent word home that Nels would barely get by. She told me of the problems that were concerning her and his father—his failure to do tasks he dislikes or to complete something he starts if he loses interest. They want Nels to be a lawyer like his father and "follow in his father's footsteps," later joining his father's law firm. But Nels wants to be an architect. The new office buildings of glass and steel fascinate him. He goes down into the city to watch them being put up. Since he has already shown some real ability in both design and mechanics, this would seem better than forcing him to be a lawyer against his wishes. But his mother would not discuss this; she was just not interested. Her parting words were, "Be sure to make him work, because we can do little with him."

Here we have a seemingly gifted boy, who is accomplishing very little, except that he is a member of the group. Yet he has much in his favor. Perhaps when he gets away from home and starts working on the things where his real interests lie, he may become motivated to use his capabilities and make some very worth-while contributions to our society.

Maureen Grady was a very different kind of child. She was so highly ambitious that she drove herself too hard, and the pressure to achieve her best almost became too much for her. One of her teachers tells us:

Maureen is a quiet, charming, lovely girl who is extremely ambitious. She wishes to please everyone. She is a talented dancer and puts in many hours practicing her techniques. At the same time, she is an excellent student in all her other subjects. Her I.Q. is 135.

She is a rather tense little girl who does not give vent to her emotions except through her dancing. She has had several serious illnesses and has shown some concern when she has talked with me about her health, not getting enough sleep, and missing too much school because she has been ill. She is well-liked by both boys and girls. She has expressed concern that she does not have enough time for fun and play. She worries a lot when she makes a mistake. Her standards are so high that even small mistakes upset her. She does work over again if she is not satisfied with it.

She is a delight to teach. She is very eager to learn. She is full of questions and brings in interesting material to report on in the classroom. It is a joy to watch her eagerness. She does not do as well as one would expect on tests. I notice a definite tenseness about her when she is taking a test. But she is without a doubt an outstanding student in the field which I teach.

She writes poems and stories that are very interesting. She always analyzes herself and is very quick to learn through her mistakes. Her thinking at times seems very adult.

But now her health seems to be failing again. The doctor has told her parents she must get more rest. Her father called the school this week to say, "That girl of mine is trying to do too much. Could you get her to let up?" Yet there is some indication that in spite of their solicitude, her parents are so proud of her successes that they do push her at home and that she is anxious to please them.

Her dance teacher reports that her same eagerness and fine technique are there, but there is a noticeable lag due to tiredness. She is also late getting her assignments in to her other classes and is becoming quite disturbed about it.

To me, the responsibility of the school is in helping to keep this child in balance by keeping her challenged but not driven. There should be more free time for her to gain recognition of her very real talent in dancing, which from all reports can be a great gift to the world, affording pleasure to many people.

MOTIVATING CHILDREN TO WANT TO LEARN

Children need to learn how to work hard, how to put out effort, how to accept and use the pressure that comes from within themselves—to press toward accomplishing something to the best of their ability. If we watch a little child learning to write, we see the effort going into the formation of his letters. But this is effort directed outward toward the accomplishment of the task, not inward toward an evaluation of the self. This pressure to achieve turned outward can be a strong incentive toward accomplishment. On the other hand, the pressure to achieve, coupled with discouragement and doubts of personal worth, can block learning.

Our own feelings about success and failure and the way in which we present a task or offer a challenge or present a standard for work to be achieved will be important factors in determining whether the child looks outward toward attacking the problem or task or inward with a sense of anxiety or failure about himself. In the first case, the push toward successful performance results in action and an ultimate release of the tension. In the second, it results only in disturbed feelings about the self.

When we look at children as individuals and try to discover the interests and strengths of each child, we can often find the clue to what will motivate the child to want to learn. Sometimes we become so burdened with large numbers of children or so intent on teaching the required subject matter that we pass by those moments in the life of a child that could have been used as incentives to learning.

Alfred was a fifth-grader who was having troubles at school. He was not interested; he was not paying attention; he was restless. But this boy had an overwhelming interest—something he loved. He spent a lot of time outdoors, gathering nature specimens. In his room at home, his collection included all kinds of fascinating bugs, praying mantis eggs, and birds' nests.

One day Alfred found a beautiful cocoon. The next day, as he left for school, he noticed a stirring in the cocoon. Carefully, he took the precious cocoon to school—his eyes shining with excitement. But when he got to school and tried to tell the teacher about it, she said, "Oh, we are far too busy for that today," and she put the cocoon away on a top shelf.

A very precious moment was lost. That teacher never did find how to motivate Alfred. However busy we are, we need to remain sensitive to those things that have meaning in the life of a child, for these interests are the keys to genuine and permanent motivation.

Sometimes there will be things that we feel children might be interested in if the doors were open to them. It may seem wise and necessary to hold children to a task or a project or a unit, in the hope that they will become interested and move ahead. There are also facts or skills that we feel children must learn because these things are basic to other learning. One cannot always motivate through interest. At times it is necessary to hold a child to a task, but teaching with some pressure is likely to succeed only if what we are asking is possible of achievement. If we put pressures on children to do that which they cannot do, then we will fail to teach, however important or necessary we feel the lesson to be. There is no greater incentive toward doing a hard task than doing the preceding task with a feeling of satisfactory accomplishment.

If a child sees no meaning in the things we want him to learn, no amount of pressure will motivate him.

Tate had been an excellent student, but in his junior year in high school, his whole personality seemed to undergo a change. His ready smile and friendly, out-going spirit were replaced with moodiness, quick impatience, and irritability. The climax came in the middle of the year when he was supposed to hand in a notebook. But the notebook was never turned in. Every time he was asked about it, he gave vague promises that he would bring it in. Finally, Tate was called into the counsellor's office. "Tate, what is this about your notebook? You've always done such fine work. What is the problem?" Tate shifted around a bit and then blurted out, "It's senseless! Why should I copy things out of a book and then put them into a notebook? The teacher can read them in the book. I've read them in the book, and I know where to find those facts if I need them. Anyway, I know all that stuff. It is plain stupid to be asked to spend time I would rather put on other things on that kind of assignment."

Mursell (9) says that if we want a child to drill or do careful work, we must give the child something to take pains about, for ". . . no one can polish a jewel if there is no jewel to polish."

HELPING CHILDREN LEARN

FROM MISTAKES

If we are to be able to help children learn how to stand up under the normal competition of life, we must think about the concept of failure we are helping them develop. Do we tend to punish the child who fails, making him feel that he is in disgrace and is a disappointment? Do we make a child ashamed of making mistakes or having errors on a paper? Or do we help him learn through the mistakes he makes? Temporary failure can be an important step in learning. If children get perfect papers, they probably do not need to do the assignments; they certainly will not need much more drill or further assignments on the same points. We might even ask whether a child who always hands in a perfect paper is not being held back to a level of work that is below his ability.

A mistake can show what a child needs to know, what his misconceptions are, where he needs clearer explanation. It is a personal matter, not one of competition with others.

The wrong use of competition in an attempt to eliminate errors may result in a discouraged child who feels that it is "bad" to fail —indeed, that perhaps it may be wiser to protect oneself by not even trying. It does not help Eliza to know that she had more spelling errors than Hank. It does help her to know that she needs to work at the words she missed. It may also help the teacher see that she has made an error, perhaps in giving Eliza words to spell that she cannot understand.

When a child fails, he does not usually see it just as a failure to learn his number facts or list of spelling words; it is much more personal. He usually feels he is failing someone, frequently his parents or his teacher. If we intensify this feeling with our blame and disappointment, with our comparisons with other children who are doing better—so that he interprets this to mean that we like the other children better than we like him—we make it harder for him to learn and grow from his failures. It is our job to help him see failure objectively and to help him *not* to interpret failure as a reflection upon himself as a person.

CHILDREN WITH SPECIAL PROBLEMS IN ACHIEVING THEIR POTENTIAL

There will always be some children who do not fit into any of the usual groupings and must have some special help and consideration if their learning needs are to be met. These are the immature children, the borderline, mentally retarded children, the handicapped children who cannot be put in special classes, or the extremely academically gifted children whose ability and quality of mind make the ordinary methods, books, and materials unsuitable for them.

These children present a dilemma for the teacher and put special demands on her. This is especially true for the teacher in a school system that does not have special classes, remedial teachers, or clinical facilities to call upon. However, limited help for these special children is better than no help at all.

What do we do in our classroom for those children who do not fit, yet for administrative reasons must remain with us?

THE SLOW-LEARNING CHILD

In almost every classroom, there will be one or two youngsters whose lack of ability makes them lag behind the rest. These children will never be able to achieve the standards normal for the grade in which they are placed, for their intelligence falls in the below-average group. If we expect them to master the work of their grade, they will be faced with continual failure. We cannot keep them from the realization that they are behind the others in their ability to read or spell or write, but we can find balancing situations in the classroom. Our attitude also is important. Very often we think of these children as nonlearners; yet even these youngsters can develop some skills and be helped to be self-respecting achievers at a level that is normal for them. Norman Beal was such a child. His teacher, Miss Cato, tells about him:

Norman was the middle child in a family of three. His family were professional people. His older brother was an outstanding student in school, and his younger sister was crowding Norman from behind. He did not learn to read in the first grade and was kept back. In the fourth grade, he hit snags again as his reading level of 2.6 made it impossible for him to keep up with the work of the group, even when he was placed in the lowest reading group and given remedial help as well. His I.Q. was· 85—too high for placement in a special class, too low for successful academic success in the ordinary classroom. He was a big boy physically and would have been socially out of place if held back in the third grade.

Yet, Norman had his strengths. His family lived in the country and his father and mother encouraged Norman to work around the small farm. He helped the hired man milk the cows; he learned to weed and hoe; and he delighted in providing the family with the fresh vegetables he had grown in his garden. They, in turn, showed full appreciation of his work and gave him as much credit for his work around the place as they gave to his older brother and sister for their school achievements. So Norman came to school with a certain self-confidence.

His family liked him and he in turn liked people. He had a puckish smile and a sense of humor, which went over in the classroom. His teacher used his skill with plants and put him in charge of the classroom plants. He weeded and watered them carefully—and visitors sometimes commented on their attractiveness. He did better in arithmetic than reading and his teacher would help him count the milk money and let him count the number of children asking for lunch. She would trust him to take the order and the milk money to the cafeteria. In reading, she worked with him alone since he was far below the level of the slow group in the fourth grade. Occasionally, he would tell a short story about the farm to the class—and they listened appreciatively, understanding his difficulties but respecting his efforts. His teacher had done a good job of conveying respect for Norman to the other children and they accepted him as she did. Norman will never achieve the levels of success open to his brother and sister but through the combined efforts of an understanding family and a school that can offer him experiences of being respected for what he can do, Norman will be able to develop sufficient self-confidence and self-respect to lead a good life, probably on a farm—a life he already loves and finds satisfying. He knows that he isn't as "good at books" as his brother and sister but neither are they as good with animals as he is. He knows he is behind the other children in school, but he can make plants grow and tell others about his cow and his garden. He will be a productive citizen.

We must accept the fact that slow-learning children, because of mental limitations, will never be able to master adequately all the tools of learning we consider important. But they can still succeed if the work given to them is geared to their needs and abilities. These children are slow in reaction time. It takes them longer to think things through. They may learn a response in one situation but have a lower ability to transfer it to another. They usually have a short attention span. They are easily distracted and do not combine ideas very readily. They must be told how and when to do things with simple, clear, specific directions. They can usually carry out simple directions but are not able to plan as well as the other children. They cannot work with abstractions—they need concrete material and experiences. They need tactile experiences in learning to write and count for a longer period than others do. The normal activity of a classroom is often quite confusing to these youngsters; the teacher must often work with these children alone or in small groups.

These boys and girls do not learn as easily from their own mistakes; they are very dependent upon guidance and encouragement. They are often easily upset and discouraged, but they can be helped to develop self-respect. Miss Cato knew this as she planned the work for Norman and made a place for him in the classroom. There is a motto it is well to remember when we work with these slow youngsters and try to give them a sense of achievement: "No matter how slow the progress may be, each at his own speed grows profitably."

It is so easy for children in this group to develop a sense of failure—a picture of themselves as someone who is "dumb" and "no good."

We must distinguish in our thinking between those who are slow learners because of mental limitations and those who are slow learners for other reasons. Sometimes, we tend to group these children together when their needs and the quality of their ability are very different. There will be children in our classrooms who are slow learners because of many other kinds of difficulties such as deafness, poor eyes, poor coordination, emotional difficulties, slow maturation, and illness. These youngsters may be of normal or superior intelligence but will need more time and more help in order to achieve.

THE IMMATURE CHILD

In most school systems, there is a definite chronological age for starting school which does not take into account the mental or emotional age of a child. It is unfortunate that we have labeled grades which are equated with age. A primary system, for instance, with no obvious promotions, lends itself much better to meeting the needs of the child who is beginning school and whose immaturities can be observed and helped. We need to spot the immature child as soon as possible before a failure is checked up and he begins to feel discouraged at the beginning of his school experience. Margy Lowe was such a child—a youngster with a difficult family situation who was not ready for school when she entered the first grade. Fortunately for Margy, her third-grade teacher realized how immature she was and was able to begin to help her. Margy was a child who was physically undeveloped. She came from a home in which the children had love and affection from their parents, but the total family situation was one that resulted in an insecurity which prevented either of the children in the family from maturing as well as one would have liked. Margy's teacher tells about it this way:

I have known Margy for almost two years. She is now nine years old; a nervous slender child of average height. Her dark complexion, straight, dark-brown hair, large brown eyes and big white teeth do not make her a pretty child at all, but she is happy, intelligent, active, healthy, and has many fine personality characteristics. These personality traits, such as generosity and thoughtfulness, more than make up for looks.

Margy was not always so. When she first came into my third-grade classroom, she was painfully shy, extremely nervous and was afraid of many things—especially herself. In spite of all her efforts, she could not seem to "catch on" to the work in any area. In group play and on the playground, she had not yet learned how to cooperate in team play. Neither was she ready to master the skills of ball handling, running, and skipping. She had very few friends. In other words, Margy came to the third grade at a time when she could best profit from second-grade work. In the middle of the year, I asked Margy's mother to come to school for a conference. She came willingly, and I was able to learn a good deal about Margy's home background from this conference.

Margy has a sister Doris who is seven years old. She is now in the first grade for the second year, experiencing many of the same difficulties Margy has had. Doris' difficulties appear to be of a greater degree, however; she cries constantly and still sucks her thumb. The two children get along very well together with only a few squabbles. They seem to enjoy sharing with each other and are proud of each other's accomplishments.

Margy's mother has been very cooperative. She is fond of her children and is concerned about them. She is most willing to help in any way she can. In our conferences at school and at home, she has given several hints, both directly and by her actions, as to why Margy, in spite of her good intelligence, has not matured as rapidly as most other children.

The family lives in a city apartment. Margy is never allowed to play outside alone. In addition, there are very few children of Margy's age for her to play with. Margy has not had very much chance to explore either herself or her environment. In her anxiety to protect her children, it appears that Mrs. Lowe may have oversupervised both the girls.

It has been a hard struggle for her father to become established in a job. For a while, he had two jobs—one part-time during the mornings and the other as a night orderly in a hospital. He now has a regular job six days a week in the very demanding and tiring field of male nurse. These situations have had their influence upon the children. First, the lack of money has meant that the family of four must live in a one bedroom apartment. The two children occupy the bedroom. They use it for everything and their activity, when they are at home, is strictly limited to this space. The back end of the small living-dining room is partitioned off for a bedroom for Mr. and Mrs. Lowe. When Mr. Lowe is working at night, it is necessary for him to sleep during the daytime. Therefore, when the children come home from school, they have to be greatly restricted to insure quiet. This need has been strongly impressed upon them.

During these difficult times, Mr. Lowe has not had either the time or energy to play with the children. However, in his spare time he makes things for them, such as a doll's house and doll furniture. He is very clever with his hands. These playthings please the children and make them very proud of their father. But in his concern for his children and his desire to see them be good and do well in school, he often sets his standards too high and expects perfection from them. This has also been a stumbling block for the youngsters.

Mrs. Lowe has had a difficult role to play in this situation. She has had to be in the middle between the children's natural desires and drives and the father's demands and necessities due to his occupation. She herself has had to forego many pleasures and shoulder many disappointments and discouragements.

Taking into account the past home and school difficulties, I have given Margy freedom to discover things for herself. She has been held only to those standards she could meet successfully. When she showed an interest in something, I tried to help her learn to accomplish it. By the end of the first year with me, she had gained a little confidence. She is friendlier with the other children now and has a few good friends. She was able to handle easily the responsibility of orienting the new children to the class and its routines. Because these children were at her emotional level and didn't know her as she had been last year, she was able to make friends more easily. Adults have become less frightening to her. In class work, she is no longer always in the lowest groups. Her papers are finished, the work is correct, and because of better eye-hand coordination, the writing is legible and fairly neat. She has made many good contributions to class discussions. School is now fun and a challenge to her. Margy appears to have solved her most pressing problems and to have gained much self-confidence. She is now mature enough for her class. She should be able to make her next adjustments with less trouble.

THE CHILD WHO IS HELD BACK

In every classroom, there are likely to be boys and girls who are really not ready for the work or the social demands of the grade in which they are placed. Sometimes it is wise and possible to hold these youngsters in the primary grades for four years, or to retain them at a later grade level. But this is not always practical. Sometimes the immature youngster or the child who is a slow learner for some other reason is large physically and would feel awkward and out of place if retained with younger and smaller children. He may have a younger brother or sister who is crowding him in school so that the emotional reaction to being held back would add to his sense of defeat, rather than help him benefit by the extra years in which to grow up. His family and friends may label him a "failure" if he repeats a grade.

Decisions concerning nonpromotion are serious ones and cannot be made without a study of the total child and his home situation—his feelings about repeating and the expressed feelings of other children and his family toward him. Sometimes, with good interpretation, a child can be retained with value, but the feelings of the child can never be ignored. They must be considered and the child must be helped to face them and work them through if a feeling of shame and defeat is to be avoided.

In the matter of whether or not to promote a child, opinions differ widely. In a recent symposium conducted by the *Journal of the National Education Association* (10), one of the participants discusses briefly five studies concerning this problem:

One study examined the progress of sixty first-grade children who were promoted, but whose ability and achievement were comparable to sixty others who were not promoted. The study showed that the promoted children made more gains in achievement in one year than the repeaters did in two.

In another study, fifty-three per cent of the children who repeated a grade above first grade did poorer work the second year. Twenty-five per cent improved their achievement the second year.

Records of nonpromoted children during a seven-year period were studied in a dis-

trict of 5000 enrollment. The study showed that the achievement of forty per cent of the children was poorer than before their failure to be promoted. Thirty-nine per cent made no progress, and twenty per cent improved.

A study of several thousand elementary-school children in Illinois showed that two-thirds of those not promoted showed no improvement the following year, many did poorer work, and less than one-third showed improvement.

In the fifth study, children "who were to be failed" were equated and divided into two groups. One group was promoted and the other retained. The results showed that children of normal ability gained more from promotion than from repetition of the grade. Children of less than average ability made very slight gains by repeating the grade.

Another participant in the same symposium said:

Research that I have seen shows that children who repeat a grade are not likely to do better the second time unless the cause of their previous failure is discovered and remedial work is accomplished.

THE EMOTIONALLY DISTURBED CHILD

Simon Potter is not as fortunate as Margy. He, too, is immature, a slow-learning child, but his emotional problems complicate the picture and raise the question, "What's ahead for Simon?" His teacher says:

Simon is a member of my sixth-grade class. He is restless and has a short attention span. He accomplishes very little academically. He wants recognition and attention. He is impeded by emotional difficulties and has little self-control. He is now twelve years old. His growth has been rapid and he is showing signs of approaching puberty. He is extremely nervous, gets excited and upset easily. When overstimulated, his mother tells me he sleeps poorly and has difficulty with self-control. He is tall and thin, in spite of the fact that he usually cleans up his plate in cafeteria and goes back for seconds. He bites his fingernails, has other tics and mannerisms. He has poor posture and muscle coordination. He has marked aggressive tendencies, which cause me concern in the classroom. He does many peculiar things to gain attention and is always playing with something.

As he has been in our school since first grade, I have talked with his other teachers about him. His problems seem to have been present even in the first grade. In the first grade, he had difficulty adjusting to groups. He had more difficulty with number concepts than with reading. He did read the pre-primer, primer, and one first reader. He had difficulty with some of the words and had to be reminded several times to keep his mind on his work. His second year report shows very slow progress in all areas of work, with poor work habits and a bad attitude toward his work.

During his third year, he showed such marked emotional maladjustment that his teacher referred him to the psychologist for testing. He was below level in all his schoolwork and his peculiar behavior of the first grade was intensified. He did not pay attention and he would sit doing no work. He scored an I.Q. of 101 on the Binet. The psychologist reported that he had good average intelligence with achievement far below grade placement and that the personality tests indicated immaturity, great insecurity, a tendency to depressive moods, an inadequacy in social relations, and a preoccupation with the more frightening aspects of reality. He seemed severely handicapped by his emotional difficulties.

When the psychologist talked with his parents, she found that they were both professional people who expected and demanded high scholastic achievement from Simon. They were not prepared to have a child of average intelligence. His father said that Simon's older brother, James, who was now in the Air Force, was a "brilliant boy who would make his mark in the world." He felt that Simon was capable of better work but that he was lazy and did not apply himself. He felt that he should be made to apply himself to his work and should show proper respect for school regula-

tions. He should not be permitted to disturb the class.

His mother showed more understanding of Simon's nervous condition and said that she felt embarrassed that her son "should act and conduct himself in such unsocial ways." But she feels very strongly that the school is to blame for all of his difficulties, and has always looked to a happening at school as a reason for anything that might go wrong. She told the psychologist that she feels he is in a very difficult position in school in that he knows that he cannot compete with his fellow classmates in any academic field and sees them leaving him farther and farther behind every year. She admitted that there was much pressure at home for academic achievement. "We just expect it in our family," she said.

In spite of his many difficulties and problems, Simon is a very likable boy. His actions sometimes make me think of a small child. He wants the kind of attention that makes him push other children out of the way so that he may sit next to me in the lunch room or by me when I am reading a story. He likes coming to school early to tell me about something that interests him. In school, we have tried to channel his need for attention to more acceptable forms of behavior by giving him individual and group responsibilities, which would still gain for him some of the attention he desires. But he always has the feeling that he is being slighted, no matter how many privileges and extra activities he is given. He is usually honest about his behavior and if he complains or tattles on anyone else, he will be quick to say, "I know. I do it, too."

He was kept back in the fourth grade. Since the third grade, he has received remedial help and each teacher has given him individual classroom instruction. He has responded well with this procedure until the past year. But, although his response was good, his progress was slow and often erratic. His attention span, even with individual teaching, continued short. The remedial teacher who worked with him this year felt that he had gained very little and that he was beginning to feel resentment toward having to attend the special class. Moreover, many learnings that had seemed fixed would appear to be entirely lost on a recheck.

This year, although he is still very far behind, he is doing a bit better. He has acquired all the basic number skills. Reading difficulties still keep him from problem solving but he can tell me orally how to solve most problems. Spelling deficiencies make it hard for him to put anything down on paper. He must have much individual help in written work. In the classroom, he makes such remarks as "I only like recess" and he counts up the time before a holiday and is always talking about when school will be out.

In spite of his restlessness, I have found that Simon responds better to a more formal class atmosphere. He seems to work better in a controlled group. He becomes overstimulated in a more permissive atmosphere, such as the times when we are working in free moving groups on projects. In such a situation, he is apt to lose his self-control and get overexcited if things do not go his way. He needs an adult to help him keep the proper perspective.

I feel Simon knows that in spite of his behavior I have a genuine liking for him. He seems to be becoming a happier child and he also is showing less need for aggressive and attention-getting behavior. Through my own acceptance of him, I think I have helped the class be more tolerant of him, and I try to help him rather than to try to battle with him about every little act of misconduct on his part, no matter how minor. Until this year, Simon had earned the name and reputation of being the "bad boy" of his class.

I feel that this year, he has gained more emotionally and socially than academically. I have encouraged him to participate orally in language arts, to try to be a good listener, to get the most he can from films and visual aids. I do not feel that he has gained much in other areas. I have tried to work individually with him, but I find his attention span still very short; the incentive must be very strong to get him to do even a short written assignment without much prodding.

He is going into junior high school next year. He is far from ready but how can such a big boy be kept back? He will still be faced with the same problems academically. He will also be faced with more problems of maturity as he goes into his thirteenth year. He will realize more emphatically that he is different and is far behind in school work. How will he get along? How can he be helped? How will he react when he reaches junior high school? What is ahead for Simon?

THE HANDICAPPED CHILD

The severely handicapped child is usually taught either at home or in a special class or school. But in our classrooms, we will have children with one kind of handicap or another—the child who does not see well, the child whose hearing is impaired, the crippled child, the epileptic child, the child with poor coordination, the hyperactive child, whose restlessness and distractibility may make him a disturbing influence in the class. Each of these youngsters will have special needs that must be recognized as we teach him—the seat near the teacher, the desk with the especially good light, opportunity for more frequent moving around for the restless child. Allowances will necessarily have to be made for the special handicap. Yet it is wholesome for these children to grow up among the normal youngsters with whom they will live and work as they grow older. It is also a wholesome experience for the other children in a classroom to help meet the needs of handicapped children, and to learn to respect them as people rather than regard them as something strange and different.

It is best to treat these children as we would treat the other youngsters in the classroom, drawing them into the group activities as much as possible. Miss Leslie found that both Marilee and Nora were able to take part in group activities and that the children learned not to laugh at Nora's stutter and to make some unconscious allowances for Marilee in their games. These children do best when normal expectations are put upon them for the mastering of skills and achievement according to their ability and within the limits of the handicap. The child with poor coordination should not be exposed to speed tests that put too much strain on him. The child with poor eyesight should not be expected to cover as many pages of reading as the other children. The restless, hyperactive youngster should be protected as far as possible from competitive situations that overexcite him. But these children can be helped to a sense of achievement and progress. They will need encouragement as they go along, the sense of making progress, the feeling of contributing to the group in ways that are compatible with their handicap. The crippled boy who cannot take part in games can learn to be a good referee or scorekeeper. The little girl who cannot jump rope may be able to learn to turn it well. The crippled child whose handicap is apparent usually elicits the sympathy of the other children. It is the child whose handicap is not so apparent—who just appears queer and awkward to the other youngsters or is hyperactive and restless—who is the most easily misunderstood.

Miss Sinclair helped her third-graders understand the problems of a little girl who had poor eyesight and poor coordination.

Judy came into the classroom from recess crying one day. Miss Sinclair drew her to her and asked her what had happened. The youngster sobbed that the girls would not allow her to jump rope with them. They said she was clumsy when she turned the rope and spoiled the game. "But I want to learn to jump," she sobbed on her teacher's shoulder. Miss Sinclair asked her what she would like her to do about it. The little girl's face brightened up and she said, "Let's talk it over. In our class, we talk things over, don't we?" Miss Sinclair thought it was a fine idea. So when the children came back into the classroom, Miss Sinclair drew up her chair and sat down in a ring of desks and said, "Judy has a problem. She doesn't jump rope as well as the rest of you because her eyesight and coordination aren't too good. This means she can't turn a rope well and is left out of the jump rope games. What do you think we should do about it?" One little girl volunteered. "I know how Judy feels —I can't run fast and I feel bad when everyone gets mad at me in our relay races." Another

youngster said, "But she does mess up the rope turning and that spoils the jumping for whoever is in." Together they talked the situation over and decided that they didn't want Judy to feel bad— they hadn't meant to be unkind—they just wanted some good jump roping. Judy accepted the situation that she couldn't turn the rope well and agreed not to turn, but the girls offered to let her have her turn jumping and to help her to learn how to jump. The situation was handled in a kindly, friendly, matter-of-fact way, as a situation that had arisen. The teacher didn't try to arouse sympathy for Judy nor did she scold the children for being unkind. "It is something we can all work out together." Judy was helped to accept realistically the limits of her handicap and the children were helped to be considerate and thoughtful of another's need and feelings—a fine learning situation for all. The next day at recess, a happy little girl ran up to her teacher and said, "Everything is all right now—I don't turn the rope but the girls are teaching me to jump."

However, while we try to treat the handicapped child as normally as possible, we do need to be aware that there may be very deep feelings of hurt and discouragement. These children will need help in a realistic acceptance of their handicap, help in finding their strengths, recognition of their courage in keeping steadily ahead, and understanding of their moods of discouragement when they may need special support and encouragement.

THE GIFTED CHILD

In many of our classrooms we will find children who are able to go beyond the curriculum as it is planned for the average child of a particular age level. These are our academically talented boys and girls among whom will be found those who make a very real contribution to our society not only in the field of academic endeavor but also in such areas as music, creative writing, graphic arts, mechanical skills, dramatics, and social leadership. These are the boys and girls who will be able to profit most by a college education or special training in the field of their individual talent. About 13 per cent of our school children fall in this grouping, beginning with an I.Q. of approximately 120. Dunlap (11) categorizes these children in this way:

The term superior *refers to children who are markedly above average in intelligence and have the potential ability to complete college and as adults to assume substantial positions in their communities. The term* gifted *is applied to the top fraction of the superior group who have good intelligence and show potential promise of making contributions of a high order to their generation. The term* extremely gifted *is used in reference to a small fraction of the gifted group who have an exceedingly high level of ability and whose potential powers should enable them to make original and significant contributions to the welfare of their own and succeeding generations. These levels of intelligence as measured by an individual mental test, such as the Stanford-Binet Scales, may be interpreted roughly in terms of intelligence quotient or I.Q. as follows:*

Superior—120 or 125 I.Q. and above, that is, the top 5 to 10 per cent of unselected school children.

Gifted—135 or 140 I.Q. and above, that is, approximately one-fifth to one-tenth of the superior group and the top 1 to 3 per cent of school children in general.

Extremely Gifted—170 or 180 I.Q. and above, that is from one-tenth to one-hundredth of the gifted group or the top one in 10,000 to 100,000 school children in a random population.

The needs of many of the superior youngsters can be met by an enriched program in the regular classroom, particularly if the kind of teachable groups discussed on page 44 are formed, but even at the elementary level some of these children will need provision and encouragement to move ahead in areas of special talent. At the secondary level, these youngsters will need a college preparatory course, with emphasis on academic achievement, if they are to be prepared for advanced work in college or in their special field.

It is much more difficult to meet adequately the needs of gifted and extremely gifted children, even with an enriched program. Gifted children need many opportunities to find answers, to reach widely in their reading, to do much individual work, to be allowed to go as far as their seeking minds take them, and to be helped to develop whatever special talent they may have. This is true, in even greater degree, of the extremely gifted. Some schools are also experimenting with special classes or groupings that cut across grade lines, in which the work is planned to meet the individual needs of these gifted children.

Gifted children need special understanding, guidance, and educational provisions if their talents are to be realized and used for the good of all. Yet because they are able to study alone or because they seem to be getting the work of the grade, we often tend to ignore them or expect too much of them. It is often thought that gifted youngsters do not have, indeed should not have, any problems achieving their potential. But we must not forget that they are children, not just minds, and that they may have as many problems achieving as do other youngsters, though some of the problems differ in kind and degree.

Many people think of gifted children as having inflated opinions of themselves or as having a high sense of achievement. But this is not always so. Even at a very young age, these children are often self-critical. They put their standards of achievement beyond what they can accomplish and become discouraged because their abstract idea of what they want to do is far ahead of their ability to put it into concrete form. Little three-year-old Sammy tore up his picture and threw himself on the floor of his nursery school in a temper tantrum. "It doesn't look like a man! See, he has no stomach, and I can't make his hair right."

Sometimes, too, the gifted child is not helped to gain a sense of achievement because he cannot communicate with other youngsters or even with his teacher. The child who asks many questions is sometimes considered rude or smart alecky. "Eager beaver" is a term of disparagement often used against a gifted child. Yet these children with the questing, curious minds usually are not trying to show off—they want to know, they want an answer, they want to gain knowledge. Too often, if their questioning attitude is misunderstood, if the teacher stops calling on them "because they know all the answers anyway" and gives no other outlet for these children to come and ask questions, they stop asking and take to daydreaming, reading, or causing a disturbance in the classroom. The burden should not be on the child alone to be able to interpret his needs to the teacher but on the teacher to find ways of understanding what is behind the child's questioning, what it is he is seeking.

In some communities and in some schools, the gifted child may be faced with a hard choice of following his real interests, which may lead him away from others of his age, or of responding to the pressures to be "like the others," which make him try to hide his abilities. Mead (12) put it this way:

Any degree of outstanding success is represented as cutting one off from the group so that it becomes fashionable not to get better grades than the others, not to be too good, not to go up too fast. These pressures for keeping on all fours with one's classmates, neighbors, business associates, which are increasing in American life, tend to be particularly felt in the school age groups, especially in the case of the child who shows intellectual or artistic gifts.

These gifted children are deprived of a sense of achievement, also, when the work we offer them does not really challenge them. If a child shows on an achievement test that his actual level of achievement is several years beyond his grade placement, we should not require him to waste his time going over routine assignments at grade level. If he reads well, with high comprehension, appropriate speed, ability to unlock new words, it is not necessary for him to go back and work through every step in the usual reading program. We may find a child, like Ralph, who turns in inadequate work because he is so bored with his assignments.

Ralph was to be retained in the fifth grade because his teacher said, "He has done absolutely nothing in arithmetic this year." But Ralph, like Phil, did not seem to be a dull boy all the time. He did well in social-studies projects—when he wanted to. He liked to read, but his written work was inadequate and sloppy. His handwriting was certainly not up to fifth-grade standards. But his ideas and questions in all his subjects were outstanding. These conflicting characteristics puzzled his teacher, but she still felt it necessary to hold him back. "His next teacher will not think he is ready for sixth-grade work," she said.

Since the school had no psychological services, Ralph's parents arranged to have him tested at the State University. It was discovered that he had an I.Q. of 165, and achievement tests placed him at ninth-grade level and above in all his subjects. Ralph had been so bored with unchallenging work that he had taken to daydreaming and fooling around instead of working. In Ralph's case, acceleration into junior high school happened to be the answer, and Ralph moved competently ahead into high school and, later, college.

It is a fallacy to think that it will not harm a gifted child to sit in a classroom conforming to daily assignments and be bored year in and year out. Such an approach to learning makes learning to conform to a given task more valuable than working at the level of one's ability and produces children who sit wasting their time in drill, which they do not need, in order to understand processes they have already grasped.

This does not mean that gifted children do not need to be helped to master skills—arithmetic, spelling, punctuation, and the like. It does mean that we should hold these children to routine tasks only as long as it takes us to see that they understand and can use the fundamental skills competently.

Miss Norton was concerned because Gregory turned in themes that were badly written and badly spelled—but the thoughts were most unusual, the expression used and the turn of the phrase showed that here was a ninth-grader who had unusual verbal ability. But day after day, Miss Norton returned his themes full of red marks and the comment, "Gregory, this is very poor work." She was so interested in the mechanics of writing that she failed to comment on the more significant part, which was the content. By the end of the semester, Gregory still handed in themes that were returned covered with red corrections, but the thought was also lacking. "What's the use," was his comment, "all she cares about are commas and spelling."

Mr. Drew, on the other hand, was also distressed by the poor mechanics in the themes Gregory handed in the following year, but he worked with Gregory on the school paper and knew that here was a boy who had something to say. So the themes came back, "This is good thinking, well-expressed. I like it—keep up your writing. But Gregory—the spelling!" Gradually, by encouragement and appreciation of the boy's ability, with some friendly and good-natured insistence that something be done about the spelling, Mr. Drew did succeed in getting some acceptance from Gregory of the need to understand the mechanics of writing. But Mr. Drew put it in terms that had meaning for the boy.

Even the gifted child has a greater sense of achievement if we appreciate and encourage his strengths and help him with his weaknesses. But it does not help to attack the weaknesses without first giving appreciation to the strengths.

THE NEED FOR A FLEXIBLE, ENRICHED PROGRAM

Gifted children are able to take initiative and plan their own work. The Terman study (13) shows us that the average extremely gifted child is held back two to three full grades below the level he has already attained in school subjects. If we are to help these children have a real sense of achievement, we must encourage them to go ahead on projects and interests of their own. These may grow out of the work of the classroom but in some cases, they will be carried far beyond the level and interest of the other children in the group. Our enthusiasm, our personal interest in their projects and hobbies, our willingness to help them obtain books and materials, the support we give through our interest will help many of these children use their own initiative and interest to go ahead.

Some of these children, particularly in the higher grades or in high school, may go beyond the knowledge that we have as classroom teacher in the field of their particular interest. A good teacher is not afraid to say sometimes, "I don't know, but let's find someone who does." One high-school science teacher of biology contacted men in his community who were willing to take an interest in boys who wanted to go ahead in fields of science in which he was not trained. These men met with the boys and helped them go ahead on projects in which they were interested. At the end of the year, the boys and their sponsors put on a science demonstration at the P.T.A. meeting of their school.

If we are to meet the needs of these gifted youngsters, we must think in terms of books, material, equipment, and projects that are geared to their level. An enrichment program, if carefully thought through, may be able to do this. But we must be careful not to think that time spent on a project automatically spells achievement; it may only spell labor. Neither is more of the same activity an answer. If a child can already do a process in arithmetic, he does not need twice as many problems to do as the child who is just learning the process. He needs only enough problems to show you that he does understand; then he should be allowed to proceed to the next step.

We may need to do much more flexible thinking about ways in which we can use the facilities of our school. Can we perhaps free these children for a workshop period? Perhaps this could be managed by grouping gifted children from several grades together for part of each day, with an especially creative teacher who could work with them as a remedial teacher works with those children who are behind. We might ask these questions, "Are there one or two teachers in our school who are especially well-prepared both in personality and training to work with these youngsters part of each day? What are our community resources? Whom could we call on to help us meet the needs of these children?"

ADVANCED HOBBIES AND OTHER SPECIAL INTERESTS SHOULD BE ENCOURAGED

Sometimes a gifted child will turn to his hobbies because in them he feels that he has accomplished something. Often such a child will put time, effort, thought, and remarkably good workmanship into a hobby. One father came to high school to talk to the guidance counselor about his son. He was deeply concerned because he felt his son did not know how to study. He would not apply himself to his Spanish and was getting a C grade when his father felt he could get an A. During the conversation, the counselor asked if the boy worked hard on anything. "Oh yes," said the father. "Every night, just as soon as he can skim through his homework, he is down in the basement working on some science experiments he is carrying on down there." He laughed and said, "We can't even pry him loose to go to bed." Here was a boy who did know how

to concentrate and study when he was motivated by genuine interest and a sense of achievement. The counselor advised the father to accept the C in Spanish and promised that he would talk with the science teacher and get all the available help for the boy in his major field.

We also have to accept the fact that even an extremely gifted child may not do equally well in all fields. There are times when it is not wise to hold him back until he has high achievement in his weakest spot. Instead, we would do better to encourage him to go ahead as far as possible with his major interest. Studies of the lives of great men have shown us that in most cases, these men and women were already showing the area of their interest and strength in their teens or even earlier.

GRADE ADVANCEMENT IN SOME CASES IS ADVISABLE

Occasionally, just as we may hold back a child who is immature, so it may be wise to put a mature and highly gifted child a grade ahead. In planning for these children, we must again ask many questions about their maturity, their physical size and development, their social ability. Terman feels that it is wise for some high I.Q. children, who are also socially mature and emotionally stable, to reach college by the time they are sixteen or seventeen. This will always have to be an individual decision with study of the individual child.

Betty Legner was a youngster who was accelerated in junior high school. In her particular school, there was not another way in which her needs could be met. Her teacher tells us about her in this way:

Betty was in my seventh-grade core class. After a few days in class, she went on a trip to Niagara Falls with her parents. Much to my amazement, upon her return, she handed in the assignment she had chosen as her project in orientation. Furthermore, she had pictures of her trip and asked that she might tell the class the many wonderful things she had seen while away. I marveled at the wealth of material she had captured in her week's trip. Being quite familiar with that part of the country, I relived my own experiences in her discussion. The class, delighted, asked many questions. It surprised me to note her poise and well-balanced personality as she described the beautiful scenery and brought out the historical facts so prevalent in that part of our country. It did not take me long to realize I had an outstanding pupil.

In core, there is ample opportunity for a capable pupil to use his talent. As time passed, I began to record and analyze situations in which Betty participated. She always had her work completed far ahead of anyone in the group and frequently volunteered to help her fellow pupils. Being talented in art, she worked on several murals during the year. She organized the material and, with others of artistic talent, produced some very fine drawings. At no time in her work did she assume a superior attitude. She just seemed to delight in creating and developing activities that were exceptional in a seventh-grade student. The amount of information she collected for her notebooks on different countries was exceptional. Not only did she illustrate particular places but would write a poem or story regarding them. She just possessed something that took her out of the realm of her classmates.

In the latter part of September of that year, the Lorge Thorndike and Stanford Achievement Tests were given. The results of these tests, regarding Betty, aged 12 years 5 months, were:

Lorge Thorndike Mental Maturity
Grade Equivalent   12 plus
I.Q. 149
Stanford Achievement Tests

Reading	11.8 (Grade Placement)
Spelling	10.5
Language	12.2
Arithmetic	11.4

Betty was progressing more rapidly than the members of her other classes. Her science teacher gave me an article she did considerable research on last year and presented to the class. It was on the "Nebular Hypothesis." She was quite interested in science and spent much of her free time in core doing research, drawing pictures, illustrat-ing experiments, and reading scientific material outside of the regular textbooks.

The report from her mathematics teacher was another example of her ability. She did not only the prescribed work, but additional work as well. She was always willing to help her fellow pupils and contributed more than her share to class discussion.

She was such an exceptional pupil that she was given the Orleans Algebra Prognosis Test, without having even studied algebra. She made a total of 60 on the test, which was excellent.

I could see her rapid development during the year I had her, and especially after she was a part of a dance group in the "musicapades" in the spring. This brought out another side of her character. She seemed so free and happy to be in the play. But not once did she neglect to keep up on all of her schoolwork, an excuse quite frequent with many pupils.

During the first nine weeks of her eighth-grade year, there were rumors of her ability to the point of promoting her to a ninth-grade section. Her core teacher felt, as I had the previous year, that Betty was the most capable student she had ever met. The same was true in mathematics. She was always doing extra work and was ready and willing to help others.

In order to advance more rapidly, she had procured an algebra book from the library during the summer and had taught herself considerable algebra.

From each and every teacher, there was a unanimous report of almost perfect attendance, conduct, and capability.

With all these factors in view, from her previous test record and seventh-grade averages which had been, Core A, Math A, Science A, Music A, Art A, Physical Education A, along with conferences with her parents, who were beginning to feel that in eighth grade, Betty was not meeting the needed challenge, she was promoted to ninth grade at the end of the marking period. Now that Betty has been accelerated to the ninth grade, her mother feels that she has something to challenge her in school and is quite happy with the arrangement.

In our eagerness to have all children achieve and in view of the special emphasis being increasingly placed on helping youngsters live up to their level of ability, we must be constantly watchful lest we put too much of the wrong kind of pressure on boys and girls. We sometimes find that children of high intellectual ability are overburdened with homework to such an extent that they do not have the necessary time for outdoor play or other wholesome activities. This can occur at both the elementary and the secondary levels. We sometimes find boys and girls of high intellectual ability who have been encouraged to enroll in a total accelerated program under such pressure that they become discouraged and defeated rather than challenged and stimulated.

There are many kinds of intellectual ability. The fact that a child is gifted in science or mathematics does not necessarily mean that he has the verbal skills to do equally well in an accelerated creative writing course; neither does it necessarily mean that a child with a high degree of creativity and originality in writing or music or art may have the necessary interest and drive or even necessary mathematical ability to carry an accelerated course in mathematics. Too much acceleration may boomerang on some intelligent youngsters and result in a loss of interest and drive or over-tension and anxiety. Good and thoughtful guidance based on an understanding of the total personality and make-up of each child is needed before academic burdens are increased over that which is normal for the age of the child.

ACHIEVEMENT IS THE RESULT OF MANY FACTORS

Whether the child is gifted, extremely gifted, an average child, or a youngster who learns slowly, we need to remind ourselves, as Kuhlen (14) says that:

Achievement is, of course, the result of many factors. It is the product of motivation, of the amount of energy that is thrown into the task at hand, of the health possessed by the subject, of his general emotional and personal and social adjustment, of the conditions of work, of his background skills both with respect to the particular task at hand and more general skills of how to work and think. All of these factors and others not easily identifiable, combine to constitute functioning intelligence. Schools and individuals might profitably examine some of these factors with a view to improving in a practical way the capacity to achieve.

Among people of exceptional accomplishment in the arts, sheer talent is only one requisite for success. Along with talent must go a strong drive, physical capacity to stand up under long hours of labor, a stimulating early environment to nurture interest, and the gaining of sufficient emotional satisfactions from the endeavor itself to maintain the motivation essential to further serious applications. Talent alone, without the drive and the physical stamina to capitalize it, does not lead to outstanding achievement.

Gardner (15) also discusses the necessity of effort directed toward the best possible performance by all of us:

... Our society cannot achieve greatness unless individuals at many levels of ability accept the need for high standards of performance and strive to achieve those stand-

ards within the limits possible for them. Democracy must foster a conception of excellence which may be applied to every level of ability and to every socially acceptable activity. . . . The whole tone and fiber of our society depends upon a pervasive and almost universal striving for good performance. . . .

What we want is a system in which youngsters at every level of ability are stretched to their best performance and get the maximum education of which they are capable. We do not want any youngster to feel that he is unworthy or lacking in human dignity because of limitations in aptitude, but we do want to see our ablest youngsters encouraged, stimulated, and inspired to reach the heights of performance of which they are capable. I like to think that we are now sufficiently mature as a people to keep both of those objectives in mind and not to slight either of them.

REFERENCES

(1) Kanner, Leo. "The Emotional Quandaries of Exceptional Children," *Helping Parents Understand the Exceptional Child.* Langhorne, Pa.: The Woods School, May 1952, pp. 23, 21-22.

(2) Erikson, Erik. "Growth and Crises of the 'Healthy Personality,'" *Symposium on the Healthy Personality,* edited by Milton J. E. Senn. New York: The Josiah Macy, Jr. Foundation, 1950, pp. 91-146.

(3) Krugman, Morris. "What Can We Test?" From *Our Children Today,* edited by Sidonie M. Gruenberg and The Child Study Association of America. Copyright 1952 by The Viking Press, Inc., and reprinted by their permission.

(4) Kuhlen, Raymond G. *The Psychology of Adolescent Development.* New York: Harper & Brothers, 1952, pp. 94, 118-119, 139, 132-133.

(5) Jersild, Arthur T. "Grouping in the Classroom," Letter No. 7 from the Committee on Academic Education, American Psychiatric Association, Feb. 1951. Unpublished material.

(6) Ilg, Frances L., and Ames, Louise Bates. *Child Behavior.* New York: Harper & Brothers, 1955, pp. 284-285.

(7) Reichert, John L. "Competitive Athletics for Pre-Teen-Age Children," *Journal of the American Medical Association,* April 1958, p. 1701.

(8) Allen, Frederick. "The Dilemmas of Growth for Parents and Children," *Child Study,* Vol. XXXV, No. 2, Spring 1958, pp. 4-7.

(9) Mursell, James L. *Developmental Teaching.* New York: McGraw-Hill Book Co., Inc., 1949, p. 70.

(10) *NEA Journal.* "Promotion Policies in Our Schools, A Symposium," *Journal of the National Education Association,* Vol. 49, No. 4, April 1960, pp. 15-21.

(11) Dunlap, James M. "The Education of Children with High Mental Ability," *Education of Exceptional Children and Youth,"* edited by W. M. Cruikshank and G. O. Johnson. Prentice-Hall, Inc., Englewood Cliffs, N.J., and Staples Press, London, 1958, p. 149.

(12) Mead, Margaret. "The Gifted Child in the American Culture of Today," *Journal of Teacher Education,* 5:211-214, September 1954.

(13) Terman, L. M. "The Discovery and Encouragement of Exceptional Talent," *American Psychologist,* 9:221-30, June 1954.

(14) Kuhlen, *op. cit.,* p. 129.

(15) Gardner, John W. "Excellence and Equality," *The Nation's Children,* 2: *Development and Education,* 1960 White House Conference on Children and Youth, edited by Eli Ginzberg. New York: Columbia University Press, 1960, pp. 225-237.

CHAPTER 3

PARTICIPATION

What difference does it really make if
a child participates or not—as long as he seems
to be getting along all right in his studies?

There is such a difference in levels of ability in my
class this year. I'm finding it difficult to see
that each child really participates in our major projects.

In our efforts to get children to work with the group,
isn't it possible that we may destroy a
child's desire and need to express his individuality?

I just don't see how teacher-pupil planning
can work. I have to teach certain things in a certain
length of time. If I let the children in
on the planning, how will we ever get anything done?

I had a class last year that never did learn to
work together. After an agonizing self-appraisal,
I decided that the component parts (meaning
the children themselves) were like oil and water—
they just didn't mix. Is that possible?

I have had cliques or gangs within my classroom groups
who cooperated among themselves beautifully but
who refused to be drawn into active participation
with the rest of the class. Just how can I
involve such groups into the larger classroom group?

PROMOTES LEARNING

RESPONSIBLE CITIZENSHIP BEGINS WITH CLASSROOM PARTICIPATION

Each country will foster the kind of education that will teach its boys and girls to follow the way of life in which it is hoped they will grow up. In an authoritarian country, it is natural that schools should prepare children to live under authority. In such schools, we are likely to find that children are not taught to think for themselves, but rather they are taught what they should think. They are taught many facts; they are taught to memorize and to recite; they may use textbooks that are distorted to uphold an ideological point of view. Challenging questions by the pupil are likely to be ignored or turned aside by the teacher, or they may cause the child to be punished for interfering with the process of education. This kind of education is likely to be, in fact, more a process of indoctrination than a process of education as we know it. A high value is placed on docility and upon the acceptance of authority. In its extreme forms such education can put more stress on erecting barriers to "dangerous or disturbing" thoughts or to free inquiry, than on developing creative and individual potentialities. In the field of science, inquiry may be demanded and encouraged toward the goals set by the state. But students are not likely to be permitted to choose the direction of their study, and their abilities and achievements must be dedicated to the preservation of the existing order.

Education in a democracy, on the other hand, is based on the assumption that we live in a changing world. It recognizes that we cannot provide our children with ready-made solutions for the problems they will meet. We must help them learn how to attack problems. A democracy needs men and women who can think for themselves, who can weigh issues intelligently, who can listen to many points of view and then make up their own minds and cast their own vote independently and thoughtfully. It needs men and women who obey the state not because it is the authority, but because they have chosen their leaders and are willing to work cooperatively with them toward common goals.

Preparation for this thoughtful, intelligent, independent citizenship requires a very different kind of education for our boys and girls than that given in an authoritarian country. It means that teachers have to think in terms of providing experiences for the children that will help them learn not only necessary facts and skills but also learn how to question, evaluate, and put into practical use that which they learn. This means that we must draw each child actively into the life of the classroom. We know that only through active participation in the learning process do boys and girls learn to be creative, self-directing citizens, willing and able to contribute to their communities.

Although children have many group experiences as they are growing up, the classroom is one group experience that is common to all children and is planned to prepare them for their roles in the adult world. In the classroom, year by year, children are learning how to live together, share together, and use their individual abilities for the good of the group.

In essence, this experience is good citizenship and not only leads to a more effective setting for learning today but also is necessary and important preparation for citizenship of tomorrow.

Thus, quite simply, because we can not permit the understanding of how to work with people to grow haphazardly, teachers have the function of not only equipping boys and girls with a body of knowledge and necessary skills but also helping them become more responsible citizens through their classroom experiences.

GROUP ACCEPTANCE IS IMPORTANT TO EMOTIONAL AND SOCIAL GROWTH

Children in our classrooms are developing an image of themselves as successful or unsuccessful in group situations. Just as a child can develop a feeling of self-doubt if he is put constantly in a position of failing in the tasks assigned him, so can he develop a serious doubt about his capacity to get along with other people if he always finds himself in a group situation he cannot handle. Children must have approval from those of their own age as well as from adults if they are to develop successfully.

We sometimes tend to overlook the importance of the social growth of the children in our rooms. Often we put more emphasis upon their mental or physical growth. We may worry if they are not learning to read or if they look fatigued and undernourished. We are often not quite so concerned if they are not getting along well with the other children in the classroom. But for successful participation in school and in later life, the ability to win acceptance by others is of the greatest importance. It also plays a significant role in the child's ability to learn. The youngster who is unhappy because he is not accepted by the other children, who does not have good friends, or who has been dropped from a group is rarely in good shape to learn to his capacity. Too often his mind is full of worries about himself and he has little energy left over to apply to his schoolwork. One intelligent ten-year-old became a repeater because his mind was so preoccupied with the problem of being too small and underdeveloped to be a real part of the boy-group.

Youngsters are not born knowing how to establish good group relationships. They learn this skill from their environment and the experiences they have. The process takes time—whether we are dealing with the little baby who is born king of his universe, or the two-year-old who is too young to understand about sharing, or the adolescent who is awkwardly trying to find his way in his relationship with his first girl friend. One of the developmental tasks of all children is to learn how to establish relationships with other people. If a person remains at the egocentric stage of the baby, he does not become a mature citizen, even though he becomes an adult in chronological age.

The otherwise competent, intelligent person can be at a major disadvantage if he has not learned how to work out his relationships with other people or to work and live comfortably with others in a group. Vocational teachers know that many people are fired from jobs not because of incompetency in their work but because they could not work with others. They could not give and take, settle differences amicably, share work, or carry their load. Many of the maladjustments of life develop because of failure in this area. The emotional and social development of the child are woven together. A child who is emotionally underdeveloped or is emotionally upset cannot work with other people as a more secure and happy individual can. We need to learn how to spot these youngsters in our classroom for it will be of little avail to urge them into situations with other children until we have found a way to meet some of their needs and to help them work through their hurts.

Amanda Durkin was "different" and became unsure of herself; she was not able to do well in her schoolwork or to become part of the group while she was troubled about her acceptance by other children.

Amanda entered my second-grade class this year. She is a pretty child with a great desire to please everyone in her classroom. She is considerate of others, loves to share experiences, and enters into class activities with enthusiasm. She tries very hard to do everything she should. In class discussion or in "Show and Tell" she always has something to say. She makes a real effort to be nice to everyone and is very fair in her work and play. The report that came with her from her previous school confirmed my opinion of a well-adjusted, attentive, happy and enthusiastic child. Her energy seemed boundless; she entered enthusiastically into games and dances and showed a good sense of rhythm. During the first week of school she got along well with other children and was often chosen as a dancing partner.

But as the year went on, Amanda's popularity died. The children are still nice to her and still choose her, but not as they did at first. Now she is seldom picked to eat or work with. She is beginning to be "alone" and her schoolwork is suffering so that she is getting far behind. She is no longer the gay, enthusiastic little girl of that first week in school.

Amanda still makes an effort to be nice to everyone. Yet as the year has gone on, her clothes are often old and unclean with the hems out. The one "good" dress with which she started school is old now, too. Her appearance, with her drooping hems, her soiled clothes, and the snarled, unbrushed appearance of her beautiful hair, is becoming noticeably different from her classmates. Her lunches are inadequate and she often begs from others. She knows better but is too hungry to care. Lunch is often one uncut sandwich, often unwrapped and in a dirty lunch box. Sometimes she has eaten the sandwich on her way to school and has had nothing for lunch. The children are beginning to notice these things and to comment on them.

It was the lunches that caused me to speak to the principal. This resulted in the visiting teacher going to see Amanda's mother. The visiting teacher found out that this year a serious change had occurred in Amanda's life just before she started school. The housing project in which they lived had been torn down. Her mother, who is separated from Amanda's father, had rented a converted garage near our school. It was the only housing she could find that she could afford. Amanda's mother is not an efficient planner or budgeter. She is working full time to support her children. Her energy does not stretch to such tasks as ironing, mending, and sewing. If she gets a dress washed that is a good

deal. She shows little concern if it is too long or the hem is half out. She is a tired, discouraged woman. In the old school in which Amanda did so well, she was not noticeably different from her classmates who came almost entirely from underprivileged homes. She loved her teacher and all her natural buoyancy found expression in her first-grade experience, but in our school her different home background separated her noticeably from the other children who all came from upper middle-class, and mostly from professional, homes.

The difference between Amanda and the other children was accentuated by the fact that the mothers of the other children became aware of Amanda's unsupervised home. Amanda was a Brownie and when she was driven home by mothers in the Brownie group, they soon noticed that there was no one at home to greet the youngster. Twice the child could not get in and the mother who was driving felt concern at leaving her sitting alone on the doorstep. Yet the child was insistent that this was what she had been told to do. The other mothers tried to be kind, but they are interested in their children's school and other activities; they go together on planned outings. Amanda cannot be part of the many neighborhood activities, nor "in on" the overnight visits the other girls have. The other children make no attempt to stop and play with Amanda, even though some of them pass her home on their way to and from school. I have the feeling they have heard their parents discuss Amanda's home and lack of supervision. It is quite possible that they may have been told that they may not stop there. Amanda is not yet aware of the difference between her home and others, I believe, but she is hurt and bewildered, I am sure, by the children's attitude toward her. Last year school was a happy experience. She was popular. She "belonged." But this year it is not the same, and I am at a loss as to how to bridge the gap.

Grace Janicek was also a youngster who would like to have made friends and wanted to be part of the class group, but her own deeply hurt feelings stood in her way. Her teacher writes:

My 32 sixth-graders came from a well-to-do suburban neighborhood. They were all, with no exceptions, children of professional people or successful businessmen. Yet, with a background of comparative ease, good clothes, and native intelligence, Grace differed so much from the others that by the end of the first week, I found myself dreading to meet the class each morning, for fear of what the day's contact with Grace would do to me.

The child's size, alone, was disconcerting. She towered over the other members of the class—and me—with her 5'10". She sat slouched in her seat, gazing out of the window or doodling. After my third or fourth reprimand for lack of attention, she looked at me as if she had not heard me before, straightened up, and went to the other extreme. For a few days, nobody but Grace had a chance to answer any questions. Her assignments came in on time and well done. I relaxed and complimented myself . . . too soon. After a few days, Grace relaxed, too—slouched, daydreamed, drew sketches, paid no attention, did no homework.

Requested to come in for a conference, Mrs. Janicek promptly complied and said, during the conference, that the situation had occurred before. She then told me that Grace was three years old when her father was in the Air Force during World War II. There was a new baby, and the mother and children followed the father from one base to another until he went overseas. After he left, they could find no suitable place to live for some time, and moved about, renting and visiting relatives. Grace went to nursery school at the age of two and to another nursery school of a different type a year later. There was no nursery school at the next place. She went to kindergarten in the North, and the teacher asked Mrs. Janicek to stop Grace from talking as the other children "never got a chance." "She's driving me crazy," the mother quoted the teacher. Grace went to first grade in the South, and the teacher asked Mrs. Janicek to keep the child home until the next move. "I can't handle her," the teacher told Grace's mother.

During the moves between towns, there were stopovers in other places and Grace went to kindergarten or first grade, for a week or two. When the war was over the father returned, but even then there were problems of finding a new job, making a new home, getting reacquainted.

"My husband said I had ruined the children," Mrs. Janicek told me frankly. "The boy was a crybaby and Grace dominated everyone or fought with them. Once she said, 'Boy, I'd like to be the old kid at school, just once, when new kids come in. Would I ever give them a rough time!' " Once when she was reproached for being pugnacious with a child and alienating the friendship of the child's parents for her own parents, Grace said, according to her mother, "What difference does it make? Next year we'll be gone—we'll never see them again."

Grace seemed to have no friends and her isolation became more apparent as the year progressed. While the class was practicing for the Christmas program, I became aware of a scuffling in the chorus. I saw that it was Grace and the boy next to her. I moved them to other positions. But they were the two tallest in the class, although he was only as high as her chin, and my original arrangement looked better than my disciplinary one. So the next day we tried it again, and this time Grace suddenly burst into tears and rushed from the room. The boy said she had kicked him and he had pushed her. Grace later said he kept trying to push her out of the line.

The teasing was resumed after the pushing incident. I now heard it myself, on the playground and after school. But this time the effect on Grace was startling. She began coming to school dressed in outlandish clothes. She wore a boy's jacket and tennis shoes.

Perhaps this new way of dressing was another attempt to attract attention, we thought, even unpleasant attention. But it wasn't the boyish, tough clothes that attracted the attention. I had a surprise visit from a representative of the student council who wanted my support in persuading Grace to wear white socks. All the girls had agreed to this months ago, I was informed. It was a sort of school trademark. Out of the whole school, only Grace wore colored socks. "She just does it to be different and make us mad," the student told me. "Perhaps you can get her to wear white."

But Grace looked at me coldly, from sullen eyes. I found myself apologizing for mentioning socks. I felt I was talking too much. When I stopped, Grace left the room without a word.

On the advice of the family pediatrician and the school psychologist, Mrs. Janicek and Grace attended a mental health clinic that spring. No miracles occurred, Grace showed no change in her work habits, but in early June she was more cheerful and her clothes were more like those of the other girls. I felt I could compliment her on her appearance the day of the class picture, and I added, laughing, "White socks, too." Grace looked down at her feet in surprise. "To match my white dress," she said. "I always wore socks to match my clothes. I never noticed everyone else wore white. I never started that mismatched sock fad on purpose either. I happened to wear them by mistake, and when people laughed, I was too embarrassed to admit it, so I pretended I did it on purpose. And lots of times when you chewed me out for daydreaming, I was planning my sewing." Sewing, what sewing? Dressmaking. Grace, it seemed, had learned how to sew when she was a small child. She had now had various private lessons in sewing, dressmaking, dress design, tailoring. I felt it was tragic that Mrs. Janicek had not mentioned the sewing. When I asked her about it, she agreed with me. As it was, Grace, with the help of the clinic, got through sixth grade with average marks achieved by balancing her very high ones against the very low ones. She emerged, on the surface, more conforming in appearance, but still determined to live within an unfriendly shell, so that no one would tease her about overfriendliness, or push her away lest they appear to be "friendly with a freak," as she put it.

There are many patterns of good social adjustment. We must not try to force all of the children in our room into many social contacts. We must instead try to know each child's temperament and the pattern of relationships he can develop—the type of participation with others in which he can be successful. Not every child can be chairman of a committee or president of a class.

A quiet child may remain a quiet person all his life. This does not mean that he is a maladjusted person. Children who are labeled quiet now may still be quiet—but not maladjusted—when they are grownup. It is much better to be a comfortably quiet person than a badly adjusted person who has been pushed into the wrong personality pattern.

We have overstressed the extroverted, outgoing personality. Sometimes an outgoing child is admired by a large number of people when in reality he is not as successful a friend as a quieter child. He may find making friends so easy that he passes from one to another without developing any real loyalty or attachment. It is the quality of the friendship, not the quantity of the friends, that counts. If a child is able to identify with other children in school affairs and other activities, if he has individual friends and interests, we do not need to be overconcerned if he does not fit into the more typical group pattern of his age.

INDIVIDUALITY IS IMPORTANT, TOO

Although most children like to do things together, we must learn to recognize the child who really likes to work alone. He may be a faster working child who is really so far beyond the other children that it takes more patience than a child can be asked to give if he must slow up to the pace of the others. Such a child should be permitted and even encouraged to follow his individual portion of the project, working alone at his own speed. There will be times when he can relate what he is doing to the work of the others and share his results with them as an integral part of the work of the class. Sometimes such a child can benefit greatly by being helped to interpret what he is doing to the others. This is a skill that most extremely gifted children will need later in life.

Seventh-grade Guy was interested in atoms and in the way they are split. He presented his material to the science class but they all became so bored and restless with his long and technically worded explanation that Mr. Wright had to say, "Guy, I think you have some good stuff here, but over the week end, see if you can put it into some form that the rest of us can understand. We don't know quite as much about this as you do." On Monday morning, Guy returned to the class with a clever chalk cartoon talk on atoms that held the attention of every child in the class. Guy had learned an important lesson in real participation.

If the child is comfortable with himself, there is no need for concern if he spends little time with others. There is a growing feeling that perhaps we have put too much stress on groups and not enough on the development of individuality. Group experience is valuable but so is the ability to be oneself. The support of the group gives the child one important kind of security. Retaining one's individuality gives another. If a child is comfortable being different or being more individualistic than others, it is wise to let him develop in his own way—providing he also has the ability to cooperate with the group when it is necessary. It is conformity not cooperation that we have too often emphasized to the detriment of the children in our classroom.

Carl was a quiet boy, well liked by the boys in the ninth grade, but he did not enter into many of the social activities of the school. He was always friendly and pleasant. He carried his share in class projects and made a good solid contribution. He seemed to enjoy what he was doing. But he had a special gift in music and preferred to go home after school and practice. He enjoyed being in the school orchestra and had a close friendship with two of the other boys who were interested in music. They met at his home to try out new pieces and listen to records. Now that they were getting older, they occasionally went to a concert together. The other boys thought them a little queer and highbrow but liked them. These boys were all right. They made their contribution to the school group through their music. They had good times together—not "boy times" perhaps—but they did things they sincerely liked. These boys were not antisocial nor were they maladjusted. They were more serious than most boys their age but they enjoyed themselves in their own ways. They knew how to be good warm friends to each other and how to be cooperative with their schoolmates. They did not fit the pattern, but they were all right within themselves.

The child who withdraws from the group in his unhappiness because he cannot get along has a real problem. Such a child needs our help. We need to learn to distinguish between the child who does not belong to a group because he is unable to do so, and the one like Carl, who is comfortable with himself and with what he is doing by himself or with a few good friends.

Some children are markedly different from the others but are able to manage their differences successfully.

Laura Prescott is a girl who found herself in a different kind of world when she entered our suburban high school, but Laura had so much inner confidence that she was able to meet the new situation, remain herself, and yet make an adequate adjustment to the school situation. Laura's family were mountain folk, but they moved down into the town at the foot of their mountain in order to make a living for the large family of nine boys and girls. Both of her parents work as carpenters, the mother as a helper with the pine paneling, the building of window boxes and shelves, and doing the cleaning for the new houses. They have hired out as a team to a contractor in the town who is enthusiastic about their efficient work. During the week the family lives in a large, old rambling house on the edge of town so that the children can go to the schools in town, which are better than the little one-room school in their mountain community. Every week end when the weather is good they go back to the mountains in their old truck. Laura's home life seems to be very pleasant and the relationship of parents and children seems to be one of congeniality and general harmony.

Laura is an attractive girl. She has a pleasant face, a winning smile, and a sweet disposition. She seems to be an easy person to get along with, although she definitely can be riled when worried and teased too much. She has reddish hair which she wears in a "pony tail." She is a large girl for her age and has developed faster than most of the girls in her class. She has large hips and bust and says that she cannot help being "big and fat." She talks freely of her interests, her likes and dislikes. She likes to read and watch television and likes the stories and programs of adventure and romance. She sings and dances, preferring the hillbilly songs and square dancing. She has a boy friend who plays in a hillbilly band. She goes with him to dances and to practices. Laura says that her mother and her twelve-year-old brother go with them. While the boy friend is busy with his playing, Laura dances with her mother and her little brother. Her boy friend is going to teach her to play the bass fiddle and when they get a television show, she will sing and "slap the bass."

Laura admits that she has never done well in school and likes almost everything she does better than going to school. But she has never failed a grade and wants to continue her schooling until the end of high school. Arithmetic is her hardest subject—she was able to do only fourth-grade work during her first year in high school. She has been doing remedial work in arithmetic all this year and seems to be very proud of the fact that for once in a long time, she is feeling success in mathematics where for so long she experienced defeat and failure. She said that her mother wanted to meet her teacher as she was the only teacher she had ever had who helped her with mathematics and who ever tried to find out why she couldn't learn it.

She is already following the trade of her parents and with her older brothers has built one small house in the woods back of their house, which they use as a clubhouse. Now she is building her little brothers and sisters a playhouse in the back-yard. She seems devoted to her family and willing to do anything for them. She talks very affectionately about the younger children and tells of incidents in their lives that show how close they are to each other. Laura is very unselfish and is most generous with the money she has. When she goes shopping, she often buys things for her mother or the younger children instead of for herself. She says she sometimes asks herself why she is not buying for herself, but when she gets home and sees the pleasure the others get and what appreciation they show, she is always glad she bought for them.

Laura's parents arrive home from work late every afternoon and she and her sisters take over all of the household duties when they get home from school. They clean the whole house—four bedrooms, living room, dining room, and kitchen; prepare dinner for the family and tend to the dogs, cats, chickens, and pigs. The father takes care of the geese, which are his pets. The two older boys have jobs after school to add to the family income.

Laura's classmates like and accept her, although she is so different from anyone they have known before. However, there are some who tease her and even make fun of her. She is very outspoken to the students and tells them what she thinks if they are doing things of which she doesn't approve. She says that often she has girls angry with her when she gives them a lecture. She has high morals and does not like anything on the shady side, although she does not mind swearing a little now and then to put emphasis where she feels emphasis is due.

She reacts very differently to different class situations. Her English teacher says that she makes very interesting reports and always includes stories or examples that make them very enjoyable. He says that the students always laugh when she gets up to talk, for she is comical, a good comedienne of the hillbilly type, and would be a "riot" on a television show. He says that she has perfect timing and the students enjoy her greatly. Of course, this is exactly where her interest lies as she says that she wants to be an entertainer.

Laura took a very active part in the Christmas party at school and volunteered to be on any committee being formed. She ended up doing much of the decorating and, as large as she is, had no trouble climbing around tacking up greens or what-

ever had to be done. She was also on the enter-
tainment committee. They planned to have a record
player, records, and dancing. This was really one
of the first chances I had had to see her in action.
Her dancing was terrific! She put her whole self
into it. The boys were rather shy and none of them
seemed to have the same interests that many of
the girls had. She would try to get the boys to enter
the fun but the girls found themselves dancing
together most of the time. Everyone got a big kick
out of watching Laura, and some of the students
remarked what a riot she could be at other times
and in her classes.

Although she appears to be rough and gruff,
Laura is also sensitive. For a while in her home
economics class, her teacher said she was dis-
interested and uncooperative. She would not bring
materials for sewing class and when the teacher
offered to furnish them, she refused the offer saying
she had the material at home. It could have been
that she did not have the money for the material
but was too proud to accept any from the teacher.
She told me how she was asked to join the junior
homemakers club but did not have the money for
the dues. She now has her material and is sewing.
She says that she has almost caught up with the
others in the class. In physical education, she was
failing because she did not have tennis shoes and
would not change for gym. Her teacher found that
the reason she would not dress was because she
did not want to take group showers. Her mother
told her she did not want her to take the group
showers as she did not think it was nice. Now she
takes an individual shower about five minutes before the period is over; consequently, she is dressing for gym now and is passing her work.

Laura's biggest problem is school success. She
responds warmly to people who take an interest
in her. She needs encouragement and needs to be
allowed to succeed as far as possible in the course
of study she pursues. She will need guidance and
warm personal contacts with the teachers. The outside world offers a challenge almost as strong and
nearly as satisfying as the school experience. Here
is a friendly girl who by a simple friendly touch
can be reached and helped with her problems.
She needs someone to have a genuine interest in
her. She needs to feel that she is succeeding in
whatever choice she makes. Lacking even some of
this, she can easily develop feelings and conflicts
that would propel her out of school into her outside
world which is warm, friendly, and satisfying.

Laura, like Carl, will always be different
from the other boys and girls in her school.
Her teachers will not be able to change her
to any great degree, but they can give her
their support and encouragement. They can
show appreciation for the contribution she
makes, in her own way, to the group. She
may not conform to all the standards of her
suburban school, but she has a personal integrity, which will be respected by her fellow students. Laura will probably never
participate fully in the life of the school for
the pull of her own world is greater, but she
will have a strength in a life of her own that
should be recognized, accepted, and appreciated. It would be unwise to try to mold
Laura, who is well adjusted in her own environment, into a partial copy of the girls
in her school.

WE CAN FOSTER WHOLESOME PARTICIPATION BY—

ESTABLISHING SOME PATTERNS FOR

WORKING TOGETHER

Real participation takes place when a class
composed of individual children becomes a
group who can work, think, share, and function together but at the same time retain
and respect their individual integrity and
shoulder their own responsibility for learning. We may have more success in creating
in our classroom an atmosphere of this kind
if we borrow some of the techniques of

group work, which closely parallel our techniques of good teaching. Hollister (1)* suggests some guides:

Each person comes to [a class] as an individual. He has his own ideas, his own feelings, his own reasons for being there. And, unless we consciously utilize that individuality, he may leave at the end of the session just as he came—a little richer in facts and ideas, perhaps, but still without the deeper emotional understandings and social experiences basic to personal growth.

Some of these deeper emotional understandings can develop if the individual has a chance to give of himself in a group setting. The separate individuals can join together, thinking *and* feeling *more and more as one, as they work toward common goals. Together, you and your group can build a climate where every member accepts every other member, where each person's contribution is considered significant.*

This is the group experience, *which is hard to describe because so much of it lies in the realm of feelings. Once you have experienced it, you can* feel *the difference— a warm, safe, secure climate which encourages a deeper sharing and often brings about important attitude changes.*

Whether or not your [class achieves] this group experience *depends to a considerable extent on you, their [teacher]. There's no blueprint for bringing it about. It depends on such intangible things as your manner, the tone of your voice, and the way you handle your position of leadership. Most of all it depends on your ability to communicate your conviction that* all *people are important [including children] . . . .*

Participation is, of course, the heart of the group experience. Helping individuals to participate is a major part of your role as [teacher].

MEET THE GROUP'S DEPENDENCY NEED

People come to groups with certain expectations. The first of these is that someone will be in charge, will start things off, and that they will have no particular responsibility. This may be called a "dependency expectation." If the [teacher] does not meet this expectation to a limited extent, the group will get anxious. Members are often so concerned with their safety in a group that they often do not even hear during the first few minutes. It is best not to outline the basic purposes of the course or plunge into concentrated content material during the first five minutes! So devise and introduce some activity that quickly gets the whole group participating in some easy task. . . .

PROVIDE EARLY GROUP SUCCESS

To help build group confidence provide for an early successful experience through easy participation. . . . A simple easy groupwide participation task leads to early confidence and readiness to work as a group in more difficult ways.

SHARE LEADERSHIP WITH THE GROUP

Leadership sharing has real potential in dramatizing that this is a group. Leadership is a group of functions, not a person. At first the roles are all in the [teacher], but it is a part of her leadership to diffuse the roles to all the group so that all have a part.

1. *Distribute the leadership*
The [teacher] suggests jobs necessary for the group success and invites other suggested roles. . . . [Later] the group can volunteer or nominate and elect to some jobs. Try to get everyone in a job that represents some leadership service to the group.

[Have many jobs in mind. Give each member a choice of roles important to the group's activity. Rotate jobs sometimes, and help with the follow-through. Children, Junior-Highers especially, need reminding. It is

---

*Full references are cited at the end of the chapter.

sometimes useful to appoint a trouble-maker as *Sergeant-at-Arms!*]

2. *Use special talent within the group*

Use special experience of [class] members as a resource. . . . [Some families may have materials that can be brought in; some pupils may have had useful experiences; some youngsters may have parents whose backgrounds would make them valuable resources of special knowledge].

HELP THE GROUP BUILD ITS OWN AGENDA: USE OF THE INTEREST SURVEY

Despite the fact that the course itself or the current topic has been previously selected, time should be taken to give the group the opportunity to outline what it especially wants to talk about within the realm of that topic. This taking an interest survey not only helps the [teacher] assess the beginning level of the discussion for this particular group on this topic, it also sets in motion a process that kindles interest and uncovers motivations (wants, concerns) at work in the group which can be used to spark the discussion. The interest survey not only provides subtopics and questions for discussion but sets in motion a contagious uncovering of feelings about these topics. Questions, concerns, curiosity or hopes expressed by one member light up similar feelings already present in others. Successfully carried out, an interest survey gets members so involved in the topic that group participation follows smoothly. Its use also dramatizes that the [teacher] is group centered and [children] will have a share in determining what happens in this group. . . .

LIMIT-SETTING TECHNIQUES

If the conversation wanders off into a difficult, uncomfortable or much too personal area, the [teacher] has a responsibility to set limits, to pull the discussion back to a safe total group activity. Limits can be set by such devices as (1) defining again the topic to be discussed, (2) redirecting the conversation to a new concern, (3) bidding in others to give other ideas, (4) moving to total group activity (listing new topics or summarizing by buzz groups), or (5) getting out of a specific personal problem of some one person to a problem more common to all by generalizing. . . .

EVALUATING OR STOCK-TAKING

To get the full value from a group experience, it is important that evaluation be built into the program. The [class] should be aware of how far they've gone and what still remains to be done, not just at the end but all the way through the experience. Reviewing your progress helps to give a feeling of accomplishment. It also helps the group to keep their self-determined goals in mind, and to modify those goals in the light of what they have learned. There are several ways to help bring about this sense of accomplishment.

1. *Give clear summaries often.* This may be simply repeating back a point somebody has made in order to honor it, but it is a major pace setting role. It gives a sense of pace and movement, and doing this is part of a [teacher's] role.
   In summarizing be sure to include not only majority but also minority opinions. All contributions are important to the group experience, even those which may seem to you, or to the group as a whole, to run against the grain.

2. *Use summaries to give clues for future progress:* "We seem to have settled our ideas about—, but we seem to need some more discussion of—." "This leads us to the place where we may well take a look at—."

3. *Emphasize the growth of the group in summaries.* "I believe we've become

*closer, more understanding of one an-
other." "We've become more of a team."
"We're thinking together more." Or other similar phrases suited to the subject
of the discussion. Help the group to build
a sense of its unity. It's also healthy to
recognize any group failures, if you do it
in a constructive way.*

4. *Set aside time for the group to evaluate
itself. What have we done? What was
worthwhile? What not so good? What
needs clarification that we've discussed?
What have we missed?*

5. *Use charts, plans, or suggestion sheets as
a stock-taking device. Record some specific accomplishments, perhaps a list of
the group's suggestions of learnings they
have discussed.*

6. *Use summaries at the beginning of a session as a device for recapturing the tone
of the last meeting. "Remember last time
we were saying . . . We felt that . . ."
Naming the feelings that went along with
the topic helps to do this and is important.*

PLANNING THE WORK WITH THE CHILDREN

In Miss Lewis' room, there was teacher-
pupil planning. Each morning, Miss Lewis
pulled up her chair and sat down for a talk
with the children about the day's work. The
"plan for the day" was written on the chalkboard. Miss Lewis knew the "goals" for the
different groups. These were put on the
board and talked about, but the children
discussed how these goals would be reached.
Committees were elected for specific jobs
that had to be carried out in the room. In
Miss Lewis' room, everyone had a chance to
help. After the committees were decided on,
children could volunteer for the committee
on which they wanted to serve. The group
set up the rules and standards for the classroom and agreed on how they would be observed. A "captain" or "chairman" of each

group was chosen for each week, but as
Miss Lewis says:

. . . with careful guidance on my part I see that it
keeps rotating until every child has a turn. There
are four main groups of tasks for the four parts of
the room. In addition to the captain, whose duty it
is to give out and put away all supplies and to
keep the group working quietly, the children choose
the host and hostess. These two take care of any
guest or if we go into another room for a special
treat they extend the appreciation for the class.
Other tasks are to dust the erasers; clean the
library; take charge of the centers of interest;
collect the milk money; look after the pets; water
the flowers; take messages to the principal's office.
These may seem unimportant but from the very
start I give the responsibility to the children. Even
my most difficult children have accepted and
carried out small responsibilities and are beginning
to feel much more a part of the class.

Toward the end of the year the youngsters were
asked to evaluate themselves as a group:

At a class meeting, I asked the president, Hetty,
if I might ask the class a question. The question
was, "What kind of a class are you?" They closed
their eyes and then in a spontaneous, eager way,
they made the following remarks:

Tony: "We are a happy class. We are kind
to visitors."
Jim: "But sometimes we forget."
Deborah: "We don't have self-control."
Billy: "We are noisy in activity period and
opening exercises."
Peggy: "We have improved a little, especially
in independent work period."
Paul: "We have teacher-pupil planning."
Jim: "We vote to decide things."
Ellen: "I think we should all be friends."
Stewart: "We are not always polite."
Markham: "We should improve when Miss
Lewis is out of the room."

In Miss Nevins' fifth-grade class, the children were taught how to plan their units
of work and how to tackle problems as they
arose. At the beginning of the year, they
formulated their "class code" and put it

on a permanent chart at the front of their classroom:

We share the planning
We make the rules
We keep the rules
We discuss our problems
We learn to understand ourselves
   and each other
We accept responsibility

Before a new unit of work was started, the class would sit down together and formulate "our plan." They would decide on the main points they would need to have answered. Children were encouraged to raise questions and to suggest things pertinent to the topic they were to study. Then the work was divided; some of the children worked together in groups or committees to look up information and put it into form for presentation to the class. Other boys and girls volunteered to bring in special reports or to undertake a special project. One child who was highly gifted in art often developed outstanding visual-aid pictures and diagrams, which made the material come to life for the other children. As the work progressed, Miss Nevins would sit down with each group, helping them evaluate what they were doing and modify or make a change in plans that were not working out effectively. Sometimes if a committee felt they were "stuck," they would ask for a class discussion so that the whole group could re-evaluate the original plans. The children themselves kept the standards high through their own criticisms and evaluations.

As they worked together, Miss Nevins tried to see that each child, even the slow learners, had an appropriate part in gathering the material. The children were helped to accept and understand each other's strengths and weaknesses and to make use of the best in everyone. This could not always be left to the judgment of the children;

sometimes Miss Nevins would need to say, "I wonder if Tony could help us on this committee." Often, too, Miss Nevins would raise the question "How do you know?" if statements were made on the basis of inadequate information. Miss Nevins found that as her boys and girls discovered a sense of achievement and satisfaction in a completed unit, they were motivated and eager to go ahead on the next project.

As the work of the group becomes meaningful, one is better able to help children understand the meaning of cooperation— the putting aside of immediate personal interests for the more vital interests of the larger group. It is sometimes necessary to discuss openly and focus upon points in human relationships that need clarifying for children. If a teacher believes in teacher-pupil planning of work and activities, she will realize that this can be done only in so far as she also helps her pupils understand each other and the ways in which they relate to one another.

ENCOURAGING EACH CHILD TO CONTRIBUTE

IN HIS OWN WAY

One of the most important steps to active participation is to encourage a child to contribute in any way he can. We remember how slow Norman took care of the plants in the classroom and received real appreciation from his teacher and classmates. A child must participate within his own capacities and use his own strengths. He should not be made to feel that he has failed because he could not contribute as someone else has done. If we make value judgments that seem to favor certain kinds of participation as more important than others, we defeat our purpose, which is for each child to make his own contribution. A little child may be able to enter into the developing of simple situations such as working out: "What do we need to do to keep our classroom neater?" This same youngster, however, may be incapable of exploring a wider field by himself.

Sometimes a project is geared at too low a level for the children who learn rapidly so that they become bored and restless. Far healthier is a blending of the skills of every child at each level of learning so that out of the group process comes more effective learning for all. For instance, if the class is putting on a play some children will be actors, some will paint the scenery, some will make tickets, some who are good at arithmetic will sell them, some will usher, and some will take the tickets. No job should receive greater value than another, for each child will give in his own way. This is an important concept of democracy.

Sometimes in our eagerness to see that each child has an opportunity to participate, we push youngsters into situations they are not yet capable of handling. Miss Miller thought that it would be very helpful for shy, intelligent Dorothy to have the experience of being class chairman for a month, so she talked with some of the more popular youngsters in the fifth grade and asked them to see that Dorothy was elected. The youngsters did so, but it didn't work out well because Dorothy was so shy and so inexperienced that in spite of all the help that Miss Miller tried to give her, she was close to tears with embarrassment when she had to lead the class.

Clearly, Miss Miller had been right in trying to draw Dorothy into more participation but wrong in choosing an activity that put so much strain on her. She could perhaps have been secretary or have taken tickets at the play.

If there is to be real participation, the opportunities must be wide enough so that children of many levels of skill and interest can find a way to participate. All boys cannot play ball, but if there are other activities such as shop or stamp collecting or a camera club, each child will be more likely to find a group of his own to which he can—and gladly—belong.

CREATING MEANINGFUL PROJECTS TO WHICH ALL CAN CONTRIBUTE

Real participation in learning takes place when teacher and children explore a subject together rather than when the teacher presents the marshaled facts to her class and the children recite them back to her. Real participation is a two-way thing, from teacher to child and from child to teacher. The teacher has much to give, but the wise teacher realizes that better learning comes through active searching than through passive receiving. She encourages the child to think and to question, to develop a genuine interest in "finding out," and to develop ideas of his own. She values his contribution and helps the class value it.

We know that even in the first grade, children are helped to learn to read by having a part in making up some of the stories and charts, so that the words take on meaning to them as an expression of incidents in their lives. We know that a child learns to count best when he can see and manipulate blocks or sticks or objects, which he can move around and combine so that counting has a meaning for him. We know that a child learns to think and use judgment by being confronted with actual situations in which he is helped to learn how to think through the issues and work toward a solution. Unless a child relates learning to his own personal experiences, unless he learns to think and use his knowledge, the learning has little permanent significance for him.

Sometimes it looks much easier to teach only the facts to children, to demand silence in the classroom, immediate obedience, and conformity of opinion. Some teachers feel that letting the children help in the planning slows up the work and that projects take up too much time and are difficult to develop in a large class. As one third-grade teacher said: "I just give them the facts. Projects are such a waste of time." In her class, the boys and girls read their textbooks and parroted the facts back to her. To these children, science was a matter of words, rather than an exciting, valuable experience in questioning, searching for an answer, and finding out. When we weigh the values, we see that teaching is more challenging and more effective when we look beyond the subject matter to be taught to the fact that the way of teaching itself has significance.

Butler (2) could have told her eight-year-olds the facts about rain, which she felt they should know, but by drawing them into discovering these same facts, the meaning of these facts came alive for the children:

By the third day of school we had started a terrarium. Cleo brought a turtle. Suzanne brought some rich black dirt and two small plants with pretty red leaves. We took one of the bright yellow doll dishes from the doll cabinet to hold some water in the terrarium. The sand, a mossy stick, and other materials for the terrarium came from the schoolyard. The teacher brought four books about terrariums to the class meeting. She read one story to the children and then called on a volunteer to read each of the other stories. These books were kept open for several days. The parts about terrariums were reviewed again and again by most of the group. New materials kept coming in for the terrarium. New bits of information were contributed by individuals.

When the terrarium was finished, the children kept a close watch to see whether the drops of moisture were forming or not. Some child was always looking to see whether it was "raining" in our terrarium. For three days, during the reading period, most of the children tried to find out why it would not rain in our terrarium. Danny had actually read every science book we had to find out why it would not "rain." He took books home from school and looked in books he had at home. Three times the group had seen the movie What Makes Rain. *Several days passed and no drops of moisture appeared on the top of the glass of our terrarium. The children made several guesses as to why the drops did not form. "Let's do it all over and read the directions in that other book. Maybe we didn't make it right," was one suggestion.*

The next day the teacher put the terrarium in the window where the sun could hit it. Drops of moisture, "of rain," as the children called it soon appeared. Jeanette was the first to see the drops and called everyone's attention to the "rain." The general conclusion had been that we had not waited long enough. That afternoon the teacher moved the terrarium away from the sun. There were no drops of rain on the glass the next morning. After two days of this moving back and forth one boy, not Danny as I had hoped, finally suggested it was the hot and cold air that helped make rain.

In the activity period two girls, who were skilled in writing, had been selected to make a chart to put by the terrarium. This was the chart they made.

RAIN

1. *The sun helps make rain by evaporation.*
2. *The wind helps make rain by moving the hot and cold air.*
3. *Animals help make rain by giving off moisture.*
4. *Plants help make rain by giving off moisture. Trees are the biggest plants.*
5. *The oceans, the rivers, the lakes, and the streams give back moisture to help make rain.*
6. *The soil gives back moisture.*

While it is true that many children, when they are well drilled, can store away facts and formulas and pass examinations, too often many of these facts are forgotten after the exam and never used again because they had no real meaning to the children. One eighth-grade boy, who had studied hard for an exam, was asked by his father, "What is it you have been studying? It must have been very interesting." "Oh, that! That was a lot of stuff we had to learn for the exam. I don't remember what it was all about."

Children begin to think for themselves and to grow in maturity of judgment when they become so involved in the topic under study that they continue to think about it outside of the classroom. Instead of doing work because it is assigned to them, children can be helped to think about and see the reasons for the work they are required to do.

We are all anxious for children to like to read, but too often reading becomes a chore rather than a pleasure. The following account tells of a teacher who lived an experience with her boys and girls that made the reading of a book and the writing of a letter become a part of each child. Nulton (3) writes:

It all began when eight-year-old Kimsey sprang to his feet, waving both arms and rhythmically swinging his body, to exclaim exuberantly, "Let's write to that man! This is the best book we've ever read. Let's write and ask him to write another one!"

The eight-year-olds and their teacher were reading aloud daily, presumably a chapter a day, though often enthusiasm prevailed and the wail, "We can't stop now!" led into another chapter. The book was E. B. White's Charlotte's Web. *We were in the middle of chapter thirteen where Wilbur was doing acrobatics to show Charlotte that he was "radiant" when Kimsey's idea hit.*

There was a stunned silence, partly at the interruption of such a good paragraph, partly at the enormity of the idea. The silence percolated. The teacher kept still, though undoubtedly her eyes must have been dancing.

Faith quietly penetrated the silence. "Mr. White might like to know how much we are enjoying this book."

"I like the way the geese talk. I'm going to tell him to put more talk like that in the next book!" Manuel chortled.

Here came the discussion.

"Could we write to him? I guess we could —just like we do to anybody else."

"What's his address?"

"Does the title page tell his address?"

"No, of course not. He might move. A title page doesn't tell that."

"It tells where the book was printed."

"Miss N., could you get his address?"

At this point the teacher explained that a letter to an author could be addressed in care of the company which published the book. The title page was consulted.

Discussion resumed, accepting fully the idea that we would write and further formulating things which they wished to say.

"I'm going to tell him I like the part where he puts in the names of so many things."

"No pig should be made to live on a manure pile. It's not fair to Wilbur. I'm going to tell him that!" Bill rebelliously exploded.

"This is not real," said Luke in scorn. "Wilbur's not a real pig."

"Is he, Miss N.? Is Wilbur a real pig?" anxiously from Susan who likes to be accurate and whose imagination chooses statistics and facts rather than fairy make-believe.

"I'm not personally acquainted with either Wilbur or Mr. E. B. White," said their teacher, "but I do remember when Mr. White went up into New England and bought a farm. He wrote about it in a magazine for grownups and I was quite disappointed because I wanted him to do more writing instead of going off to a farm. So perhaps Wilbur is real.

"It sounds real."

"I think Lurvy's queer. I'm sure Fern's real.

"The best part of the whole book is where..........."

Now there are times when it is best to act in the enthusiasm of the moment with young children. . . . There are other times in our progress toward maturity when we can learn to wait a little, withhold judgment, season our enjoyment with a mellow perspective of the whole. To all the factors of maturity and ability in such a situation the teacher must be sensitively attuned.

Had we better write now while this enthusiasm and discussion are running high or can we risk having enough maturity to be able to hold purpose, ideas and enthusiasm until we have read the whole and can write with perspective?

Will it kill the enjoyment of the book—put a plodding, have-to-work hex upon it if we labor over writing letters now?

Have we the ability to sharpen our judgments and make deeper interpretations if we let this idea of writing letters simmer a while? Can the simmering stimulate us to do that?

Do they all want keenly enough to do this that the idea will not pass with the enthusiastic moment and the letters level off to an uninspired and unexpressive exercise?

These were the questions racing through the teacher's mind as she watched and listened to the group discussion. Now, with the comment,

"The best part of the book is where—" decision must be swift. The teacher plunged. Maturity is worth taking risks.

"How do you know where the best part of the book is when we've only read about half of it?" she asked.

A surprised silence. Here we'd been so busy talking we'd forgotten there was more story! But not one child said, "Let's go on with the story." The letters were important.

After a moment Pat spoke. "We'd better wait. No telling how good it's going to be before the end."

"We could still say what we wanted to after we finish the book."

"I'll still like the way the geese talk."

"You might like some other things, too." . . .

"Let's keep reminding ourselves of the things we want to say, then write when we finish the whole book," came the constructive suggestion from June. . . .

"We could take June's suggestion," the teacher reinforced the line of planning, and "try to remember the things we especially want to say. We might have other things we'd like to say after we've read the whole, then if we'd already written we'd be sorry we hadn't known about that part. Can you each remember for a few days the things you'd like to say to Mr. White? Shall we keep thinking of the things we'd like to say as we go on with the book?"

Thus it was decided.

Then came the day when . . . emotion was powerful. Eyes were filled, though eight-year dignity held tears within the lids. Teacher began to wonder if we had better stop reading.

"I'm going to tell Mr. White I'm sorry Charlotte died," Nita mumbled with a sniff.

"Maybe she won't after all," suggested the teacher.

"It will all turn out happily after all," spoke Sandra. "Don't you know how they always get married and live happily ever after?"

"No, it won't! That's just in movies. It's not like that in real life and in good books!" from Kit.

"Is a sense of literary values developing!" exclaimed the teacher to herself. 'Not like that in good books,' that child can never be satisfied with trashy, ungenuine writing!"

There followed speculation as to how the book might turn out; what endings would make a good book out of it. Teacher took care there wasn't time to read further just then. Insights could ripen.

They did. As suspense mounted insights were heightened. Comments were continuous and penetrating, yet balanced by restraint and reserved waiting for conclusion of the whole. At times the teacher wondered, however, if so much had been said that at the end there would be no need to express in writing.

Not so. The book was finished in a satisfied silence which remained satisfactory for the long breathless moment that follows all good reading aloud.

"There, it has ended just right," said Nita, groping in her mind to try to find why it was just right although Charlotte had died after all.

"Yes! Now tomorrow we will write to Mr. White and tell him." Decisive James! So right that his decision was accepted and the children turned immediately to other activities.

"How did these children come by their maturity?" wondered the teacher. To have attempted writing the letters now would have been surfeit. The letters would have been empty. "How did they know?" Gratefully she watched their strenuous physical activity. "I shall wait," she concluded, "until they, themselves, bring up the matter of writing letters. Then we can discuss it and plan what we want to say—at least discuss and plan enough to stimulate them to carry through." . . .

The next day at the hour usually reserved for children to choose worthwhile activities, first one child, then another, finally the whole group, got pencil and paper without comment. And lo! suddenly, we were all writing. No remarks had been made. No plans were needed. Each person knew what he wanted to say.

"How do you spell 'manure pile'?" from Bill, then a mutter, "It just isn't fair!"

"How do you spell 'goo-goo-goose'?" giggled Manuel. "I'm telling him I like the way he made the goo-goo-goose talk!" Manuel never realized he had transposed the technique.

The letters, although longer than usual and full of unaccustomed vocabulary, were quickly written. They were spontaneous and varied. In most cases the writer expressed one point which apparently, he considered most important. The quick, spontaneous illustrations and marginal decorations were as expressive as the writing. Every letter had some decorations: webs, spiders, a pig, a mouse, running vines, or a cleverly drawn episode.

We did not actually dare let ourselves hope for a reply. Repeatedly we reminded ourselves, "He is a very busy person. He has many important things to do."

One month later came the reply from Mr. E. B. White.

"Dear Third Graders:

"I didn't mean to be so slow in answering your letters. It is almost a month since you wrote them. I loved getting them and I am very pleased to know that you liked Charlotte's Web, and I am glad that you told me your reasons. . . .

"Thank you again for your wonderful letters and the drawings that you made for me.

"Sincerely yours,
"E. B. White"

"Oh——oooh!" The long release of suspended satisfaction.

"Read it again!"

The teacher did. Then a child read it aloud.

"It is just right," from Lucia. (In other words, "He didn't talk down to us or patronize us and he put in the right things.")

. . . It had been, indeed, an experience that was "just right." We had discovered a new book and to us a new author. . . . We had realized that authors are real, living people; that they, too, like letters; that they may even be encouraged to make more books.

The one book discovered and enjoyed had led us on to another by the same author—to further insights, comparisons, and heightened critical reading. Very rarely, indeed, had they missed any of the subtle implications in Charlotte's Web.

. . . Certainly, valuations of books and insights into literature were increasingly clear-sighted. Taste developed. Writing skills and techniques were recognized and pinned down with unabashed comment. Their own letter writing was spontaneous *and victorious over technical difficulties. Nor is it mere unrelated happen-so that the eight-year-olds are now revelling in writing stories, stories, stories of their own."*

Some children have never done "active" learning before and will need a chance to get the "feel" of a new kind of learning situation. Some are afraid of their own abilities or have never been taught how to gather information and work with a group on a project. These children must be helped slowly to gain confidence. Other children respond with enthusiasm as one high-school girl did when she said: "In my old school all the pressures came from outside. You had to do your work not because it meant anything to you but because you were told to do it. I was bored most of the time. But here the pressures come from inside me—I work because if I don't, I won't be able to enter into the class discussions—and they're keen. I don't want to sit on the sidelines."

Although participation is our goal, there will be situations in which we must be willing to go slowly and involve children gradually. We will sometimes be discouraged at the results of the participation. Learning to accept responsibility for one's own share in the learning process takes time. The process can be encouraged but it cannot be hurried.

ENCOURAGING CONSTRUCTIVE

COMMUNICATION AND COMMON PURPOSES

The silent classroom in which children work always as individuals fails to develop a constructive group interchange. Children need many opportunities to discuss projects and problems, to get to know one another better, and to learn to help each other. We often speak of the cruelty of children to each other and fail to recognize the kindly help they are often willing to give—help that is forbidden in so many classrooms. If we expect boys and girls to have only formal communication between one another during a school day, we must expect that emotions will spill over and children will vent their tensions and antagonisms on one another when the bell rings. When youngsters have the normal outlet of discussion and purposeful movement, their feelings and energy tensions are less bottled up and less likely to explode in unhealthy, unfriendly ways. When children are real participants in the learning process, they usually surprise us with the quality of their thinking and the interest they show in their individual work and in each other's progress.

One of our tasks is to help the children to pool their skills for the joint effort, to supplement one another and discover the fact that one person can make one kind of contribution and the next another. As they are able to talk with one another and work through differences together, youngsters often find that in some situations they can achieve a purpose better together than one person could alone.

KEEPING IN MIND THAT EACH CLASS HAS ITS OWN PERSONALITY

As each child is different, so is each combination of children different. Each class has its own "personality," and we must also try to understand its needs and problems. For the personality of the group as a whole, the way it works together, the feeling that exists in the classroom, may profoundly affect the ability of an individual child to do his best. Butler (4) put it this way:

It was the first three weeks of a new term at the beginning of a new year. The teacher, although experienced, was new in the district and had never seen the children before; nor did she know a single parent. Some of the group were used to a rich activity program while others for various reasons were used to a rather formal drill in skills-type of work. The children came from homes varying in economic stability. One father was a doctor, another a student, another a teacher, and still another in the jargon of his son, "cuts gwass fer peoples." The differences in background of first-hand experiences were even wider. One child had only two books of his own. Some children had had many travel experiences and excursions with understanding parents who helped them make their own generalizations about their surroundings. They were all very active, responsive children.

Few of these children knew each other. Those seven children who had been in the same group before naturally stayed pretty close together and tended to exclude others. They felt secure. They knew how to go ahead and make plans and carry them out. Yes, they knew also how to choose the more challenging and interesting jobs and how to talk someone else into doing those less attractive, necessary jobs. Most of the children, however, did not know each other at all. When individuals know little of each other, they sometimes tend to be suspicious of each other. Because these children didn't know each other well and had no common background of standards on which to base their actions, there was much arguing at the first of school about such problems as who gets the typewriter first, who gets the swing first, who has the best picture, and who gets to be pilot. If one child went to the piano, they all went and wanted to play now!

The crying need at the beginning was to develop a better group feeling—a we, us, our feeling.

. . . If you have been used to working with children who are well acquainted and have had a common background, it is hard to imagine how big the problem of developing a group feeling of oneness can be. The teacher was sure of one thing—the group needed to carry on many activities together!

. . . Of course, if the teacher sets up the standards and doles out the punishment for those who do not adhere, for one reason or another, then perhaps there is less confusion, less arguing, and less reasoning; but there is also less learning-how-to-get-along together.

. . . Until children feel a part of the group to the extent they want to bring something back to the group; until children have something they consider important to say and want to say it; until children have something to write and want to write it, or an idea to put on paper, how can the teacher help them improve their oral delivery, their written communication, or their art?

Miss Butler knew that every class does not automatically become a group. Sometimes a teacher will have a class that does not seem to work together at all, for it is not the teacher alone who determines the success of the group process in her classroom but the interaction between these particular children. Sometimes we expect the children in our classrooms to have a greater ability to accept one another than they have been helped to develop. If we are to plan for the intelligent participation of the children, we will need to find out what we can expect of them, the point of social development each youngster has reached, and some of the problems they are facing as they learn to live and work together. Miss Frank knew this when she said, "At the beginning of the year, no two members of the class could work together without trouble. Much of the class time at first was spent in discussion and evaluation periods to find out just why the group could not work peacefully together." But by the end of the year, she could say, "We are just now beginning to live together as one happy group. There has been growth in group feeling but it has only been attained by sincere effort on the parts of the pupils, the parents, and the teacher."

As teachers, we have a dual responsibility. We teach individual children, but we must teach them in a classroom situation. Usually, a cooperative feeling can gradually be helped to develop if we are willing to study the children, to notice their natural alignments and friendships, and to utilize these as work is planned and carried out.

USING THE NATURAL GROUPINGS IN THE
CLASSROOM TO THE BEST ADVANTAGE

Children need to belong to their own small and very special groups. This is all right as long as they learn also how to step out of these groups and work with members of other groups in the classroom and school situation.

At the beginning of the year it may be necessary and wise to accept the natural groups and gradually to work toward greater participation and acceptance of the other members of the class. We begin by working with the natural leaders, but we must also try to develop leadership. As the year progresses and confidence develops between teacher and students, the problem can often be attacked by rational and conscious methods, for although it is not possible and would not be desirable to try and make every child a friend of every other child, it is possible to increase understanding and respect for one another. It is also possible to put work for a common end above individual preferences.

The groupings among the children may have very little to do with the teacher or even the atmosphere of the school. Children, like adults, are drawn to one another for reasons that are not always obvious— but what happens to these groups as they meet in the classroom is often determined by their relationship to the teacher. If, for instance, a group of children feels that their teacher has little use for them, that she "picks on" them, they will probably retaliate by difficult behavior—slouching in their seats, talking and giggling, and being generally disruptive. In turn, they will make fun of and often run down the children who are interested in their work and are cooperative with the teacher. With names and effective gestures, their opinions of these "creeps" is soon spread through the school.

Even an excellent teacher may sometimes encounter difficulties in helping a class develop any real feeling of cooperation. Sometimes it is because of the crosscurrents between the children in the group. A teacher may find two strong centers of attraction— two groupings around different leaders who feel an antagonism or rivalry for one another. The other boys and girls in the room may tend to separate and take sides, as they cluster around the leader whom they most admire.

Sometimes the qualities of leadership are not as desirable as we might like. But we must try and find out the values of the children in our particular class so that we may better understand the group motivation. In one area, it may be the boy who is the toughest and can hold his own in a fight who commands respect; in another, it may be social skill and glamour—the boy who has the social know-how or the girl who is surrounded by admirers. In still another setting, it may be the school activity leaders or the star athletes who command the most informal leadership. It is not always easy to be quite sure who is the real leader, but it is important to try to know. By means of a sociogram designed to find out with whom the children would most like to work, with whom they would choose to eat lunch or sit, we can get much insight into the small groupings within the large group. Then we will be better able to see the kind of interests that will be needed to bring the group into a common focus upon a common interest. At first we may find that the two or three major groups attack one another in rivalry for positions on committees, or in accepting or attacking ideas, that they work on an emotional level, as so many adults do, rather than a thinking level. But if we make work challenging and interesting, it will cut across cliques naturally—one child selecting this part of the work, another that particular job.

Although we will often have to begin by getting to know the natural leaders and working for their interest and cooperation, it is sometimes hard to accept the kind of leadership that a group has chosen for itself, particularly at the junior high school level.

Sometimes we find that the class may have rejected some of the finest students in the room because the class places little value on scholastic ability or quiet charm or gentleness—and turns rather to the person who has the indefinable something called "it." As one teacher put it, "I can't understand why Tom is never chosen as a chairman. He has so much ability, but he just doesn't seem to have the qualities the others value at the moment."

We do not know enough about the formation of groups or what makes one group dominate another, but if the focus of the group is on a project that has meaning for them, the group will usually be drawn away from individual cliques toward a common purpose. The integration of the group will be less difficult. Where work is meaningless to the children, the focus remains on being with one's best friends or becoming a member of a popular group. These shifting interplays of individual personalities can become quite disrupting to the classroom situation. Where cliques are dominant and the interplay competitive and full of rivalry, it is usually an indication that the work of the classroom is neither challenging nor meaningful enough to make students divert their attention from their immediate personal affairs.

It is unfortunate if the classroom or the social life of the school is dominated by one or two particular cliques who are interested in themselves alone and have not related themselves to the larger life of the school. In one school, a socially sophisticated group of ninth-graders so dominated the school parties that the other boys and girls began to stop coming for as one girl put it, "They make me feel as if I'm not worth anything at all." It is important to see that extracurricular activities, parties, and other school activities are run as cooperative enterprises and not as the property of one "clique."

Sometimes a group seems to run counter to what we think is advisable or desirable. If this is really true, then a wise teacher will work with the whole group and try to redirect the group pattern, rather than try to solve the problem by removing a particular child from a group to which he is deeply attached, unless the group has a really delinquent pattern or the friendship an obviously unfortunate influence. Even then, it is best to try to redirect the child's attachment toward another group and other activities. Simply to forbid the child to see his friends is not likely to be either wise or successful.

A child will often follow his group even if it does go counter to what he knows he should do. If such a child is forbidden to associate with his "gang," he may find ways to do so when no one is observing him—so strong is the group loyalty.

We must be sure that our criticism of children's group activities is valid—that we do not misinterpret what they are doing. Sometimes we feel children are doing something wrong because they are noisy, seem to have secrets, or huddle together in solemn conclave on the playground. Sometimes we are against children's activities because they are troublesome to us, not because they are really harmful to the children.

HELPING LEFT-OUT CHILDREN FIND THEIR PLACE IN THE GROUP

Often we expect too much of children in their social contacts. In every classroom, there will be children who are immature for their age and do not fit readily into a group; there will be sensitive children who find it hard to take the noisy activity of a playground; there will be children of different backgrounds and interests who may find the group difficult to understand and be "understood by." There will also be children whose parents have made it difficult for them to make friends with other youngsters because of the belittling comments they are continually making about the neighborhood group or the prejudices they express so openly. Youngsters will make many mistakes; they will often be crude. We must give them time and encouragement, and we must not laugh at them, scold them, or tease them, or force them, as shy Dorothy was forced, into situations they are not ready to handle.

During his school years a child will learn a lot about getting along with other people. He will learn to hold his own on the playground. He will find out about the skills he must master to compete in the child group and the kind of friendliness that gets across to other boys and girls. He will learn a lot about choosing friends and, except in rare situations, he should be permitted to choose them himself. Sometimes his experiences will not be very happy ones. He will learn that some friendships break up, that others prove disappointing. Sometimes he will be at fault because he did not give his share in the relationship; sometimes because of troublesome feelings, he may keep friends away. There are times when his friends will fail him or a group of children will reject him. Gradually he learns how to choose friends with whom he can have satisfying relationships. Through these experiences, he is learning about human relationships and his share in them.

A child cannot be protected from these experiences; they are part of growing up. But as teachers we should be aware of them and try to help the child keep the balance on the side of satisfying friendships. If a child is continually failing in his friendships with other children, we should quietly observe him and see why he is not able to get along with others and try to give him help where it is needed. This is not a deliberate failing on his part. We must seek the cause, not blame the child, for his inability to get along or be friendly.

Our attitude is important at these times. If a child is having difficulty or being pushed aside or being ignored by others—"We don't want to work with her"—we shall need to be supporting to the child—warm and kindly. But we should not make too much of the situation or let the child feel we attach too much importance to it. We might say, "The children don't mean to be unkind. They don't know you very well yet," or "Jim and Ned have been friendly with each other for a long time. They just didn't think when they would not let you join their group." Or even quite matter-of-factly, "Nobody is liked by everyone. There will always be some people who like us and some who don't. Why don't you work with the group over here?" If we show anxiety about a child's experience, he will sense our concern and be less able to take it in stride. If a child is really an isolate in the class, we may have to find more direct ways of including him in the children's activities, while at the same time we try to help the basic problem. Sometimes by using the natural groupings wherever possible, so that the children enjoy their working relationships, we can gradually find spots for the isolates in groups that are strong enough to accept and begin to understand the needs of these individual youngsters. Often a group of children around a friendly child are willing to work as a group to help another youngster who needs friends, whereas asking one child to stand alone in such a capacity might be asking too much.

These are good spots, too, for sociodrama. Through role-playing, we can help children talk over and analyze together what happens in playground situations, in quarrels between friends, in groups that do not want to work together, or in cases when a child is left out. In this way, it is possible to help the children understand the common experiences many people have. Role-playing offers an excellent starting point for discussion without attaching personal blame in either direction.

Some teachers feel that it is best to seat children apart from their friends to "avoid trouble." This is sometimes best, but often it works in the other direction. The children then can hardly wait to get into the halls, to throw notes, or to talk to a "best" friend when the teacher is out of the room.

We may find that a child's work improves greatly when he is permitted to work with a friend instead of being separated from him. Often children who are alike will get along better together than a mixture of all kinds of youngsters in a group. A shy child, asked to work with a socially sophisticated youngster, may feel so completely ill at ease that she withdraws into herself. Or a well-behaved little girl placed between two talkative boys in order to keep them apart may find herself made a scapegoat.

One has to be very sensitive to the undercurrents within the classroom and play such things as seating or the formation of committees almost by ear. Usually, it is wise to let children's interest be the criterion in forming a committee. Naturally formed groupings are usually better than forced groupings. Wise placement of the one or two isolates, after encouragement to choose a group in which they are interested, may be necessary. But where children sit and with whom they choose to work is not nearly as important for growth as the purposiveness of their work. This will depend upon whether the work has meaning for them and gives them a chance to be successful in it.

COOPERATION—NOT CONFORMITY—IS THE GOAL OF PARTICIPATION*

As we try to think through the problem of participation, difficulty may arise when we find that the very group membership so necessary for the growth of responsibility in one direction seems to stunt it in another. In our realization that we must work together to survive, we have in recent years been focusing on the group. We speak in terms of group interaction, of acceptance by the group, of arriving at group decisions. Somehow we feel we must reach a unanimous agreement by compromising here and there. We may look askance at the individual who stands out and says, "I don't agree." And at the same time we decry the fact that we seem to be losing our ability to stand out as individuals. We ask, "Where are our leaders?" "Where are our thinkers?" We are sometimes concerned when fine children do not seem to have the strength of character to stand out against the group when its actions go counter to what adults consider desirable.

Have we perhaps tended to confuse good group membership with conformity to group opinion, asking in essence that the individual sacrifice some of his integrity in order to be accepted? Have we perhaps drawn back from the boy or girl who, in all sincerity, has questioned a statement or an opinion or has said, "I don't agree with the conclusions we have reached"? Is there a difference between trying to get conformity of opinion as it relates to a subject under discussion for which no action is required, and agreement as to a course of action the group must follow as a unit? Is the minority opinion sometimes an indication that real participation has taken place in the thinking of the group? Can a minority opinion or point of view often be a most valuable and stimulating contribution, ultimately carrying the group further forward than a unanimous opinion would have done?

Can we really discuss responsible participation and set the goals toward which we want to help our boys and girls unless we also rethink the kind of premium which has, too frequently, been put on acceptance by the group? Should it be cooperation rather than conformity that each member of our class can be expected to give—expecting in return the right to retain his personal integrity of action and thought?

*Much of the material in this section is taken from the author's article "Responsibility in Children: The Contribution of the Home." *Child Study,* summer 1956. It is reprinted here with permission of the publishers.

If acceptance by the group and participation in classroom activities become ends in themselves, we cannot expect that our children will be prepared for responsible citizenship. Only as the group is able to tolerate, and even appreciate, differences among its members can group membership and participation be an essential and genuine preliminary experience to the responsible individualism so necessary for adult citizenship.

REFERENCES

(1) Hollister, William G. *Suggested Techniques for Leading Group Discussions.* Department of Mental Health, National Institute of Health. Unpublished material.

(2) Butler, Elsie. "Living Together in the Third Grade," *Elementary English,* Vol. XXVIII, Jan. 1951, pp. 3-5.

(3) Nulton, Lucy. "Eight-Year-Olds Tangled in *Charlotte's Web,*" *Elementary English,* Vol. XXXI, Jan. 1954, pp. 11-16.

(4) Butler, *op. cit.,* pp. 1-2, 55.

CHAPTER 4

EXPRESSION

OF FEELINGS

We read so much about curbing strong
emotions, in one way or another. But nobody
can be serene and happy all the time.
How can we strike a reasonably good balance here?

When you know a child is troubled
about something, how do you go about finding
out what it is so that you can help?

Whenever anyone says to me that I should foster my
children's creativity, I get panic-stricken.
I'm not even a passable artist or musician so how can
I help youngsters express themselves creatively?

When I listen to confidences
children offer, I sometimes hear things
I know the children shouldn't be
telling me. How do I handle these situations?

Suppose Johnnie is angry about something and wants
to hit anyone within arm's length. He will be
expressing his hostile feelings—but is this good?

I have hesitated to use role-playing
in my classes. I'm not at all sure that I can
handle the feelings that may come out.

FOR EMOTIONAL GROWTH

TO BE ALIVE IS TO FEEL

Emotions and feelings are the driving force of life. Even strong emotions such as anger, fear, and unhappiness have their place in life. It is our task not to forbid or deny children's emotions but to help them understand that everybody has such feelings at times and that it is how we learn to cope with our feelings that is most important.

It is well for all of us to remember that anger, for example, is the right emotion to feel when you or someone else has been unfairly treated. Some of the great achievements of mankind have been developed because men were angry. Anger against unfair taxation brought about the birth of our own country. Anger at the treatment of children during the early days of the industrial revolution brought about reforms and the Child Labor Laws. Anger against the loss of mothers in childbirth contributed to the development of the hygienic conditions of the modern maternity hospital.

Our job is not to forbid anger and its manifestations, but rather to help the children in our classrooms to a greater tolerance of frustration and gradually more selectivity in what they become angry about. We can help them, too, to learn how to use anger in appropriate action instead of in simple emotional explosion. Very little children hit when they are angry. When they are about four, they hit with words and call one another names. As children grow older, they learn better ways to express their anger in words, and gradually, we hope, they learn to meet obstacles through considered action instead of in anger.

Fear, too, is necessary for it often warns us of danger. It keeps a child from running in front of a car or climbing to a dangerous place. We can help a child see that all of us have fear but that we must try to develop the courage to face certain situations instead of running away from them. There are other situations that require the wisdom of knowing when it is time to run away. For instance, we have to teach children that it is not courageous to take a dare that may result in injury to themselves or to someone else. These are the times it takes more courage to say "no" than to say "yes."

Even the emotion of unhappiness cannot and should not always be avoided. One cannot really know happiness without having experienced the contrasting emotion of unhappiness. Just as life cannot be painless, physically speaking, so it cannot be painless emotionally. An artist tells the story of his teen-age daughter, who came home utterly inconsolable over an unfortunate incident that had happened at school. The incident was of such a nature that nothing could really be done about it and the only solution was to learn to accept it and hope the hurt would soon pass. As his daughter finished sobbing out her tale, her father took paint brush in hand and, alternately dipping it in various colors, made broad swatches and swirls of color on paper. He then asked his daughter what she thought of the picture. Since the picture was devoid of any outline or form, his daughter told him it didn't mean anything to her. Her father then filled in the picture with black paint, creating a handsome picture of a ship at sea. He said, "Now you see that black is necessary to a picture—just as some 'blackness' is necessary to life itself. It gives form, vividness, and meaning to life. Without the black, this picture (and your life, too) would be spiritless and drab."

Too often, as grownups, we act as if feelings were something to be discouraged. A little boy is taught that he mustn't cry if he is afraid or hurt or unhappy. A child is often admonished to "Sit still" or "Don't get so excited" when he is literally "wiggling all over" with excitement or enthusiasm. With some children, we may teach control so effectively that they lose their spontaneity—

their capacity to respond directly to their feelings.

By forbidding or denying a child his feelings—"That didn't hurt, did it?" "Everyone is happy now, isn't he?" or "A big boy like you shouldn't be afraid of the dark"—we are teaching the child to hide his feelings instead of learning how to use them constructively. The child who has been told it is wrong to be afraid or it is wrong not to like mother or teacher does not have a change of feelings—he simply learns to keep his feelings to himself. Then they come out in irritability, anger, timidness, sullenness, temper tantrums, hostility. Or the feelings may come out in physical symptoms—headaches, stomach aches, nausea, general feelings of being unwell. Modern medical findings have made us, as adults, well aware of the part our feelings play in our physical well-being —the headache that suddenly comes on after an unpleasant interview with an irate parent, the stomach ache that threatens to prevent you from making a speech at the PTA meeting. Both adults and children need to find constructive ways of coping with their feelings.

An atmosphere that cultivates courage, sympathy, understanding of other people, joy in a job well done will help reduce such destructive emotions as jealousy, greed, and revenge. If children are made to feel insecure, less wanted, less skillful than other children, we can expect that some of these more destructive emotions will be aroused.

ALL KINDS OF FEELINGS

MUST BE ACCEPTED

Sometimes when we discover a child's real feelings, we are shocked. We feel we must do something—we must not let a child hate like that. Such an approach will frighten the child away and push his feelings down deeply, for he will read in our reaction that this kind of feeling is not allowed. "I hate my mother—I hate her," sobbed out in a moment of emotion may put a barrier between child and shocked teacher. Yet we know that all of us have strong feelings of hate and love, that at one time or another, the hate may temporarily (or permanently) overbalance the love feelings. Shock at such feelings will not help a child face them but will drive them below the surface. A quiet "We all feel that way sometimes" can reduce the anxiety and ease the child into talking more about it. We must accept feelings while we limit action, and then try to help the child clarify his feelings.

Often the junior or senior high school teacher will find herself the recipient of a confidence that she feels should have gone to the child's parents. Its intimacy, or what it reveals of the child's home and his relationship with his parents, embarrasses her. But we need to remember that as children grow into adolescents, they are struggling to find their way out of the home circle, and the guidance of their parents seems temporarily unacceptable. Yet, adolescent boys and girls still want to know what an adult thinks. They are trying to identify with the adult world but are often in conflict and confusion, hardly knowing what they want or what to do with their feelings. It is sometimes easier for teen-agers to talk to a teacher whom they feel they can trust with their mixed-up feelings and ideas than to a parent. A teacher accepts these confidences, but, in doing so, she also accepts the obligation not to take these confidences to the teachers' room and spread them out for laughter. She accepts them with the same sincerity with which they were offered. A betrayed confidence can cause a sensitive adolescent to shut up within himself and hesitate, ever again, to share his thoughts and feelings with another, especially an adult. Whatever needs to be done in the way of action should be done without revealing the confidence the child has shared to anyone but those professionally equipped to help with the situation. Even then, confidences that are not pertinent to the situation should be respected.

We can destroy a confidence by using this moment as a time for moralizing; a "lecture" can make a youngster "pull away." Support can be given, the talk can be directed into the handling of the feelings or of the situation, choices can be suggested but not presented as "musts." Shock or anger at the revelations must be avoided; even too much sympathy may destroy the flow of the confidence.

ACCEPTING FEELINGS DOES NOT MEAN
ENDORSING ALL KINDS OF BEHAVIOR

We must distinguish between talking with a child to try to get out feelings, and talking with him or reasoning with him about his behavior, in order to get him to change it. Our attitude to the first is one of greater sensitivity. We are not trying to change the child or put demands on him; instead, we are trying to help him free himself of his tensions and hurt, knowing that he cannot think clearly about a problem as long as his feelings are mixed up. That is our goal.

In the second case, we are trying to get the child to *act,* to behave differently. We can understand the reason behind difficult behavior but we cannot permit expressions of anger and frustration that are harmful and disrupting. We do not say, "You must not feel that way." But we can say, "You may not act that way." We cannot always solve a child's problem, but we may be able to help him find a solution.

If the general atmosphere of the classroom is one in which children feel they are accepted and understood, there will be many ways in which we can help our boys and girls understand their feelings better. In such a classroom, children will have less need to give vent to their feelings by lying, stealing, hitting out at other children, or shutting up inside themselves, for they will learn to know that they may talk things over with a teacher who will listen.

FEELINGS CAN CHANGE

As we try to help children grow up and use their feelings more constructively, we must begin where they are with the needs they show. It is useless to tell a child to "be your age" if he is still reacting emotionally at the level of a much younger child. Mrs. Tripp knew this when she tried to help immature little Karen Williams grow up enough to leave her mother and take part in the life of the first grade.

Karen, although she lived close to the school, arrived at school each morning with her mother. As soon as her mother started to leave her, Karen would burst into tears and cry as if her heart would break. They were not tears that just welled up in her eyes, but sobs that seemed to say, "I can't bear to let you leave me." Mrs. Tripp's report says:

Karen was only five years and eight months when she came crying into my classroom on that first day of school. She was the youngest member of the group. She was an attractive little girl, scrupulously clean. Her dress was really far too frilly for school. She was small-boned and tiny—giving the impression of a very small and very young child. This impression was later confirmed; through actual height and weight measurements, she was physically the smallest member of the class. She had one little brother, eighteen months old.

I realized that the immediate problem was to handle Karen's tears in such a way that she need feel no embarrassment about them. I didn't want to add feelings of shame. I felt that I must accept the reality of the pain of separation, and at the same time, make some start on replacing the crying responses with new responses that would be satisfying to Karen and, at the same time, would be socially acceptable. I tried to accept the fact that the crying was appropriate to the pain this child was experiencing through separation. I was also aware that other children were experiencing the same pain, but they were handling it in a different way. I had some fear that Karen's crying, which was loud, might induce a sympathetic reaction in the hearts of her schoolmates. One, I could handle, a dozen—not very easily!

On that first day of school, Karen arrived clutching a bouquet for her teacher. Her mother was trying to help her bridge the gap between home and school. She had helped Karen pick the flowers that morning. I was happy about this for it gave the child something to do as soon as she arrived at school. Karen's mother kissed her good-bye and hurried out of the room, leaving the youngster clutching her bouquet of flowers. I said, "Good-bye, Mrs. Williams. Good morning, Karen." I took her hand and noticed that she didn't withdraw even though the sobs had started. "Let's find a vase for those pretty flowers so that we can show the children what you brought to school this morning." We went to the sink, which had low broad drainboards so Karen could easily reach the faucet. I got a vase and showed Karen how to turn on the water and helped her arrange the flowers and place them on the window sill. During this activity, the youngster stopped crying. I then showed her where to put her jacket and led her to her desk.

Each day, I handled the crying in a similar fashion as soon as I saw Karen come into the classroom. There were, of course, variations. The role I tried to play was that of another kind, female person who could satisfy Karen's need for warmth and affection.

This pattern continued until the tears gradually lessened. During my absence one day, Karen cried bitterly again and was taken to the principal's office. She complained of a stomach ache. The principal rubbed her stomach but, knowing the situation, kept Karen at school. Next day, Karen arrived without tears, complaining of a stomach ache. She told me about her experience of the previous day with the principal. As she told me, she started crying harder than she had at any other time since the first day of school.

I explained that I was sorry that I was not at school on the previous day and that I had missed being with Karen and her classmates. I also suggested that sometimes stomach aches accompanied crying and wondered if Karen would like to see if the pain disappeared if she tried to stop sobbing. If this did not work, I said, I would be willing to call her mother if it appeared that Karen were

really ill. During recess Karen confided that she felt better. At lunch time, Karen said, "Teacher, I think you are right. When I stopped crying, my tummy stopped hurting. Now I'm hungry." And Karen ate the lunch her mother had packed.

Karen gradually became divided in her loyalty between home and school. She came to me when she felt the flood coming on again as it often did at recess or at lunch time.

I tried to help Karen by initiating a classroom discussion of "How did you come to school?" "Some come by bus. All of us share the experience of separation from home." I wrote a chalkboard story of "How Did We Come to School?" I initiated further discussion of "How did you feel about coming to school?"

Tim said, "I was scared."

Nina said, "I wanted to come."

Many said they were frightened; others, like Nina, were eager, and some did not respond at all. Karen listened and found that she was not alone in experiencing the pain of separation and fear of a new situation.

I went on to say, "Some of us feel like crying when we come to school because this is new and different. Many of you did not know what to expect. One of your first jobs is to learn to be happy here. What are some of the things here which you have seen and touched that make you happy?"

I wrote what the children said on the chalkboard:

"We like the toys."

"We like the little desks."

"We like the water fountain."

"We like the pretty pictures."

One child said, "I like the other children."

I said, "These things are yours this year. Your mother and father have helped pay for them." Then I said, "Let's see how many children we have." The children helped count noses. Most of them could count to ten; some continued through all the twenty-seven.

Once the crying was stopped, Karen participated in group activities. She had come out of herself enough to experience pleasure in the classroom. At no point was there a recurrence of tears during the actual teaching time. The child smiled and even raised her hand to make remarks.

Karen was coming to school not in response to

any felt need she had but to a felt need of the society in which she happened to be born. My task was to supply enough things that Karen liked to do so that she actually felt that she wanted to come to school. To find out whether I was succeeding in moving the child in this direction, after four weeks I took the calculated risk and suggested the following to the child. This conversation occurred at the conclusion of school just before Karen went home.

"Karen, you seem to like school so much that I'm wondering if you might not enjoy coming to school with your friend, Betty Michael."

Karen did not show any signs of distress and said, "I think I will talk to my Mommy about that."

The next morning, Karen came to school alone. She cried all the way but she got there. I greeted her, "I am so glad to see you." I took special care that morning to help her remove her jacket, blow her nose, and make her physically comfortable before we started class activities. At recess that morning, Karen asked if she could take the big ball outside. I asked another very kindly and friendly little girl if she would play ball with Karen.

I believe tremendous effort went into this child's arrival under her own power. I think it is interesting to note that it was followed by a burst of initiative on her part. On the playground that day, I noticed that Karen asked another child if it were time to go in and purchase ice cream. (The school sells ice cream at lunch time.) Although she lives within walking distance of home, Karen has been content to stay at school for the lunch period.

Karen talks freely now. She brings things to school for "Show and Tell." She laughs and seems, on the whole, relaxed. She talks to the other children in the room. She volunteers information and answers questions. She does not show any signs of overdependence on me. She has been taught how to zip up her jacket and does this easily. She has also learned how to put her own shoes on. Children have noticed her and welcome her in play. She is willing to be last in line to take a turn at jump rope. (She wanted to learn how and actually performed well on her first try. She is an enthusiastic rope-jumper.) She does well on all seatwork. She listens attentively and follows directions well. She shows good eye-hand coordi-

nation with beginning handwriting. She loves and learns poetry easily. She is not ashamed of her errors and does not try to conceal them from me. Although the Lee-Clarke readiness tests given at the end of four weeks indicated an expected delay in reading readiness of six months, Karen has already learned eight color words and can recognize the number symbols 1-6. She can discriminate quantities and attach the proper symbol to the amount. Karen's adjustment indicates that she will be ready in the fall to move from a reading readiness group to a pre-primer. She is eager and confident.

Often the job of the teacher is to try gradually to replace one feeling tone with another, as Mrs. Tripp tried to help Karen. A child who has been hurt, who has been laughed at, or who has had repeated experiences with failure or rejection will often stand on the side lines—anxious to enter into the discussion or the game or activity, but afraid to do so.

Miss Leslie helped little Nora, who had drawn into herself, enter into the games and laugh with the children. She helped Mark, who had been hurt by adults, gradually to feel that here was someone he could trust.

Often we must try to replace a feeling of "I can't do it," based on experiences of frustration and failure that anticipate, "I shall fail," "I always spoil everything," with the beginning of a feeling of "I can." This happened to Phil when Miss Phelps began to show him that he could succeed. The road back from discouragement is long; it takes patience to help a child change the feeling tones about himself so that he is able to learn how to go ahead.

Sometimes the tension based on anxiety is so great that a child cannot transform the tension into activity. One little girl, who was a perfectionist, could not bring herself to write for fear she would make a mistake. Sometimes a child becomes so tense in his failure to read that he cannot get out the word. These children need special help; direct commands to write or read will not produce results.

WE CAN HELP CHILDREN GROW TOWARD EMOTIONAL MATURITY BY—

KEEPING COMMUNICATION CHANNELS OPEN

It is important to keep the channels of communication open between teachers and children so that boys and girls feel free to come and talk or just to sit close. Communication need not be through words alone; a smile, a tone of voice, a kindly look, a hand on the shoulder of the older child, an arm around the younger one, will go a long way toward communicating a friendly understanding. Many children have built up their defenses so high to protect themselves from the hurts they have felt that it is hard to break through to the point where communication becomes a possibility. Mrs. Tripp said, "I'm not afraid for those who cry, but I wonder how to reach those who come in each morning with a wooden expression and no 'hello.'"

Communication cannot be forced. A child is likely to open up only as he observes you with other children, sees that you do not burst out in anger with him because he is "dumb," slow, awkward, behind the rest of the class, or even seriously disturbed. Even when we realize that a child's behavior is probably an indication that he needs help, we may not be able to help him immediately. Rarely can we help a child by a direct attack. It is not helpful to probe and question and try to force a child to talk about his feelings. It takes sensitivity and a willingness to wait for the child to feel free to come to us or to show that he needs us now.

Larrick (1)* tells about a third-grade teacher who "realized that individual children often had something to say to her at a time when the rush of the day's schedule made her too busy to listen. 'Write me a note,' she would tell them, 'and put it in the second drawer of my desk so I can read it later'. Evidently her sincerity showed in the tone of her voice, for notes poured in—some

*Full references are cited at the end of the chapter.

that were gay and exuberant, some wistful and lonely, a few that were genuinely troubled and anxious. Thus out of the mouths of her third-graders, she learned to know what they were thinking as she would never have learned otherwise."

Here are the statements a group of children gave when they were asked by Larrick to write about the things they wondered about.

I wonder if I am going to get my work in on time. I wish I could be faster than I am.

I wonder why school doesn't end. It is tiresome just sitting in these wiggly desks and having to do tests and do arithmetic. But worst of all is spelling. I wish summer would come.

I have been wondering, do teachers have pets. They say they don't but it seems that there are two or three girls in my room that always get to do everything.

I wonder why the teacher always scolds you when you don't have your lessons done or when you don't get a few problems right.

I wonder how old my teacher is. . . . I like teachers that laugh. My first-grade teacher never laughed. But my third-grade teacher laughs a lot.

Sometimes I wonder if anyone likes me. They act as if they don't . . . They just go off and leave me behind. Then I seem to wonder if they like me.

I wonder why I always get blamed all the time when I tease my brother. He always starts it. I wonder why I always want to tease him.

I wonder why I am not as pretty as the other girls I know. If I was as pretty as Dorothy everyone would like me. She may have straight hair but she is still prettier than me.

I wonder if I am good or bad . . . When my aunt or uncle come over they say I have been nice when they leave. But my mother and father say that I'm just a worry. That's why I don't know.

I wonder how come all big children blame things on little children that little children didn't do. I wonder about playing on Saturday because I have no one to play with and I don't know where to go.

I wonder why do some children be so mean all the time.

I wonder why my mother divorced my dad.

BEING SENSITIVE TO TROUBLED FEELINGS

Our basic emotions may be universal. We may all be equipped in the same way to respond to fear, anger, sorrow, or happiness. But what causes these emotions is personal to each one of us, dependent upon our life experiences and/or the meanings and associations they have given to us. An experience that gives rise to unhappy feelings in one child may "roll off the back" of another.

In one case Tommy, feeling secure within himself, might shrug his shoulders and boycott baseball, because to him and to his parents, his interest in the microscope might be much more satisfying than an interest in baseball or "what the other boys think." But if Tommy were not sure of himself, if he did not feel that his parents approved of his deep interest in his microscope, if he himself were a lonely little boy, his interest might still draw him away from baseball toward the microscope, but he would be hurt, uncertain, and uncomfortable because he realized that the others thought him odd. The first Tommy could safely be left to go his way In his own inner security, he would be able to handle the situation and make a choice of what he wanted to do. The second Tommy would need encouragement and support in developing his real interest in science, but at the same time, he would need help in feeling greater personal security and

the sense of belonging that he deeply wants. Otherwise, he would be turning to his microscope for solace, because he could not work out his other problems satisfactorily while inside he would carry the gnawing feeling that he wanted to belong, that he wanted to be like other boys and do the things they were doing.

AGGRESSIVENESS MAY BE A SIGNAL

Children cannot always tell us of their real feelings. Words do not come easily to all youngsters. Neither are they always conscious of why they are quarrelsome, unhappy, or restless. Feelings run very deep and the motives behind them are not always apparent, even to the one who is experiencing them. But a child's behavior is a signal to us of the feelings that may lie beneath the surface.

Miss Nesbit realized this as she got to know Ray Severson, a well-built, good-looking sixteen-year-old in her sophomore English class:

I became interested in Ray because he seemed to have a temper that grew red-hot quickly over small things—an error pointed out in his work, his grades, the "right answer," a definition, the use of a new word, the way I conducted the class, or the behavior of another student. He had a spark in his eye that flashed when he listened to the opinions of others. I learned to watch for the moment when the spark got a little too bright and Ray began to flush with anger. His temper caused him trouble in the halls and in his extracurricular activities, too.

However, whenever he had said something out of the way in the class, he always came in between classes or after school to apologize to me. And he often stopped in to lean on my desk and chat about affairs of the day. When his temper was under control, he was an interesting, alert boy. He was an average student who had many interests and took part in the activities of the school, although, as in class, he had some very definite opinions about these, too.

This year, his temper led him into three serious fights. In the early part of the semester, Ray knocked down a boy in a one-sided fist fight. I witnessed the fight but was too surprised to prevent it. As I saw it, Ray had just been looking at the boy—then, without a word, knocked him down with one blow.

I took the two boys to the office. The principal told me that this had happened often during the past year and that Ray had an uncontrollable temper. He also said that Ray had acquired a reputation of being hard to handle. I was surprised because up to this moment, there had been nothing that smacked of problems that couldn't be solved. Now, knowing what had happened the year before, I could see that this fight might be deeply related to the rest of Ray's personality, as I had seen it in the classroom.

Later, I talked with Ray, presenting my view that we can never fight in the school building or really hurt anyone, no matter what the other person has done.

Ray kept saying, "I had to. I just had to. You don't understand."

"You mean you had to prove yourself in some way?"

"Yes, I had to. You don't understand. People don't think I'll fight."

"But Ray, if you were small and people picked on you, then you might feel that way. Nobody can take advantage of you, however, because you are tall and strong."

"But you don't know what has happened. People think I won't fight, and I've got to do it."

"All right, Ray. You've proved that you will fight. Everybody knows it now, and you don't have to do it any more. In the school buildings, it is never allowed."

After the next school dance, however, Ray knocked down another boy as they came out of the school building. It appeared that the boy had teased Ray at the dance, and Ray had refused to fight then. He had, instead, waited to fight until after the school function was over.

A week later, Ray grew violent in the study hall. Someone had thrown a paper wad at him. Ray jumped from his seat and fixed the blame on a boy who is usually in trouble but who was innocent this time. Ray grabbed the wad and the boy, looking terribly angry. When I approached them, Ray threw the paper wad at me and said, "Here, throw this in the waste-paper basket."

"You put it in the wastebasket, Ray," I replied.

"I'm sorry, Miss Nesbit, but I can't do that."

"Ray, we can't settle this right now, but you go to the office and wait for me there and we will talk."

"I'm sorry, Miss Nesbit, I can't go."

After this conversation, I had to ask for help from the assistant principal. Even with him, Ray was cool and repeated that he couldn't go to the office. Then suddenly, he burst into open anger again—grabbing another boy and saying, "You're the one who threw that wad at me. I'm going to beat you up!" Ray was finally taken to the office, under protest.

I called up Ray's mother and had a revealing conversation with her. She told me that Ray, as a child, had never been in a fight at all and that all the children in the neighborhood picked on him and teased him because he would not defend himself. His older brother had told him that he had to fight back and finally became annoyed with Ray for being a "coward." Ray had finally learned to defend himself a year before, and in the following months he had got into a number of fist fights. He didn't seem sure about when he was expected to fight and when he was not. Once he challenged a boy to step outside and fight. When the boy came out, Ray refused to fight after all. He was very ashamed of himself and told his mother that now everybody would know he was a coward. His mother felt that his strong build made Ray think of himself as more of a coward than he otherwise would, because he looked like a person who would never be afraid.

Ray was a "mixed-up" boy. He seemed to be trying to prove through his arguing and his fighting that his doubts about himself were false. He presented a complex picture. As his teacher realized, it would be difficult to work out the deeper reasons for his tensions without knowing much more about the relationships within his home, particularly with his father and his brother. Ray was apparently a boy who felt deeply hurt within himself.

There was probably much more behind his feeling of lack of courage than his early inability to fight. Miss Nesbit could not get all of the information she would have liked about Ray within the limitations of the teacher-pupil-home relationship, but she did find out enough to know that here was a boy whose behavior was a signal that all was not well. Ray was not a "bad boy," as some of his teachers had already labeled him. Ray was a disturber—but even more, he was disturbed.

Miss Nesbit was not able to help Ray work through his deeper problems, but he did respond to her as an understanding person and he continued to turn to her for support and guidance. In this way, she was able to give Ray some help, even though it would require the guidance personnel to work more deeply into an adjustment of the real cause of his upset feelings and disturbing behavior.

We must always remember that we have not just one child, but many children, to consider in the classroom. Uncontrolled behavior on the part of one child can run like a wave through the classroom. Children like Karen, who sobs her heart out, and Ray, who starts a fight, can affect the others so that all enter in. Other children become restless and unhappy or take sides. One cannot permit feelings to be expressed to the extent that they are too disturbing to the others in the class. Such behavior can result in embarrassment and guilt for the one who let himself go and in antagonism on the part of the other children. It may be good for inhibited Sally to shout angry names at the girls who have excluded her, but we cannot let her do it in the schoolroom.

When we experience an outbreak of aggressive behavior in our classrooms, we might well take a look at our classroom situation as a whole. Is competition encouraged to the extent that some youngsters experience so many failures, aggressiveness becomes their only outlet? Have we set up such rigid standards of class behavior that children's normal need for communication and movement is being overlooked? Is there a possibility that some of these aggressive children need more challenging work to which their energy would be better directed?

OVERLY QUIET BEHAVIOR MAY BE A SIGNAL, TOO

We recognize the feelings of a Ray because they are so disturbing and obvious that we cannot avoid them. But very often we overlook the feelings of a boy like Phil who was so conforming and quiet that it was as if "he weren't there." As far as his teachers were concerned, he might just as well not have been there until his senior year when Miss Phelps "found him." A child like Phil may conform on the surface to the requirements of being a "good, well-behaved child" who never upsets the classroom, does what is required of him, and causes no trouble. Such a child may not show his real feelings to us at all because he is "on guard." He has learned, perhaps from his parents or from an earlier school experience, that it is safer to behave well. As little Toby, a kindergartner, said, "If I sit very quietly and don't speak unless she asks me something and just do everything she wants, no one will notice me. Then I'll be all right."

It takes a sensitive teacher to realize that such a good, cooperative child may not be all right. Such a youngster may be afraid and anxious and insecure—he may be tense and strained but afraid of the consequences if he should let go of his feelings and show them openly. Toby showed his feelings of anxiety by biting his fingernails to the quick by the end of the second week of school.

Some children have deep feelings, which they are not able to express or release outwardly. Little Toby was able to tell his mother, but Phil sat year after year in the classroom, keeping his feelings to himself. The quiet child, the withdrawn child, the very "good" child who is too anxious to please, is often a child who is in great need of help in getting his real feelings out in the open.

The child whose signals of distress we have passed by until he bursts out in rebellious or aggressive behavior is at least, like Ray, trying to meet the situation himself. *His way may be wrong but his spirit is right.* He may be hard to live with but his personality will have a better chance to develop toward ultimate maturity than the child who learns to meet a difficult situation by shutting up inside himself. He also stands a better chance of having his unhappiness recognized and having something done about it.

The overly good, the overly conforming child is too often considered desirable by teachers, who find a child "who is seen but not heard" ideal to live with—"He is no bother at all." His signals are sometimes not recognized until serious damage has been done.

Such a child frequently becomes the youngster who does not learn how to play and work and live with other children. He is the child, like Phil, who may retire so deeply into his daydreams that he almost loses touch with reality. He may tend, like Toby, to do what he is told as the best means of avoiding trouble. He is likely to feel deep guilt, like Phil, if he does do something he feels he should not have done. Such children often grow up unable to make the many necessary decisions of adult life without strain—or they may be so dependent that they rarely can make them at all and will turn toward another adult or toward whoever is in authority to know what they must do. Their sense of personal worth is frequently very low.

OTHER SIGNALS WE SHOULD BE AWARE OF

There are other signals that children give us when they have had too much to take, either at home or at school, or through a combination of both. Most of these manifestations are normal to children in some measure, but when they are done in excess of normal or when they become a pattern that keeps a child from mixing with others, then they are signals of trouble ahead.

Restlessness is a very common outlet for tension. If we have a restless child in the classroom, we should not look upon him as a "bad" child but as one who needs to be studied to find out what is behind the restlessness. Sometimes we have a period of general restlessness in the classroom. It would not make sense to command a restless group of children to "sit still," deprive them of recess or keep them in longer. Such restrictions would ignore the reasons behind the restlessness. Instead, we need to provide outlets in physical activity.

Overeating, especially in an older child, is often a signal that something is wrong. We will see such a child, day after day, nibbling candy from a bag on the playground or furtively eating candy from his desk, hoping what he is doing will go unnoticed.

Crying without much provocation is another signal. The child who buries her head on her desk and cries when her teacher makes a slight suggestion or correction is often exhibiting deeply hurt feelings.

Daydreaming is sometimes a signal of trouble ahead. When a child constantly withdraws into daydreams or window-gazing, when he escapes too often from reality into his own thoughts, we can be sure he needs understanding help from us. However, all daydreaming should not be suspect. Daydreams can be a wonderful escape from the humdrum, the worries, and the feelings of failure we all have now and then. The child who takes time to think and dream may be building up ideas that someday will come out productively. It is necessary, however, for the child to learn to keep fantasy and reality in balance.

AVOIDING RECRIMINATIONS

The reasons for a child's actions are not always conscious, rational, and deliberate.

Inner tensions may make a child misbehave in spite of the fact that he knows better. "I don't know why I did it, I just did." We often say with exasperation, "He knows better." Sometimes we confront a child with the question, "Why did you do that?" The change in Rita's disposition was not a conscious one. She probably did not know why she hit out at her little sister, who still received the warm, kindly attention of her much-loved parents, while Rita was feeling the pressure of sudden, new disciplinary demands. Neither was Rita conscious of why she no longer complied with what her parents wished. Children who are under stress often act impulsively and under the pressure or tension of the moment. They do not know why. Ray would apologize after class to his teacher when he had had time to think over what he had said impulsively in class.

It rarely helps to try to extract a promise from a child, "You will never do that again, will you, Bill?" or "You will be less disturbing to please me, won't you?" Such verbal promises may be made under force of pressure of the situation, or because the child cannot avoid them, but they do nothing to change the real feelings of the child.

Anita, a third-grader, in the excitement of a hide-and-seek game on the playground, knocked over the plants that had been placed out-of-doors on the fourth-grade window sill. Her teacher scolded her for being careless and not looking where she was going. She sent her to say she was sorry to the fourth-grade teacher. Anita rushed into the fourth-grade room, red-faced with embarrassment, and blurted out, "I broke your plants—I'm sorry." Then she dashed from the room muttering to herself, "I'm not sorry, I'm not sorry, the mean old thing shouldn't have left them outside." Lip service is of little value. Again it does not mirror the real feelings. It happened that Anita was a youngster whose mother was a very precise person. Anita had suffered more than once from her mother's anger over an accident, a broken cup, a spilled dish. She

saw in the frequent anger of her mother, feelings of hostility to herself. This hurt had left her an unhappy little girl. The new accident at school frightened her and aroused all her hurt feelings toward her mother. She was not sorry. She was angry at people who hurt her in this way.

Pressuring and probing are not the way to get feelings out. Making a child admit feelings rarely works. Listening and then asking questions is often helpful—but not if there are strings attached in the form of promises to be good or do better. "You will do better, won't you?" is often beyond the child's ability to carry through. You may have discovered the cause of the feeling, but the feeling is still there.

TAKING TIME FOR PLAY AND LAUGHTER

Children's play not only sometimes gives us a clear lead to a center of anxiety, but it is also a wonderful release for the feelings of children of all ages. Running, shouting, climbing, swinging, playing baseball and football, hitting a tennis or a golf ball, running in a race, playing "Cops and Robbers," punching and wrestling can give children a release of strain and tension, an outlet for the overflow of energy and restlessness, and just plain fun. The child who has fun, who enjoys himself with his friends or even playing by himself, has an outlet that keeps him in balance and gives good feelings to balance the tension everyone develops at times.

Perhaps one reason children enjoy playing so much is that this is an area in which grownups leave them more or less alone. If children are playing, we don't often enter into this area in their lives. It belongs to them. For this reason, although we must have certain aims in teaching children the skills they need and in helping them learn good sportsmanship, we must not make of games such a serious business that they are no longer fun. For fun is the main purpose of games. Recreation should remain what the words mean, *re-creation*—a chance to create ourselves again, or refresh ourselves. If games become too competitive so that children are afraid to take part, if too much is made of winning or of the necessary skill—the most important part of the play for each child is lost. Children should play because they love it, not because they must play.

And where there is play, there should be laughter. There is nothing sadder than to see a group of children put through the formalities of a "game" in a situation in which they must not make any noise for fear they will get out of hand.

There is a place for the team sport—for the game that challenges and involves the use of one's mind and nerves and muscles. We know that tension can be pleasurable if it is followed by a satisfactory release. We know, too, that older children need some excitement and competition. But when this means that most children become spectators and do not enter in or when winning becomes so important that tension results in a bitter strain if one loses, then the value of play as recreation has been lost.

Just as children in our classrooms need time for play, so should we welcome the release that comes with laughter. Some teachers are afraid of laughter because children sometimes let their good emotions as well as their negative ones get out of control. But if the tension that preceded the laughter has not been out of control, the laughter will be normal and spontaneous and will recede when the joke is over. Uncontrolled laughter is usually an indication of overcontrol in the classroom or tension that has piled up. The suppressed giggling that develops at the back of the classroom or in the assembly hall is usually a release for pent-up feelings, for children giggle when they are nervous or afraid. But friendly, spontaneous laughter in a classroom, which wells up from the teacher or the children, is normal and wholesome. Laughing *with* someone is good. Laughing *at* someone can cause hurt. If gig-

gling develops as a sign of tension or if laughter gets out of control, the wise teacher will change the pace of the activity, turning to something new to re-focus attention.

Prime Minister Jawaharlal Nehru (2) of India wrote this open letter to the children of the world for *Shankar's Weekly* of New Delhi. When he was asked for permission to reproduce it in America, he consented readily. "When it is something for children," he said, "you don't even need to ask."

I like being with children and talking to them and, even more, playing with them. For a moment I forget that I am terribly old and that it is a very long time ago since I was a child. But when I sit down to write to you, I cannot forget my age and the distance that separates you from me.

Old people have a habit of delivering sermons and good advice to the young. I remember that I disliked this very much long, long ago when I was a boy. So I suppose you do not like it very much either.

Grownups have also a habit of appearing to be very wise, even though very few of them possess much wisdom. I have not quite made up my mind yet whether I am wise or not. Sometimes, listening to others, I feel I must be very wise and brilliant and important. Then, looking at myself, I begin to doubt this. In any event people who are wise do not talk about their wisdom and do not behave as if they were very superior persons.

So I must not give you a string of good advice as to what you should do and what you should not do. I suppose you have enough of this from your teachers and others. Nor must I presume to be a superior person.

What, then, shall I write about? If you were with me, I would love to talk to you about this beautiful world of ours, about flowers and trees and birds and animals, and stars, and mountains and glaciers, and all the other wonderful things that surround us in this world. We have all this beauty around us and yet we, who are grownups, often forget about it and lose ourselves in our affairs and imagine that we are doing very important work.

I hope you will be more sensible and open your eyes and ears to this beauty and life that surround you. Can you recognize the flowers by their names and the birds by their singing? How easy it is to make friends with them and with everything in nature, if you go to them affectionately and with friendship.

You must have read many fairy tales and stories of long ago. But the world itself is the greatest fairy tale and story of adventure that has ever been written. Only we must have eyes to see and ears to hear and a mind that opens out to the life and beauty of the world.

Grownups have a strange way of putting themselves in compartments and groups. They build up barriers and then they think that those outside their particular barrier are strangers whom they must dislike. There are barriers of religion, of caste, of color, of party, of nation, of province, of language, of custom and of wealth and poverty. Thus they live in prisons of their own making.

I have recently been to the United States of America, to Canada and to England. It was a long journey, right on the other side of the world. I found the children there very like the children here and so I easily made friends with them, and whenever I had the chance I played with them a little. That was much more interesting than many of my talks with the grownups, who imagine they are very different, and deliberately make themselves so.

You know that we had a very great man amongst us in India. He was called Mahatma Gandhi. But we used to call him affectionately, Bapuji. He was very wise but he did not show off his wisdom.

He was a friend not only to all the people of India but also to all the people in the rest of the world. He taught us not to hate anybody, not to quarrel but to play with one another and to cooperate in the service of our country. He taught us also not to be afraid of anything and to face the world cheerfully and with laughter.

As I write I think of the vast army of children all over the world, outwardly different in many ways, speaking different in many ways, speaking different languages, wearing different kinds of clothes and yet so very like one another. If you bring them together, they play or quarrel. But even their quarreling is some kind of play.

They do not think of differences amongst themselves, differences of class or caste or color or status. They are wiser than their fathers and mothers. As they grow up, unfortunately, their natural wisdom is often eclipsed by the teaching and behavior of their elders.

At school they learn many things which are no doubt useful but they gradually forget that the essential thing is to be human and kind and playful and to make life richer for ourselves and others.

We live in a wonderful world that is full of beauty and charm and adventure. There is no end to the adventures that we can have if only we seek them with our eyes open. So many people seem to go about their life's business with their eyes shut. Indeed, they object to other people keeping their eyes open. Unable to play themselves, they dislike the play of others.

Animals have keener instincts than man. If a man goes to them with murder in his heart, they are afraid of him and run away. But if he has any love for animals, they do not mind him. If you are full of fear yourself, then the animal is afraid, too, and might attack you in self-defense. The fearless person is seldom, if ever, attacked.

Perhaps that lesson might be applied to human beings also. If we meet other people in a friendly way, they also become friendly. But if we are afraid of them or if we show our dislike to them, they behave in the same manner.

These are the simple truths which the world has known for ages. But even so, the world forgets and the people of one country hate and fear the people of another country; and because they are afraid, they are sometimes foolish enough to fight each other.

Children should be wiser. At any rate, I hope the children who read this will be more sensible.

FINDING WAYS FOR CHILDREN TO EXPRESS THEIR FEELINGS CONSTRUCTIVELY

GROUP DISCUSSIONS

Miss Hillary frequently talked things over with the children in her first grade. She would sit quietly with her group and ask the children to shut their eyes and answer a question such as "What kind of a class are we?" She called it "thinking out loud."

Miss Sinclair did this, too, when she followed Judy's suggestion, "Let's talk it over" and a happier solution was reached for Judy's problem.

Conversation of this kind will help children learn how to approach their problems and differences of opinion. They learn that feelings are acceptable and a part of us and that other boys and girls have them, too. Children are helped to realize that most people, at one time or another, have such feelings as "My thoughts are bad," "I must not feel afraid," "It is bad to feel angry," or "I feel so ashamed."

In such talks, however, we must be careful to keep the discussion on the common level of "This is how many of us feel" and avoid putting the spotlight on one child and his particular anxieties. Mrs. Tripp helped Karen through her "talking it over" period, but she did not attempt to encourage Karen to talk about her own deep anxiety in front of the other children. Class discussions, especially with older boys and girls, may at times lead into more private talks in which more intimate feelings or problems may come out. Here again we should not probe but be receptive listeners, asking a question now and then, expressing a word of understanding or encouragement, helping the child tell us "how he feels about it," accepting the feelings, and helping the child, when possible, to work toward a better solution of his problem. If the feelings seem too deep and the child seriously disturbed, we will need to find a way for the youngster to receive real counseling help.

Sometimes class discussions also stimulate boys and girls to talk over their problems together. Children can release many feelings by talking to their friends. The "bull sessions" of high-school boys and girls, the shared confidences of the two eighth-graders walking home from school, the give-and-take of small boys on the way to the baseball lot, are all wholesome ways of letting out feelings. Often children feel that those of the same age are closer to their problems and more satisfactory listeners than grownups.

ROLE PLAYING

Role playing or acting out situations, is another way of releasing feelings. But the same limitations should apply to this area as to the group conversation. We can work with ways of meeting surface behavior, with the understanding of feelings and their cause, but we must stay within the framework of the common experiences of the children and not focus on playing out the feelings of a particular child. For instance, all the children may have troubles with brothers and sisters at home. We can play out the ways in which the situations could be met. We can discuss the angry, the jealous, the hurt feelings many boys and girls experience and discuss the reasons for those feelings; but we do not ask a particular child to act out his own feelings and what he would like to do to a brother or sister. We know that such feelings, when unleashed, can be very upsetting to a child. In a room alone with a therapist, these feelings may come out, but a teacher in the classroom might have great difficulty in handling the outburst. There is also always the danger that a child may feel acutely embarrassed or overwhelmed with guilt and withdraw from the situation.

The important function of role playing is to help children see that they can explore a problem together, break it down and look at it, and work out together a better way of meeting it. Miss Sinclair might have used "acting it out" to help the children handle Judy's problem.

Neither group conversations nor role playing will be effective in a classroom in which a group spirit has not been developed. If these techniques are used simply as another class exercise, they will either fall flat or become a negative experience. Many children, particularly the older ones, resent being asked to act and take part in something that has no meaning for them.

Group conversations and role playing offer a great temptation to a teacher to talk *to* her boys and girls instead of *with* them. Feelings do not come out in a situation in which a teacher "tells" children how they should feel or what they should do. "You must all be friendly to one another in our class," has little effect except to cover up feelings, unless the idea has been reached by the children themselves in the way in which they had worked through a situation such as that of Judy's.

WRITING

Many children find it difficult to talk about their feelings, but they can be helped to write them down. It may be a little poem or a few lines of a composition that will spell release to the child. Sometimes it may be a happy feeling or a little story about something they have enjoyed doing together.

Cole (3) taught a group of nine-, ten-, and eleven-year-old children during their fourth grade and the first half of the fifth. Half of the group were Mexican, a quarter Chinese, and the rest Japanese and American. She says:

Their I.Q.'s would have consigned many of them to a rather meager existence, but I *found plenty to work with and felt they stopped only where I stopped in my ability and understanding....*

Howard ... started writing about the circus. He wrote on and on straight through recess time, the children according him respect for his interest.

Speedy light and cloudy dust—make way, for here comes Silver, carrying latest story from Room 13.

Once when we went to the circus and we seen a fat lady that weighed 745 pounds and I just wondered how it felt to be that fat, and I said to my mother, "How would you like to be that fat?" And she said, "I don't think I would like it very much." And we seen the skinniest man in the world and the fattest man in the world and the tallest man in the world and the smallest midgets in the world. We seen the monkey lady and she was real funny. She looked like a monkey. And the fattest man weighed 445 pounds and the tallest man in the world was 16 feet high. We seen a lady that let snakes crawl on her and I thought it might bite her but it never. And we seen a man that would burn fire in his hand and the man with two mouths. He had a mouth in his face and a mouth under his wing bone. And we seen the lady with the iron tongue and she could hook a chain in her tongue and on the other end of her tongue was a twelve pound cannon and she held it off the floor with her tongue and shot a gun shell out of the cannon. And then we seen the half man and the half woman, but I never got to see it.

We seen the man that could swallow swords and we seen the man that fought a alligator and the alligator was wild too. And we seen the lady that was only half there and still alive and we seen the girl in the fish bowl and she could stay there fifteen minutes.

And we rode the electric cars and the merry-go-round and the ferris wheel and I bought some of the flavored ice and I rode the ponies.... And we shot guns and threw balls and shot sling shots and had a lot of fun. And they sold the best ice cream at the circus that I ever ate in my whole life, unless it was when I was a little baby and I can't remember.

Well, so long, nice dreams.

And I like to write and that is why I have written such a long story.

Next morning I read the story out loud quickly, all in one gulp. The children liked it. It was rather amusing that Howard, after having invented most of the story from his wishful thinking, should have strained his conscience over the ice cream. When I saw him alone I smiled at him and asked casually, "Did you really do some of those things, Howard, or is it all just a make-believe story?"

"Oh sure," he said, hunching his shoulders in a nervous way he had. "I did some of 'em, not all of them, but some of 'em."

When children and teacher know each other well, the written expression may be about something that is troubling one of them. As Cole (4) writes:

When children are encouraged to write that which has real meaning, they find release from what is bothering them. Let me tell the story about little Japanese Yoshiko.... From being very capable she suddenly changed and contributed little to the group. At story-writing time she handed in her paper with next to nothing on it. Then it was discovered that Ming Chan and little Yon Lee had been bothering her. Yoshiko hadn't complained. She had just closed up. The teasing was stopped. Yoshiko, much relieved, wrote page after page at writing time:

Today we are writing our own report cards. We must be intelligent, wide-awake, kind, and loving to learn things. When people are mean to you, or are not kind to you, just ignore them, but be as kind as you could be. We should not think we are the smartest one, but think you are learning every day. No one is too smart; even the best one in the world will be dumb sometime. We should be dependable and obedient.... I try to be as kind as I could, but I do not be kind to people that are mean to me. But I should be kind to them and just ignore, but when people hit me or call me names I like to hit them back or call them back. Some children thinks I am a Chinese and the Mexicans call me "China," but I am not. Lots of people know I am a Japanese and call me "Jap," but I do not like it. Sometimes they hit me and call me names, but I can't help it if I am a Japanese or Chinese or Mexican, Korean, or any kind of nationality. So I can't stop the war in China, because I did not start it, and I don't like war, but I don't care if they are warring, just so I am not in it. ... The old man who works for my father, he tells me he had some experience and tells me what to do and what I shouldn't. Every time I bring my paper home I show it to him, then he says, "Good." And he says I write better than he could, and he says, "You write like my wife did, but she's dead now."

He says that he thinks about his wife when he sees my writing. He said, "Your sister writes good but too small." He hisself used to write good but now he writes like this: "J. A. Trupp," that is his name. ... That man was at the gambling house when his wife died and his girl could not do anything....

This had been as clear a case of emotional blocking as one could hope to see. How would Yoshiko have fared in an intelligence test during this troubled period? How many times is seeming stupidity only a symptom of some very real worry in the life of the child?

Notice, too, the influence of a chance old man in the life of this child, filling a hunger for recognition and appreciation.

Children of all ages should have the privilege of not revealing themselves if they do not wish to do so. They should also have the privilege of saying whether their work should or should not be read aloud. With older children, "The Story of My Life" may be a very real release of feelings or just a stereotype. This we will need to expect and accept for the written expression of feelings can never be forced. It is the spontaneity that is valuable.

If writing is to be used creatively or for a release of feelings, we cannot use it as a lesson in correct English, punctuation, or spelling. Cole never expected her boys and girls to stay within the framework of correct spelling; instead, she encouraged the children to ask for words, which she spelled on the board. However, she found that through asking, or through a discussion of the meaning of a word, other children listened and vocabulary did increase as a by-product. But if a child has poured his feelings out in a poem or a composition or a story and finds it returned to him covered with red marks for spelling, punctuation, and sentence structure, he may learn the techniques of writing but will not learn to use writing as a release for his feelings—either those that make him happy or those that hurt.

PAINTING, DRAWING, CLAY MODELING

Children can express their feelings in many ways through their hands. Painting, drawing, pounding on clay, using a hammer and nails to make things, can release many kinds of feelings.

The little angry child who sweeps his paint brush across the paper paints out of himself some of his tensions and anger at the world. The small boy pounding away vigorously is getting over his feelings of anger because mother had "kept at him all morning."

As Cole (5) puts it:

The teacher can use creative painting to help the problem child, or "child with problems" as we are admonished now to say.

She will feel her tiredness leave like magic when she sees a picture well done, and mounts it for all the world to see that Johnny isn't the "pain-in-the-neck" that the world, and, most unfortunately, Johnny himself have been thinking. What this child's underlying difficulty may be, a teacher with a roomful can hardly determine readily. But ten to one, whatever it is, he's trying to convince himself and the world that he's Somebody. He's so shaky, so insecure within that he has to be calling for attention to sustain himself. It matters not whether the attention is favorable or otherwise.

Now, properly interested, even the problem child likes to paint. If through the power of suggestion or some other means the teacher can get the child to make a good picture, she has made a big start. She can confront him with the tangible proof that he is a worth-while person, able to make a worth-while contribution.

The teacher can prove her faith in him and his picture by mounting it handsomely and putting it alone on a great wall space for him and all to see. As long as it remains, there is the constant reminder that he is a very fine person or he couldn't have made such a picture. The proof is on the wall. . . .

I have watched a child actually keep the corner of his eye turned on his picture a good part of the day, his efforts to show unconcern to the contrary. But having his mind off his lessons didn't bother me a bit. I knew that this was the one great lesson he needed to learn; that he was an all-right sort of person; that he was accepted and so don't have to worry any more about his place among us. What this can do for the problem child it can do for all children.

But so often in our classrooms, we steal from the child the chance to use his art period for a real expression of himself by insisting that each child conform to our conception of what he should do. Just as in writing, we may kill the spirit for the technique. Some children never satisfactorily learn technique but could have obtained great and positive release in self-expression through the use of their hands. Most children turn eagerly to clay and paint and wood, eager to create, but far too many grownups have lost the feeling for the use of these materials because the "right way" of doing things has been stressed rather than the joy of using the materials.

Sometimes, we may kill a child's spontaneity by trying to touch up his work or show him how he could do better. One child, absorbed in his painting, tore it up and threw it away when his teacher took a brush and "touched up" a corner to make a tree "look better." "It's not mine—it's hers now —I hate it," he cried. It was a long time before that little boy picked up his brush willingly again. The joy of creation had gone. "It's a poor thing but mine own" is still a very applicable quotation to what many children feel.

Criticism and laughter at a child's attempts to create can also block expression and release. Jimmy, in second grade, drew a picture of Indians. He could see and feel those Indians doing war dances—throwing their strong bodies in the air, their feathers quivering! As he painted, he lived the scene. But he froze when his teacher stopped behind his shoulder and laughed, "I never saw Indians look like that, Jimmy. This is the way you draw an Indian." The moment was gone. After that, Jimmy carefully copied the pictures of the "best" painters in the room. Never again in that classroom did he capture the thrill of that moment of creation.

Sometimes a child will have an inner need to paint something different from the class. Miss Norris had in her classroom a little boy, Jeff, who loved horses. He drew them beautifully—running horses, prancing horses; still horses. He drew and drew, while his mind left behind the crowded home in which he lived, the quarreling and fighting of his family, while he ranged the hills with his favorite pinto pony. But Miss Norris felt that her fourth-grade children must learn techniques. Today they must have a still

life. She carefully arranged the bowl, the flowers, the fruit, and said, "Today, children we will draw a still life. Notice the color and the shape. First, we begin with a circle—so—now all draw your circles." Jeff sat quietly in his seat presumably following directions but he produced—a horse. Miss Norris angrily snatched it up—"Jeff, I told you today we draw a still life." Jeff quietly insisted, "I did—the horse is dead."

Much has been said about the use we can make of a child's pictures or models or dancing to give us clues to the child's problems and personality. Children's drawings are often very revealing. We are told that the use of black or muddy paint expresses unhappiness on the part of the child. A constant use of red is interpreted as anger. But here again, we must be careful not to jump to conclusions. All children who "draw small" are not inhibited personalities. Some youngsters like to experiment—or like Ted are "copying Daddy."

Johnnie painted a picture all muddy, brown-black one morning and his teacher began to wonder what was the matter with Johnnie. But Johnnie put her mind at rest by chanting, "It's raining, it's raining— see my big rain clouds."

We must avoid making problems where problems do not exist by grasping at superficial interpretations or single incidents that may express a passing mood of a child. If Johnnie's pictures had been consistently gloomy, or if Ted could never release himself to swing a paint brush or draw sweeping lines—then we would question and add this impression of his art work to our accumulated record as a possible source of information about the feelings of the youngster.

DANCING

Children like to express their feelings through their bodies with dance and rhythm, and it is possible for us to learn much about the feeling needs of our children as we watch them dance. Cole (6) says that dancing can be an "emotional index". Cole points out that the teacher can often use the response of a child to a dance situation as a key to that child's inner feelings and that this key, properly used, can be of great aid in unlocking the inner resources of the child.

The teacher will learn to judge her children more surely through their dancing. It can serve as an emotional index. For instance, I would never have known how very sensitive and self-conscious Mee Lee was, had I not watched her clinging close to the wall, like Chuchundra, the Muskrat, with never the courage to go out in the middle of the room. Here was a child, I saw, with whom I must use great sympathy and understanding. . . .

Joy and abandon are only gained through working from within. It is the emotions that control the deep muscles inside us that govern our breath and being. The child's body is free only when we have set it free through giving faith and confidence to the child emotionally. . . .

I remember a bright little Chinese boy, who came to our fourth grade direct from China. He was very sensitive and easily embarrassed. His whole background seemed to suggest that such wasn't the thing for boys to do—in China at least. Although he knew little or no English, it didn't take him long to learn to say, "Sissy, sissy," in self-defense at the boys dancing. I soon felt the odds were too much against me and gave up pressing him.

During the whole year and a half he was with us, never once did he dance. Then the last week or two his friends got him up, took him by the hands, patted him on the back, made a great to-do about his coming, for they were very fond of him. Naturally he was embarrassed, but very proud and happy to have gathered the bravery to do as the others did at last.

The time was over before he fairly got

started. It has troubled me ever since that I did not find a way somehow to get him out of his seat sooner. I had accepted defeat until it was too late. He, the one child who had needed it above all others I was content to pass over, supposing it to be the impossible.

Maybe he could have danced some of the soreness out of his poor little self, so he would have been saved the big trouble he got into by learning to say "Japanese pipple no good. Japanese pipple bah!" and tormenting our timid little Yoshiko. . . .

There are many kinds of dancing, but the most beautiful dancing of all is that dancing which is inside us already—that we don't have to go anywhere to take lessons to learn. We don't have to have ever danced before in our lives. All we have to do is let it come out of us. It comes out as we feel the music. . . .

Yet many of the children in our classroom have already had this means of release taken away from them. Already they are embarrassed, self-conscious, unable to let go and express themselves through their hands or their bodies.

Tibby was a high-strung little girl who found great joy and release in her dancing. She danced on the grass. She danced on the beach. She danced her way to bed. Her mother, noticing the beauty of her movement, thought she should take lessons and she found a truly creative teacher under whose help Tibby's self-expression, through her dance, continued to be a joy and to unfold. Tibby would dance the music that her teacher played, pouring herself into it. One day, her mother said to her teacher, "Tibby loves her lessons with you—but she isn't learning anything. Couldn't you teach her a little dance to do when we have visitors?" Her teacher demurred and Tibby was transferred to a "teacher who taught her something." The lovely quality of her dance was lost as she was taught to do what the others in the class were doing, step by step. But her mother was pleased—Tibby had been taught to dance.

A CREATIVE APPROACH TO LIFE AND LEARNING

We must be careful not to use art and music and writing only as ways to release pent-up negative feelings, for in them is a great source of expression for the creative feelings of children. Children want to take the experiences of life and mold and shape and learn from them. They want to discover and explore and make things. With their fingers in clay, a paint brush in their hands, their bodies swaying to the rhythm of music, or their thoughts struggling to get on paper, they are experiencing some of the creative joys of life.

CREATIVITY COMES FROM WITHIN

If we are to be honest in our thinking, we must recognize that we *cannot* give our boys and girls creative experiences. A creative experience has reality and meaning only as it comes from within the individual. It is important for us to remember this; otherwise, we are in danger of misinterpreting what we are doing in our classrooms. We can open doors through our creative teaching, but the experience the child will have as he passes through the door will be his own and must come from within himself. And there will be some children, too, who will either close the door or pass by on the wrong side, afraid to go in. Perhaps they were not ready and could not pass through at the time when we opened the door. These children we may be able to help come back and enter in later on.

We know very little about the nature of creativity. Why do some people seem to be endowed with qualities that seem to make it possible for them to be more creative than others? Certainly, there are those with great creative gifts who paint pictures, mold beauty of form with their hands, compose music, use their bodies exquisitely in dance, have the gift of words, or explore the world through science. There do seem to be differences in innate ability to see color and form, in the ear for music, in the coordination of the body, which make creative expression easier for some than for others. Yet we do not know the qualities of mind that are behind such creative expression, whether they exist only in a few or are present in quantitative differences, but dormant, in the many. But we do know that even though the highest expressions of creativity may not be possible for all of us, each one of us can have creative moments of depth and meaning. Probably, too, these moments could be more frequent in our lives and in the lives of the children in our classrooms if we knew better how to release the creative powers that are within us all.

CREATIVITY GOES BEYOND THE "ARTS"

Creativity means many different things to different people. Often we think of creative people as being only those who can express themselves through the fine arts. We value this kind of creativity. We covet it for children and encourage them to express themselves in this way. Yet we sometimes forget that there are other ways of being creative, such as the putting together of ideas into a scientific formula or the combining of tools and materials. The boy who takes the parts of an old car out and puts them together so that the car works again, or peps up an old car so that it makes a fine "hot rod," may cause his parents understandable worry but he may be showing creativity.

Some people, too, are creative as they work with people. In their day-by-day relationships, they are able to blend together their feelings for people with their knowledge about them and work out relationships that were not achieved with such skill by others.

If we think of creativity as a synthesis, or a putting together of ideas and concepts, we can see more fully the relationship of creativity to our individual lives and those of our children.

All of us will not be able to express ourselves creatively through the arts in ways that will be fully satisfying to us, although all of us can find some self-expression through the use of our hands and bodies. But most of us have had the experience of having ideas come together, often suddenly, giving us a solution for which we have been seeking. Creative experience does not need to result in an original discovery, in a new idea or combination of ideas, to be of value. It is the rare and gifted person who produces the inspiring work of art or the new combination of ideas that results in scientific discovery. But the little child, messing around with his paints, who finds that he can make green out of blue and yellow, can experience the thrill of creativity, which is as satisfying to him at the moment as it may have been to the first person who made such a discovery. The child who, after studying the beautiful form of a shell, wonderingly thinks, "There must be something I do not understand that could make this so perfect. Is this what they mean by God?" is passing through a creative experience many others have had but that has new and vivid meanings for him.

WE CAN HELP CHILDREN APPROACH LIFE

WITH A CREATIVE SPIRIT BY—

ENCOURAGING THE QUESTING MIND

If we give the children in our classes the authoritarian answer instead of helping them *find* the answer, we block the further play of their ideas. We deprive them of the opportunity for the increasing search for ideas that mesh and produce a satisfying whole. We should encourage questions, for honest, sincere questioning leads to creative thinking. Yet we must remember again that children need the security of a warm, personal relationship with an adult whom they can use as a sounding board. They need

someone to whom they can turn for reassurance, when for the moment they are overwhelmed by a new thought about the immensity of the universe, the reality of the stars, the immensity of the task that confronts them as they seek for knowledge. We should not open the doors too wide too soon, pouring out information beyond the comprehension of the child, for here the usefulness of knowledge ceases and the child is overwhelmed by the impossibility of his task. We give as the child is ready to receive, following his lead as his questions move ahead.

Bob's father recognized the intellectual capacity of his boy and wanted to be sure that it was well-fed. He read widely to his youngster many facts about many things. The boy grew up to be a walking encyclopedia. In school, as the years went by, Bob could pull facts and dates and names out of his mind like a magician pulling a rabbit out of a hat. But he was not creative; he rarely sought knowledge on his own; he rarely initiated a project or played with ideas. He did not experiment; he listened. He absorbed information, but he did not make it a usable part of his life. He knew many facts, but he did not know what to do with them.

Jacob's father, on the other hand, met the interests of his youngster. Together father and son would go to the museum when an interest in rocks was stimulated by stones and different kinds of sand, which they picked up on the beach one summer. Step-by-step, the father helped Jacob broaden his knowledge, discuss his ideas, and experience the *wonder of discovery*. He gave as the child was ready to receive, following his lead as his questions moved ahead.

We can find many ways to open up new areas of thinking for a child when he seems ready for them. We can produce the book, the trip to the museum, the chance to try out an idea in an experiment, at the moment when he is seeking for an answer. We can give him facts on which to build. We can supply the missing knowledge, the method of approach, the skill or technique, as the child asks for it. And even more, we can show him how and where to find what he wants to know.

There are times when it is wise to let children turn aside and follow their own thoughts. Often we ask that children think the thoughts we want them to think at a particular moment in the class period. The teacher who builds, for a little while, on the thoughts of the children and then brings attention back into the pattern of the day's work often finds the time well spent. As one intelligent girl said, "I have to choose all the time between listening to the teacher and being bored by going over again and again work that I know, or following my own thoughts and finding new ideas that fascinate me. If I think my own thoughts for a while, then when I am called on, I feel stupid because I don't know what they are talking about."

Sometimes it is wise to pause entirely in a planned lesson to capitalize on a much more creative moment that has occurred. We may prevent creativity in our children if we fill the school day so full of "must be dones" that there are no moments for dreaming or free activity or talking things over or doing something that captures the interest and the imagination, even if these activities are not on the day's calendar. We need to be willing to wait until children think their own thoughts and try to work out their answers. We should not be afraid of the silences that come when we talk and work with children. Sometimes, too, in our eagerness to supply opportunities for children to learn, or even for them to be creative, we fill their lives so full of opportunity that they are too busy keeping up with assignments or extracurricular responsibilities to be really creative.

We cannot say to children, "This is your time to be creative," and expect that all the children in the class will get busy—even with fascinating materials about them—and have a truly creative experience. Creative experiences are much more subtle and unpredictable. We can introduce a child to materials and ideas. We can teach skills. We can show the joy of expression through the use of one's hands or one's body. But the child himself must put these things together within himself to achieve a creative experience.

Sometimes we stifle a truly creative experience by our interruptions, even by our desire to be helpful. The child sitting at his table in the kindergarten trying to fit together the pieces of a picture puzzle may lose his moment of creativity if his teacher swoops down on him and says, "Time to put the puzzles away." A little more sensitivity to what is happening in the mind of a child a recognition of the complete absorption that is possible, might make it possible to delay the interruption for a little while. The teacher might enter into the child's consciousness more slowly with, "In a little while, we will need to put the puzzles away." The child who is strumming on the piano, trying to make a tune of his own, may not be practicing his piece, but he may be experiencing something much more important. The high-school boy of unusual ability who resented interruption of his thoughts because the bell rang, burst out, "Just as I am getting somewhere, I have to stop and do something else." He was voicing his resentment against administrative procedures which, though perhaps necessary, often block real mental creativity.

As was mentioned earlier, to many children a mistake is a disaster. It means that they have failed to achieve what was expected of them. A failure is something to be ashamed of. But frustration and even failure are often the steps toward a really creative experience. A mistake need not be a final, unhappy ending, but a beginning, something on which to build, to work. One channel was found to be closed, perhaps, but there are other channels to follow, other directions to try. The positive approach, which we help a child develop toward mistakes, frustration, and failure, may be important indeed in helping him toward creative experiences. We should help children realize that most creativity includes a period of tension and frustration that may be very painful. This should be expected.

The moment of resolution often comes as a flash when the ideas seem to fall into place, tumbling over one another. The picture is painted, the poem is written, the solution to the problem is found. It may be after we have had a few hours' sleep or when we are stretched out apparently doing nothing that the moment is there, the tension is gone. Too rarely in the classroom do we give time for a child to let his problem drop, to stop the struggle with his reading, to recreate himself through play and laughter, until the moment comes when he can go on again. Pushing and pressure at the point of struggle rarely helps.

It takes courage to put things together creatively—whether it be ideas, or words, or clay and paint, or a bar of music. It is an art on the part of the teacher to help a child correct a mistake and grow in skill without criticizing his expressed thoughts or his product in such a way that he feels they are small and of no value.

Our feeling about the mistakes children make can also be important in providing situations in which they can release their feelings through creativity. Derrick came home from a new art class with his eyes shining, "Mother, do you know our teacher doesn't mind if we tear up a picture and start all over again?" To many of us, the saving of paper or the neat working out of a picture in a given space, or the proper commas mean more than the child's at-tempts to get his feelings out. In any piece of creativity, there may be many starts and stops and tearings up and starting over again. This is true for adults; why not expect it for children, too? When ideas begin to flow, whether in the writing of a story or the painting of a picture or molding with clay, we cannot always capture right away just what we want.

Of course, children do need help and direction in mastering skills, too. If we can ask the question or make the quiet remark that helps the child want to find the better way, we will be really teaching. "Have you thought of this?" "Yes, I see your point, but what about this?" "I wonder whether this tree would make a shadow." We must try to lead the child toward the direction that will help his thinking, help him go ahead, help him develop the skills he needs. "Helen, that was a delightful story you handed in. Would you like me to help you a bit with spelling so that you could send it to the school paper?"

The time will come when the child wants to draw in perspective. It will have meaning for him. He will want to find a better and more accurate way of fitting the corners of the birdhouse together. We must criticize to build up rather than to tear down; we must develop the capacity in a child to evaluate his own work. We should judge a child's products by what he is able to do, not necessarily by whether he has done it the way we wanted it done. Our criticisms, our suggestions, our knowledge, and the skills we offer to teach a child must be within the capacity and readiness of the child to accept and use for himself.

Help and criticism must be offered with sensitivity to encourage, not defeat the further attempts of the child. We want the child to feel that school may be a growing experience for him—so that he knows it is not just a matter of "learning a lot of stuff the teacher tells you." He, too, can ask and search for the answers. We want him to know that we, his teachers, are also still seeking as we build on the knowledge and vital experiences of the past and scan the future to find the answers about the amazing universe in which we live.

ENCOURAGING INDIVIDUALITY IN THE WAYS CHILDREN EXPRESS THEMSELVES

One of the great scientific minds of our day tells of one of his first memories of trying to create—an effort that was met with anger and irritation rather than understanding and encouragement.

One day when I was in the first grade, I went into the home of a friend whose father was a draftsman. I was fascinated by the blueprint paper. Blueprint paper exposed to the light turns blue when wet. My friend and I were allowed to make handprints on some of the paper by dipping our hands in water and placing them on the paper. I wanted blueprint paper like that.

In school the next day, I puzzled over how I could make it. I remembered that the mark of an indelible pencil turns blue when it is wet. So when the teacher left the room, I borrowed her indelible pencil and spent the time when I should have been doing numbers coloring a sheet of white paper with the indelible pencil. The teacher returned and, in anger, took the pencil away, scolded me for wasting my time in school. But I clung to my idea, took the paper home, and, dipping my hand in water, made a messy handprint on the paper! To me it was a great achievement—even though the results were not perfect.

The child who has been helped to be free to paint or make things or write in his own way has an outlet for his feelings that becomes closed to him if he is taught to feel that he must learn to paint, learn to mold, learn to write according to a "proper way."

As Cole (7) goes on to say:

The teacher should watch for the child with a very individual way of making his figures and things. From him will come the pictures of character and distinction. She should never try to show him how the hu-

man figure actually is, but rather build up his strength and surety.

"Make your picture your own way, Teresa. Don't ever try to paint like anyone else. We want to be able to look at your picture and say, 'That's Teresa's picture!'" ...

From among the most timid will come some of the finest painters. The timid child is apt to be the most creative child, the one most sensitive to beauty.

The teacher should give the children a confidence and respect for their painting as children's painting.

"It's wonderful the way you children can start right out and paint anything. You don't worry and stew around like grown-ups. You just go ahead and paint it. Grown-ups would be fussing around about how to paint one little thing while you have the whole picture painted beautifully.

"Children can paint pictures that 'feel' like the thing they're painting. Any little old camera can take pictures of things as they really look."

Later they will say, "He shouldn't try to paint like grown-ups, should he? He should paint in his own way." Children are intelligent. They can grasp truths that we adults stumble over.

A teacher like Miss Gold would have difficulty in helping free the creativity in children for she was heard to say: "I can't help it but I like my room to look nice. I don't feel comfortable unless the pictures on the walls look right to me. I have to like them myself. I do put up some of the better paintings of the children—but most of the time, I choose pictures from the magazines and mount them. They appeal to me so much more."

The teacher's job is to find the real child in his work—and the meaning of his work to him. We must allow good, strong expression in rhythm or art, not just pretty, graceful things. Children can paint and model intense feelings as well as "pretty" ones. The angry paintings, the angry stories, the angry dancing should not be discouraged for these feelings need a wholesome way out, too. Cole (8) knew this. She knew that a child can even dance the "silly-business" out of himself:

Try never to say the negative word in this dancing. Remember again that very likely the one who is annoying is really the one who is caring most about it, but has to go through a show of not caring to prove he is not a sissy.

When a child is giggling and bumping into others, it is a sure give-away that he is not free of embarrassment, but is trying to cover his inner feelings by these outer overt actions. They are symptoms that all is not right as yet within.

Of course if someone just fails to respond and makes himself too much of a nuisance, we can say very casually, "Oh Albert, come on back. You're just being silly. You're not ready to dance yet." But don't let us put an edge to our voice. Remember we're going to see these first few weeks through to something fine and beautiful. We can't afford to let anything annoy us.

If we continue positive—just praising the good and ignoring the evil, he will surprise us by falling in line. As sincere effort and expression receive the recognition and praise, there will be no object in continuing the other.

Just as we can dig a channel to control the direction of a stream, we can control the direction of our children's activities through praise and recognition.

[Remember Howard who wrote the vivid account of a day at the circus on page 112?] *. . . We noticed in his dancing that he had wonderful rhythm but preferred to act silly —mimicking and acting the fool. So we asked him to dance for us.*

"Dance funny," the children begged all over the room. The boy was clever! He showed real talent. Soon a funny little American boy who had been adopted and raised in Mexico and couldn't speak English beckoned if he, too, could go.

Together they went through antics as well as if they had been a well-rehearsed vaudeville team. Of course one had to loosen up and put himself into the spirit of the occasion. While one looked the other way, the other kicked him in the pants and then glided innocently off to pluck a flower from the desk and dance, gazing at it in the most aesthetic fashion.

Through some kind of intuitive agreement they came forward as a singing duo. One started out trustfully in an affected falsetto voice, only to have the other fail to accompany him. Then the first mix-up over, he started again in seeming faith, only to have such happen again. The children loved it. There was time off to get tuned up with important clearings of the throat and voices jumping unexpectedly into squeaks. Then one directed the other with great flourishing movements and long-held notes. They patted each other on the cheek. Then they danced again, finally the one stooping over for the other to ride on his neck. Out one door they went, and in the other, with elaborate bows from the one on top, to the delighted audience.

"Why did you tolerate such?" Ah—I had my good reasons. In the first place, these boys had a gift for this type of thing. Everyone should have a chance to express and develop himself according to his gifts. Actually this is a rather rare and highly compensated commodity. No doubt there are those in Hollywood not half so gifted making many times the board superintendent's salary.

But the real reason we had these two boys clown was that they had it in their systems and were using it in negative fashion to bother and disrupt. It was an unspoken agreement that in exchange for the one they dispensed with the other. Or maybe it was just that they got the other out of their systems or found it unnecessary now that they were being recognized as popular members of the group.

We had some company one day and we thought we could risk having the "Funny Dance." I guess it was too much to expect. One visitor said to my principal very seriously, "I sat wondering what the boys were trying to express." The principal said she thought quickly, groped for some educational principle in my defense, and then told them, "Well, you know they say we are supposed to start with the children right where we find them, and that was undeniably where she found them."

The need to observe carefully, to listen attentively, to "read between the lines"—in order that we may *really* understand children's needs and help free their capacity to learn—is well stated by Gardner and Lois Murphy (9):

... We are concerned ... not only with the unusual child but with the everyday child whose individual pattern of weaknesses, strengths, talents, limitations, individual drives, and social belongingness requires ... skilled guidance and understanding. ...

... Let us begin by noting and studying what the child can tell us ... through all his inarticulateness, his nonverbal communication, his gestures, tears, clenched fist, sleeplessness, or, on the other hand, radiant joy and deep relaxed absorption into himself—he can point the direction in which we might give him more of what he seems to need in order to grow in a balanced, resilient, creative way. ... The child may in his anguish seem first of all to need self-justification or even revenge, a need which would be slight or nonexistent if somehow his life could be better structured. Our thesis is simply that it is better to let the child tell us what he positively craves; in-

deed, if we do not respond to his joys and resentments, if we do not take his feelings seriously, we have no full or clear picture. We must be alert to notice signs of his cravings for companionship, for social understanding, for skills, for an understanding of the physical world, the living world, the esthetic and scientific world, the social and personal world. If his mind is not free to reach out and immerse itself in the things which mean most to him, we are unlikely to be able to guide him well.

REFERENCES

(1) Larrick, Nancy. "Let's Find Out What Children Think," *Childhood Education*, Jan. 1954, Vol. 30, pp. 222-224. Reprinted by permission of the Association for Childhood Education International, 3615 Wisconsin Avenue, N.W., Washington 16, D.C.

(2) Nehru, Jawaharlal. "The Brave Are Never Attacked," from *Shankar's Weekly*, New Delhi, 1950, Children's Number, pp. 6-7.

(3) Reprinted from *The Arts in the Classroom* by Natalie Robinson Cole by permission of The John Day Company, Inc., publisher. Copyright 1940 by Natalie Robinson.

(4) *Ibid.*, pp. 124-125.

(5) *Ibid.*, pp. 20-21.

(6) *Ibid.*, pp. 93, 70, 75, 71-72.

(7) *Ibid.*, pp. 7-8.

(8) *Ibid.*, pp. 86-87, 87-88.

(9) Murphy, Gardner and Lois. "The Child as Potential," *The Nation's Children*, 2: *Development and Education*, 1960 White House Conference on Children and Youth, edited by Eli Ginzberg. New York: Columbia University Press, 1960, pp. 208, 209-210.

CHAPTER 5

SELF-DISCIPLINE

Why is it that a seemingly well-behaved class
can turn into a group of wild Indians
when the teacher leaves the room for a moment?

How can we reach children whose
standards, values, and aims in life are
entirely different from our own?

Self-government sounds like an ideal way for children
to attain self-discipline. Yet, I have been
reluctant to use it because I'm not sure how far I
can allow children to handle their own affairs.

Aren't there times when a teacher is
justified in punishing a child? What kind of
punishment is appropriate in the classroom?

I would like to allow my youngsters
more freedom to move about in the classroom.
But I dread having it seem to outsiders
that my room is disorderly and uncontrolled.

What can I do with a child who seems seriously
disturbed—in need of almost constant attention and
watchfulness? How much time should I give this
one child—at the expense of the rest of the group?

IS THE REAL GOAL

WHAT DO WE MEAN BY DISCIPLINE?

There is much confusion about the meaning of *discipline.* Many teachers think of it only in negative terms such as "I must discipline Johnny. He is getting out of hand." To others, it means punishing for wrong doing, insisting on obedience; making a child or a group of children *behave.* These concepts of discipline have grown out of our past. They go back in our own history to the days of our Pilgrim Fathers, when adults were impressed with the idea that a child was born sinful and that it was the duty of parents and teachers to make him good. From this premise came the old adage "spare the rod and spoil the child." It is comparatively recent that the attitude of helping a child attain a healthy, socialized, adulthood by guidance rather than by reliance primarily on coercion or punishment has been accepted by any large number of people. There are still many people today who feel that the authoritarian approach to children is the best one, "Do this and do it now because I tell you to," backed up by punishment if the child is not immediately obedient or the job is not done. Such an authoritarian approach may be convenient to adults but usually fails to develop the child's inner control.

Another confusion in our thinking is the notion that freedom and discipline cannot exist at the same time, that one precludes the other. There is still a fear among many teachers today that if children are permitted freedom to move about, or freedom to speak to one another, confusion will result and they will have "poor discipline." As one principal of a school said, "I control every movement of the children so that they know just what to do. Then we avoid noise and difficulties." Such a concept of discipline develops children who obey orders but are not encouraged to think, to be creative, or to use judgment.

"Good" discipline is not an end in itself but a means toward providing a healthy atmosphere in which children may grow and learn. Good discipline is neither too much freedom nor too little freedom, neither complete lack of control nor authoritarianism. It is a way of living in a classroom group by which we help our children develop slowly and step-by-step from the complete and necessary control by the adult in babyhood, to the point at the end of adolescence when the young person steps over into self-controlled adulthood, able to use judgment based on a sense of values. Discipline should be thought of in terms of teaching and learning rather than punishment and restraint. A self-disciplined person is one who has learned to cooperate with others without losing the ability to think and judge for himself.

Much of our success as teachers will depend upon our attitude toward discipline. This question has been posed for us by Sheviakov and Redl (1).*

What do you want to be, anyway, an educator, or an "angel with the flaming sword"? It is upon your answer to this question that your decisions about discipline techniques will finally depend. For it requires one type of person to be the proud avenger of infantile wrongs and sins against defied "rules and regulations," and another to be the guide of human beings through the turmoil of growth. You have to make up your mind.

If as educators we are on the side of guidance that leads toward self-control, we shall need to think through this matter of discipline and ask ourselves some questions. What are our behavior goals? What kinds of

*Full references are cited at the end of the chapter.

behavior do we consider desirable for boys and girls? Can behavior goals be the same for all children? Our thinking will need to follow two channels for we will need to consider not only the kind of guidance and control that will help children behave acceptably in the group situation of the classroom, but also the kind of guidance that will lead boys and girls toward the development of values, standards, and the use of individual judgment which will influence their behavior in life situations. A child may behave well in a directed classroom situation, but his behavior here may have no relationship to what he does outside of school or later in his adult life. This is poor discipline even though the child may be conforming to the outward standards of the classroom.

THE ROOTS OF DISCIPLINE LIE IN EARLY CHILDHOOD

When a baby is born, he knows neither right nor wrong. At first, his needs revolve around the self-satisfaction that comes from sucking, the comfort of being warm and dry, the discomfort of being hungry, wet, or cold. He begins to recognize his mother as the source of his comfort. As he grows older, he gradually realizes that his mother approves of some things and disapproves of others. It is nicer when she approves. In his desire to please mother, and later father, he accepts what his parents permit as "right," what they do not permit as "wrong." Little children have primitive impulses to which they give free expression. They have a bowel movement when and where they feel like it. They kick. They bite. They snatch what they want. They explore the world by touching and putting in the mouth anything within reach. Gradually their parents and other adults around them have to help children express these impulses in socially acceptable ways. But a little child likes to do many of these things. They give him satisfaction. He will not easily change his ways unless the grownup provides an equal satisfaction in exchange. With little children this is the attention and love they receive from their parents. If a child is not sure of his parents' affection in return for conforming to their wishes, it becomes more difficult to teach him. Although the range of ways of obtaining satisfaction increases as boys and girls grow older, the stamp of genuine approval from those whom they love or admire remains the strongest incentive for social approval.

Somewhere between four and six years of age, most youngsters have absorbed a pattern of behavior from their parents and are beginning to understand what it means. At this point, the standards of the parents are taken over by the child and used when his parents are not present, and inner or self-control has begun to develop. If the experiences he has are not too difficult for him to handle, this inner control will mature as the child matures, and he will gradually develop standards within himself to fit his growing needs. This inner control, in the language we usually use, is called the *conscience*. In Freudian or psychoanalytic terms, it is called the *superego*. If this point were not reached, the child would know right from wrong only when his parents, or another adult who could serve as his conscience, were present.

We will sometimes find a youngster in our class who has not yet developed to this point of being able to begin to take responsibility for his own actions. Occasionally we find an older child or an adult who has never achieved inner control. Such a person is considered in need of treatment.

As we get to know the boys and girls in our classrooms we realize that some of them are able to use self-control and self-direction to a much greater extent than others. We find also that some are overconscientious. They worry too much if work is not completed, if it is not well done, or if they make a mistake in behavior.

Learning about behavior is tied up with the feelings a child has about the people who are teaching him. The way in which parents have impressed a youngster with a pattern of right and wrong is important to his mental health and his subsequent behavior in school. If the mother and the father patterns have been good, the child is likely to be able to become a well-adjusted school child.

If parents have been too severe, the youngster may be in too much conflict between the things he wants to do and the restraints he has been forced to learn to put upon himself. Too much pressure or pressure put on too soon—before a child can understand the reasons for what he is asked to do—may result in an inhibited personality. Such a child has become too obedient to his conscience. As one psychiatrist said, "His halo is too tight."

On the other hand, insufficient guidance, control, and pressure toward acceptable behavior may result in a child who is not sufficiently socialized and has great difficulty in meeting the give-and-take of the child group and the necessary requirements of the classroom situation. Such a child may have too little inner control or conscience because no one has ever taught him how to behave.

Overindulgent or overpermissive parents who do not set enough limits or offer enough guidance, but who do show warmth and acceptance and affection for their youngsters, may have boys and girls with pleasant, happy, but sometimes irresponsible, personalities. Inconsistent parents may leave their youngsters with feelings of confusion because they lack a pattern to follow. Such children often have trouble making up their minds. They lack direction and frequently are in conflict over decisions. Rita's parents were like this, happy and gay with her at one time, then scolding and demanding about her reading, so that Rita did not know what to expect. She became a confused little girl.

CHILDREN BRING DIFFERENT STANDARDS AND VALUES TO SCHOOL

THERE MAY BE CONFLICT BETWEEN HOME STANDARDS AND THOSE OF THE OUTSIDE WORLD

The first and most important step, then, in establishing patterns of behavior is the relationship between the child and his mother and father. The young child does what his parents wish out of attachment to them. But when children come to school, the emphasis shifts from attachment to parents to identification with other admired adults.

Phil found that behavior such as dancing, which was considered acceptable by people whom he could admire in his school, was considered unacceptable and wrong by his father and his minister. In his struggle between these two standards of conduct and his own desire to dance, Phil developed overwhelming feelings of guilt that interfered with his work in school and his adjustment to other boys and girls.

During the elementary-school years, the child looks more and more outward for his values. He is trying to find out what adult standards are, what he must do, how he must behave in order to be accepted as he is growing up. He is concerned as to whether he is "doing it right." When the standards of the home and the school do not match one another, a child can be thrown into confusion. The difference a child encounters in adult standards during his school years is one of the first value conflicts he feels.

In the preschool years, the child had to establish relationships only with his parents; now he must establish relationships with many adults and with the different authorities they represent—the school, the church, the policeman on the corner, the TV hero, the scout leader, the neighbor, and his best friend's parents. All these adults have positions of prestige in the eyes of the child. But they do not all agree on what is right and wrong. Who is right and who is wrong? David is allowed to stay up until ten thirty on Saturday night; Nora does not have to wash the dishes; Bill's father encourages him to fight; Jim's mother says fighting is wrong. Then, when a youngster leaves the primary grades, he becomes increasingly aware of the standards of his peers. Sometimes he finds that they are not the same as those of grownups. The boys admire Duncan who swears and smokes sometimes—"He's a pretty big shot"; Carl takes home "words" and tries them out and is jumped on—but the boys at school use those words and pass them around. Len's "gang" think it's fun and exciting to break the school windows if they can get away with it. Len goes along feeling uncomfortable but gets excited and hurls a rock, too. Elizabeth goes to Young Peoples' group and Sunday School, but her best friend thinks that's boring stuff—"My family doesn't go to church." Who is right and who is wrong?

As children mature physically and become adolescent, their groping for standards begins to turn in as well as out. They wrestle with ideas. Sometimes they try them out in the classroom or at home and meet with shocked response from adults—just as Phil met with stern reproof from his father. In their attempt to think for themselves and develop standards of their own, they often make mistakes—some inconsequential, some serious. But they are trying to find out many things, "What do I believe?" "Who am I?" "Where do I belong?" "What should I do?" Often during these adolescent years, boys and girls will pull away from their parents and from any grownup who acts in a parental fashion, saying, "You're behind the times." "People don't think that way now." "Look at the mess your generation made of this world." And so the struggle goes on to find what is acceptable behavior, what is unacceptable, what is good, what is wrong, and why all this confusion about it among the adults who should know.

It is also easy to forget that all of our boys and girls do not come from the same social class.

Senn (2) says that:

. . . *social class and other cultural influences are often responsible for the differences in behavior among children of various groups. Child behavior which is encouraged and rewarded by one social class may be worried about, disapproved and punished by another. Therefore professional persons appraising both the normality of a trait and methods of dealing with it must take into consideration the cultural background of the child.*

For instance, as teachers, we value education, getting ahead and doing well, and looking ahead and building for the future. We often try to help boys and girls see that it is necessary to do tasks they dislike today because they will lead toward goals that will bring them satisfaction in years ahead. "You must get good grades in high school so that you can get into college and enter the career of your choice." But many "lower-class" families place no particular value on education. High school is sometimes looked on as unnecessary and "book learning" as a waste of time. The satisfactions of the present—food and clothes today, a bit of pleasure while there is money in the pocket—seem much more important than looking toward an uncertain future.

The verbal discipline that is customary in the middle-class home often has no effect on lower-class children, who are used to more direct action—being beaten or sworn at. They do not understand the horrified objection some teachers show toward swear words, which are everyday words to them. The emphasis in the lower class is not on being good and conforming but rather on being able to stand up for oneself. The lower-class boy is expected to be a good fighter; indeed he must be, if he is to be able to exist in his "slum culture." The middle-class boy, on the other hand, is not expected to be openly aggressive, though he may be taught to fight in self-defense. A group of adolescent boys who would have been considered normal in their native Puerto Rico became juvenile delinquents in New York City. Twenty-one such boys in a state training school all showed the common characteristic of "extreme preoccupation with the concept of dignity." They had all got into trouble because of their attacks on other persons when they felt their "dignity" had been damaged.

Havighurst (3) says:

The moral rules of various societies differ, and so a highly "moral" person in one society might transgress many moral rules if he was transplanted to another society. Moral rules differ even between social classes in American society, as Kinsey has demonstrated in the sexual area of behavior, which is more thoroughly permeated by moral considerations than any other one. Consequently children of lower socio-economic status often seem highly immoral to middle-class teachers when they are really following the mores of their own social group.

There are also cultural differences in the strength of conscience between various social groups. In many societies there is very little of the punishing "Puritan" conscience that we know so well in America. Even in lower class American society there is probably a less severe conscience, on the average, than in middle-class Americans.

Social experimentation with the opposite sex (in the lower class) nearly always involves sexual experience. Marriage tends to come earlier, terminating the adolescent social life earlier. In the cities there is a good deal of informal social organization into corner gangs and neighborhood social clubs which are analogous to middle-class clubs and fraternities. The lower-class social groups more often become involved in stealing and sexual immorality, and therefore tend to get a bad name.

SOME STANDARDS AND VALUES
ARE UNIVERSAL

We must look beneath the surface values that sometimes distress us for the more universal values which can be found among all kinds of people of whatever social level. On these values we will be able to build.

Cole (4) describes how she helped the children in her room develop values. She says:

Stressing social values is the most important work of the teacher today. What the child expresses orally or puts in writing becomes part of him, especially as he receives praise and recognition for it. Attitudes toward society and work and family are the deciding factors in the life of the individual. These we must effect early. They are infinitely more important than any abstract subject could ever be. A morning spent dealing with a problem in honesty or kindliness or responsibility is spent in the best "activity" in the world.

Actually, whether deliberately or not, we are teaching values day in and day out, not only specifically and directly through content but also as our own values and standards show up in our personal reactions to situations that arise.

Laycock (5) put it this way·

One of the chief purposes of education . . . is to help boys and girls to incorporate into their beliefs and into their daily living democratic attitudes and forms of behavior. First of all there is the democratic belief that every human being, no matter what his race, creed, class, age, or intelligence is of infinite worth. To mean anything this belief must be expressed in holding to and living out the values of honesty, goodwill, tolerance, sincerity, co-operation and unselfishness. Another democratic belief is that man can solve his problems of living together in the modern world by the application of reason if accompanied by tolerance and goodwill. . . .

While teachers should not be expected to be paragons of virtue, the values which are their own guides to living inevitably affect their pupils. Certainly they will be effective in developing democratic values in their pupils only to the extent to which they themselves have embodied these values in their everyday living in school, home, and community.

While exhortation, stories, and reading are more effective at the verbal than the action level, there is still a place for group and individual guidance and counselling in helping pupils to accept values as their own, providing that practice is also provided. The classroom and playground experiences as well as family and community experiences should give boys and girls practice in socially co-operative living. They should constitute laboratory experiences in unselfishness, tolerance, goodwill, honesty, and the other democratic values. . . .

If pupils are to learn to solve community social problems they must have practice in doing so. Pupils should go out into the community and gather the facts regarding the problems of promoting the health, welfare, and beauty of the community. Having obtained the facts about the social problems of their local community, their [state], or their nation, the pupils should take steps to bring the problems to the attention of the proper authorities and also to participate with adults in the solution of these problems. This may involve anything from sharing in the improvement of the school grounds to making an effective contribution to a world organization.

CERTAIN VALUES ARE DIFFICULT TO INTERPRET

There are three areas in which we sometimes find it particularly difficult to work out our own values and interpret these values to boys and girls. We wonder what we should say, how far we should go. These three areas are: (1) prejudice; (2) religion; (3) sex education. We cannot avoid these areas in the school for all of them are part of the thread of life. They are realities that we must constantly face day by day in real situations with our boys and girls. In many schools, we may not guide directly in these areas, but indirectly boys and girls absorb our attitudes and those of the other adults of the community, and their attitudes, in turn, are formed.

PREJUDICE

Prejudice is a word that covers many areas. It may be prejudice toward a minority group, toward people who have more or less money than ourselves, toward people with less intelligence, toward people of a different religious belief, or toward people of another race or skin color. The roots of prejudice are deep. They go way down into our own childhood experiences and the attitudes of the people with whom we grew up. We were not born with prejudices.

Anyone may dislike certain people because of qualities of personality. But prejudice is not a rational dislike. Prejudice causes us to refuse to look at an individual not because of dislike toward him as an individual, but as a member of a group.

Children will bring their prejudices and social attitudes right into our classrooms. Cole (6) writes:

Then there was Tommie. . . . He came to our room, took one look at all our Mexican and Chinese children, and told his mother, out loud for us to hear, "I don't like it here." He stayed, and the first day or two brought us such trouble in the yard that the children took him to task.

"Why did you sass two teachers in one day?" they asked.

"Why did you call the principal an old Sour Puss behind her back?"

"Because I felt like it," was the best thing Tommie would say.

The children were wild. "What if everybody did what they felt like doing?"

Time passed and things went better with Tommie, but not so with Ming Chan. So one day the children put him on the spot.

"Why did you hit Yoshiko?"

"Why did you coach Yon Lee to say 'Japanese people no good'?" they demanded of him.

"Because I wanted to," repeated poor Ming, making a weak show at defiance, although tears were running down his cheeks.

Then, joy of joys, who was it coming up in front to champion the cause of decency and fair play? It was Tommie, and he said, "Now Ming, remember how I talked back the first time I was up here, and I found it didn't do no good."

Oh happy moment for all of us! When recess bell rang, I stood at the door, shook his hand, and said, "From now on you're tops with me, Tommie."

The way in which we meet the situations that arise from the very intense feelings some of the children have already developed will be important in helping them learn more democratic values. Here again we need to face ourselves and evaluate our own prejudices, for few of us are without them. Often they unconsciously affect our own sense of democratic values and prevent us from helping the children develop theirs.

Prejudice is not an individual problem. It is a social problem of wide dimensions affecting the lives and well-being of many individuals, both those who are prejudiced and those who are the object of prejudice. It is the product not only of the home but also of the wider social community in which a child has grown up. As Myrdal (7) has pointed out, there is a gulf between the American ideals of democracy and brotherhood on the one hand, and the existence of racial prejudice, discrimination, and segregation on the other. The "American Creed," which emphasizes the essential dignity of the human personality, the fundamental equality of man, and the inalienable rights to freedom, justice, and equal opportunity, is clearly contradicted by the denial of these to certain human beings because of religion, race, or national background. The group against whom prejudices are directed may vary according to the part of the country in which a youngster grew up. According to Witmer and Kotinsky (8), "Negroes, Jews, Latin Americans, Orientals, Southern and Eastern Europeans, Indians, migrants, and all of those whose economic status is very low are likely to be regarded as socially inferior and to be discriminated against."

As teachers, we cannot afford to be unaware of this conflict. We may elect to keep our own personal attitude of prejudice toward groups other than our own. We may find it too difficult to be able to change feelings that have become deeply embedded in our personality. But we can be expected to be able to control our personal feelings. We must be so aware of them that we do not let them intrude into our classrooms in such a way that could prevent a child from feeling welcome and accepted. We must also be careful not to excuse or condone unkindness or rejection by the class of a child purely upon the basis of a difference in religion, race, nationality, or economic status. Even if we cannot change our personal feelings or change the feelings of children in our class, we can help them see the common elements in people everywhere, become sensitive to the welfare of others, understand the reasons behind prejudiced feelings, and treat others with justice, fair play, and respect.

A teacher once asked the following question:

"We study and talk and read a great deal about the mental, physical, social, and emotional growth of boys and girls, but it is much more difficult to find material which is helpful to us in trying to understand moral and spiritual growth. Why is it that in our texts and in our classes the spiritual development of children is rarely considered—or if it is mentioned it is passed by casually? Isn't religion an important element in the spiritual growth of children?"

If we are interested in value guidance, we cannot ignore the spiritual growth of children nor the role religion plays in this. Each day in the classroom, as we are helping children build values and learn relationships toward other people, reverently appreciate the wonders of the world in which they are living, and seek for further knowledge and understanding of its meaning, we are adding to our children's spiritual growth and to their understanding of religion.

Religion is universal. It is man's search through all the ages for some spiritual entity that is bigger than himself. Men today are still seeking for the answers. But there are many ways in which men carry on this great search. Through the ages, in every part of the world, men have organized their way of seeking and formulating the answers that they feel they have found into systems of theology. It is *theology* that we are not permitted to teach in the schools, unless we are teaching in a church school in which a certain theological approach to God is accepted by the parents whose children attend the school. If we were to teach formal theology in our public schools, we might not be able to give to children an approach to God that would be acceptable either to their parents or to the churches which they represent.

We might also seriously confuse a child if we gave him our own religious beliefs, when they are in conflict with those of his own home and church. But we can give the children in our classroom a realization of the importance of religion; an understanding of the history of religion as man's search for God; information about the different theological groups and how they have developed; what they believe and stand for; and a deep respect for the right of every man to seek God in his own way, for this is one of the basic beliefs of the Founding Fathers of our country. It is written into our Constitution. With such understanding comes mutual respect for one another's beliefs, or even lack of belief. This in itself is a basic element in spiritual growth.

A child is helped to grow spiritually when he lives among people who themselves have found meaning in their lives, who meet the question marks of life with serenity and courage, who have a deep belief that although all the answers to the riddles of the universe have not been found, there is a challenge in the search. If children are to grow spiritually, they need the leadership of adults who are not afraid to go on seeking, are not afraid to give honest answers to questions about life and death, and help children feel that they, too, have a right to search for an understanding of what is goodness and who and what is God. If we take this approach to the spiritual growth in our children, religion takes its place in our schools. But specific theological guidance and training is a personal matter to be decided upon by each family and carried out in the home and in the church, the meeting house, the temple, or the synagogue.

Another area of guidance in which the classroom teacher often finds it difficult to know what to do is that of sex education.

Perhaps the difficulty lies in the fact that many people think of sex education as only answering children's questions about procreation and birth or giving them information about the reproductive systems of their bodies. This factual material is important in helping children understand their bodies and the physical role they will play, but the giving of physical facts is only a very small part of sex education. Whether this material is included in the curriculum of the school system or is permitted to be discussed in the classroom is usually determined by the school board or the superintendent of schools, for this is a field in which there is much controversy. Some school systems feel that it is a proper function of the school to give the boys and girls information on reproduction just as it is the function of the school to see that the child has adequate knowledge and information in other areas. In other communities this is considered such a personal and intimate part of life that it should be discussed only in the home between parent and child. Where the latter view prevails, the teaching of the facts of reproduction is not permitted in the school.

Actually, regardless of whether we teach the physiological facts, we are giving sex education to boys and girls in our classrooms every day of our lives. And many teachers are doing it well. The children learn from us through our attitudes toward and our adjustment to sex in the whole life pattern. This attitude, which the child absorbs as he lives with it day by day, will have great influence upon his total life adjustment and the values he places upon the roles of men and women.

The things boys and girls learn from life around them—their home life, the marital adjustment of their parents; the lives of the neighbors; comments, discussions, and talks about literature, history, science, social problems; books, newspapers, comics, TV, and movies—are daily teaching them how men and women treat one another and what they think about each other. As they watch and listen and absorb, boys and girls are forming value judgments. They are piecing together the pattern of our culture for men and women. Are boys in the home valued more than girls? Are there subtle differences in the way people feel about boys and girls? How do we speak of a teacher who is pregnant? What is the attitude of the school toward her? Is she allowed to teach or must she give up her job right away? Do adults make of pregnancy a mystery to discuss in whispers or side-step if questions are asked, or is it accepted as natural for a woman to bear a child? If questions are met with confusion and embarrassment, the girl who is listening is less sure of her role as a potential wife and mother; the boy is confused about his responsibility as a potential father. Day by day, boys and girls are learning about sex and its place in life, its relationship to them as they grow toward manhood and womanhood—learning well or learning with confusion.

It is not always possible to answer questions when they come up in the schoolroom, but the comfortable matter-of-fact way in which we accept them, and the simple reply we are able to give, or the comment we make that shows we have accepted the question, are almost as important as the full answer we would like to have given. Sometimes, if we know the child's family, we can suggest that his mother would like to tell him about this, or that he ask her to give him a book from the library. Occasionally when lack of information is leading a youngster into real trouble and the home will not face the problem, it may be necessary to talk with the principal and see whether the school is willing to take the responsibility of giving the child the information he must have and the special guidance he needs if he is to avoid serious trouble. Many school systems, in which direct teaching or discussion in the classroom are not permitted, see the necessity for individual help.

The ways in which we meet the situations that arise in every school and in every classroom are also significant in developing wholesome values and attitudes in the children—both in those who are actively concerned and in those who are bystanders, or who pick up information through the school grapevine. The boy who shows himself, the little girl who lifts her skirts, the youngster who masturbates in the classroom, the passing of off-color notes, the boy and girl caught together under the stairs at the school dance, the girl in the too tight sweater, the boy in revealing levis, the porno-graphic pictures and literature, the lurid sex magazines and comics, the girl who becomes pregnant—all these are part of the life of every school. They are more prevalent in some communities than others. But rare is the teacher who does not have to meet such situations and decide what to do when they arise. In many cases, the final decision, the intimate discussions with the child or the children involved are carried on by the principal or the guidance teacher. Yet the "discovery," or the first talk or contact, and sometimes the whole situation, must be met by the classroom teacher.

WE CAN TEACH SELF-DISCIPLINE BY—

KEEPING A BALANCE BETWEEN

RESTRAINT AND FREEDOM

Children can be controlled through the authority of the teacher; most children can learn to conform and obey. We can control children because we are stronger than they are and because we spell "authority" to them, but the results of such control may not be those that serve best in educating a child for self-control and cooperation. A child needs help in understanding the reasonableness behind rules and laws, to see that they are essential for group living, and to learn that he may have a part in making the rules. If our goal is to help a child grow toward ultimate self-control, we must not constantly control him in situations in which he is able to learn to accept responsibility for his own control. If a child has not had enough experience as he is growing up to help him control himself, he will have real difficulty in achieving this goal.

If we make obedience to authority an end in itself, instead of a means to an end, we have a tool that may work as long as an adult is there to see that it works, but we leave the child defenseless if there is no one to obey. We have kept temporary order in the classroom, but we have not been educators; we have not helped the children grow toward self-discipline and cooperation with others in the group.

Anderson (9) has been carrying out studies on dominative and integrative behavior. He thinks of these as two techniques of response between individuals. Dominative behavior uses commands, threats, force. It is the behavior of an insecure person who fears change and expends his energy *against* another. Such behavior adds to the insecurity of the other person. It incites resistance. If the imbalance of power is too great, it leads to submission, a fear response not related to growth. Integrative behavior allows a growth process. It involves the acceptance of another as he is, finds common purpose out of differences, gives security and makes it possible for the other person to be himself, expends energy *with* another, not *against* another. It is found in the relationships of children to each other and of the teacher toward the children.

Miss Burman showed dominative behavior toward the children in her kindergarten —an approach that could not be completely offset by many of the fine things she did. The effect of the domination on the children prevented their full growth. A student teacher who observed her class made this report:

There were good things about her room. It was beautiful, cheerful, and bright—with flowers, fish, and plants which give a pleasant feeling as you open the door. Miss Burman is an attractive looking, middle-aged woman. She has a low pleasant voice and talks and sings to the children pleasantly. She teaches a cute little song almost daily, with good finger play and counting songs. She gives rhythms in an exercise period in which she beats on a drum for signaling ups and downs, running, walking, tapping, clicking, etc. She leads from these foot sounds into the "quiet feet" necessary for the library trip and from that into library etiquette. She managed the milk distribution magnificently by having two youngsters set the tables while she led the group in singing.

Yet the children may only speak in answer to a question. Not one other word may be uttered at any time. The day I observed, some of the children were highly excited about a night fire on their street. Their parents had served hot coffee to the soaked firemen. When they gathered in the circle about Miss Burman, they were so excited they wanted to tell all about it. But she said "We don't talk here. I am going to talk to you." When she talks to them, the children sit on the floor; it makes a very attractive learning picture; her control and her attention-holding are perfect. But if a child uncrosses his legs and crosses them the other way he is "twitching." It reminded me of Japanese kids "squatting" motionless as a discipline of focusing attention. "We" don't tie a loose shoelace during exercises—and not during listening time either. "We" don't utter a sound during the milk and crackers break.

The trip upstairs to the library was accomplished to perfection—single file, no one spoke. They followed instructions to the letter, noiselessly found places in the otherwise unoccupied library and then had their first freedom—to get whatever book they wished, return it, and get others. During the entire period they were watched but not otherwise talked to. No reading aloud, no storytelling, no comments, no contact, not even whispered comments between the children about their books were permitted. When the period was over the children were told, by suggestion, to say good-bye to the librarian and "thank you"—which they did gaily—first sounds that I'd heard since 9 A.M. which went unnoticed. It was then about ten thirty.

The children don't appear unhappy except when they get shushed. They love the singing. There seems to be no outdoor recess, perhaps because of the short time they are there—9:00 to 11:15 A.M. But there was no spontaneity—not even in the rhythms. If a child went to get something in the room or if they were all moving together as to the tables for their snacks, everyone went on tiptoe, praised for "not making a sound." Miss Burman feels that if children are taught to conform in the kindergarten through firmness, they will not have trouble in later years.

Miss Burman believed in making children conform at the very beginning of their school years. She knew that a certain degree of conformity to routine is necessary in any group which must live and work together. But Miss Burman told her children what to do, she did not let them talk over together and share in the making of some of the rules for living and working together in the kindergarten group.

Those who use the dominative or authoritarian approach in the classroom will usually have these results. To the outside, the classroom will give the appearance of running smoothly and being under excellent control. The authoritative teacher feels she knows how to train and discipline her children. She rarely questions her own methods—certain things are *good* for children in the schoolroom. She usually sees the children as a group. The children, like little Toby who bit his nails to the quick, must learn to conform. The children are governed by fear. Toby's remark, "I must keep quiet," indicated this. The children's normal activity is inhibited rather than redirected into constructive channels. The teacher decides what the children will do. Miss Burman's youngsters were not permitted to talk about the fire because she had other things to talk about that day.

In such a group, some children commonly have nightmares or become tense and nervous like Toby. The individual is sacrificed for the group. Some of the children become submissive and obedient; seemingly, they conform and they are praised for their conformity. Such submission, if impressed upon a child with sufficient pressure coupled with praise and approval, stunts growth and initiative and develops a child who does conform, but who, later in life, may show little ability to think and act on his own. He is afraid he will get into trouble. He does not trust his own judgment in handling situations. He always needs an authority to turn to to reassure him that he is right. He will often find it difficult to make decisions of his own. On the other hand, there are children who respond to such treatment by becoming rebellious and self-assertive. In the classroom, such a youngster will receive disapproval and probably be punished if he does not smother his rebellion and conform outwardly. When this happens, the rebellion is still there. If the child does not dare show it to his teacher, it will still come out in his aggressive behavior toward other children or in destruction of property. This is the child who chases and hits other children on the playground or on the way home from school, trips them up in the aisle, or hits out at them on the slightest provocation. The authoritarian teacher is likely always to assign work to each child rather than sometimes to permit a choice of project or even a choice of those with whom one will work. She does not like questions that might seem to challenge any statement she has made or that a child has read in a book, and she does not like deviations from the tasks she has set.

It is necessary to maintain a classroom atmosphere in which children are not distracted from the main task of learning, and this means that some planning and organization is important. But it does not mean rigid, inflexible organization that prevents a teacher from turning aside from the scheduled work of the day to have her children watch the beauty of a moth as it emerges from its chrysalis and unfolds its wings. Neither does it mean a rigidity of planning that does not permit a child to bring in ideas leading to a discussion which temporarily turns away from the class assignment. It does mean that the teacher will know her goals. She will be well prepared in her lesson plans and will know the direction in which her class is moving. Such planning allows for the changing of plans, the changing of pace, the involvement of the children, but the teacher still knows what is happening to her class.

As one teacher wrote in an evaluation of her work, "I hope to maintain in my room a good balance between self-restraint and freedom so that the children may learn the skills they need to learn. Quiet concentration must regularly give place to active participation; work and play must have their place." No child can learn well in a room full of confusion. This teacher recognized the fact that children need predictability and regularity.

The way in which the teacher conducts the class will determine whether the guide lines are drawn with an understanding of the needs of children and the goals toward which the group is working, or whether they are drawn for the personal security of the teacher. Does she rule out movement and activity and misinterpret silence, obedience, and orderliness to mean that she has created an effective atmosphere for learning? Miss Burman had a reputation in her school for having exceptionally good control in her kindergarten classroom. She never seemed to have any "discipline problems." As she put it to the other teachers, "My children always obey me."

In contrast to Miss Burman's class are the evaluations of Miss Harper's class, which were made at the end of the year by a neighboring teacher, the speech therapist, a parent, the supervisor, and the principal. Their evaluations of her class testify to the kind of experiences children received in her room. The perplexing, difficult group of youngsters who faced her on the first day of school seem to have learned to work together and to make progress as individuals.

The second-grade teacher:

The "room across the hall" seems to be a part of my room. Those first-graders are almost as familiar with our second grade as they are with their own room. Our ungraded primary program provides many opportunities for sharing and working in many different groups.

In September, my first visits into the first grade made me aware that this was a group of distinct individuals. Each child seemed to be concerned with his interests and determined to pursue them regardless of the effect on others. Any attempt to impede his progress was reported to his teacher in loud and belligerent tones. "Miss Harper, he won't let me play with the blocks!" "But I had them first." "I know but I need them!"

What a challenge to a first-grade teacher! Energies and creativeness of the group must be directed toward maturity. An experienced teacher recognizes this and puts first things first. I have watched as this group has been led toward the idea of sharing. The concept of interrelationships between the group and the individual has been developed. I do not know how the transition was accomplished, but I recognize the many evidences of growing maturity in that room.

Children are working together for the good of the group. They are recognizing their problems and solving them on their own level day by day. They are concerned with each other. I hear such remarks as "Come see the good picture that Bobby made today" or "Betty is such a good helper that we have chosen her to be a captain this week!" or "Someone forgot to put away his game. Who will help him get it together so we can leave the play corner neat before we go home today?"

It is evident that the teacher is aware of the background of each child. She varies the techniques to encourage the most acceptable responses. Through her careful study of the children in her class, her patience and willingness to follow a democratic procedure, she has aided each child in his growth toward social maturity.

Speech therapist:

Frequently during the term, I visited Miss Harper's classroom. Besides the general atmosphere of harmony and restraint, there was obvious to even the most casual observer, several other attitudes that deserve mention here. There was apparently an ideal relationship between the teacher and students. The children were openly affectionate toward the teacher and she, in turn, always seemed keenly interested in them. They would happily approach her with matters dear to them and she would warmly encourage them to express themselves freely and to share their experience with the group.

I couldn't help noticing, too, the interest the children took in their room. They seemed to realize that it was important to them and that they were in great part responsible for its care. Habits of tidiness and responsibility were observed among the group.

It also came to my attention that the children, as a group, were highly creative. They expressed themselves in a variety of ways: finger paints, clay modeling, water colors, crayon drawings, paper cutouts, pictures and bulletin-board displays. There seemed to me to be a high degree of creative ability among these children.

In summing up my observations and impressions, the class has been:

1. A group that consistently exhibited a remarkable display of poise and self-restraint

2. A group that was courteous and attentive to visitors

3. A group that worked and played together with a maximum of cooperation and a minimum of confusion and noise

4. A group that observed habits of tidiness, respect for school property

5. A group that was expressive and creative in a variety of ways

6. A group that demonstrated a fine teacher-student relationship, yet it was a group that had a background of varied experiences

Parent:

To visit Miss Harper's class is something like visiting one big family. The children take each other for granted and seem well acquainted with each other's habits and attitudes. I have been interested in the matter-of-fact discharge of their duties in room management. To this casual visitor, individual differences in social adjustment were more noticeable earlier in the year. Then the timid child and the glib, for example, could be spotted more quickly. Was this because they had not yet found their places in the class setting?

Supervisor:

Here is a group who move out to a visitor in their room with warmth, friendliness, and spontaneity. They meet one naturally with a feeling of responsibility and concern to include the outsider in whatever they are doing and to see that he is made comfortable right away. Inside the room, one senses that children are living with affection and wise guidance from an adult who knows each child very well and who is concerned with the total growth of the individual. To repeat in a few words, here are children who live with a sense of humor, much warmth, and spontaneity.

Principal:

I get the impression that no child in the room feels ill at ease. Miss Harper's manner with her class is natural and friendly. There is freedom from coercion and undue restraint, but there is also an atmosphere of endeavor and hard but interesting work being done. Most of the pupils are maturing pleasantly in such habits as self-control; consideration for others; neatness; ability to think clearly; courtesy toward their teacher, toward each other, toward visitors, when delivering messages; etc.

The room is humming most of the time—but it seems to be a busy hum, with now and then a squeak when sudden interest discovers something unexpected.

These pupils are not paragons but are very human little individuals. They even slip up now and then, as when in art period they may drop crumbs of modeling clay on the floor and be too busy to notice it before it gets mashed in.

They show pride in their work and especial pride in certain parts of their classroom; for instance, the combination reading room and game room, separated from the classroom itself by sectional bookcases.

In this class, the teacher not only feels responsible for the development of tangible concepts—information, skills, and habits—but also is doing a fine job for her little six-year-olds in the development of appreciations, interests, powers of thinking, and social adaptability.

Sometimes we find a teacher who has too little control and guidance in the management of her classroom. She lets the children run away with the program. In a different way, this is as undesirable as Miss Burman's authoritarianism. In such a classroom the children are at a loss for direction. Certain children dominate the others. Some withdraw and are pushed aside because they cannot compete. Projects are often started with enthusiasm, but when snags are reached, the children do not always know how to get over them. The ones who want to do a good job often become frustrated and confused or are prevented from carrying out their projects by lack of cooperation from the rest of their group. One mother who visited such a classroom beat a hasty retreat, for she reported that the noise was deafening when she opened the door. It was not only deafening, but it was purposeless and confused. Her little girl, who was overstimulated by the noise and lack of control, was later placed in another room. Her first comment was, "It is so nice and quiet here. I can get my work done now." When we leave it to children to set all the controls, we are giving them a task beyond their ability to handle. They are not capable of dealing alone with the various personality needs and levels of learning experience in the classroom. Such an experience neither provides an atmosphere in which a child can learn, nor helps a child learn ways of working cooperatively with others and of attacking his own tasks.

Although there is no blueprint to which we can turn—no methods that are infallible in all classroom situations—there are some points to remember as guideposts. Children usually respond best:

When there is a good feeling in the classroom. The children feel that their teacher is fair.

When directions are given simply and clearly so that the children know what is expected of them.

When the reasons for requests are given so that the children can see why they should do what the teacher has asked. Reasons should not be elaborate but, like directions, simple and straightforward.

When the children may feel free to ask questions about the reasons and to talk over why they do not agree or not want to comply. Freedom to "talk it over" with the knowledge that what they say will be listened to and considered will help boys and girls be more accepting of the "Yes, I see your point of view, but this time I am afraid we must go ahead and do it this way."

When they know that if a teacher says "yes" or "no" she means it and will stand by it unless circumstances make it wise to change the decision.

When they help plan the classroom organization and the way in which their projects will be developed and carried out.

When they are given a chance to make and manipulate things. When freedom of body movement is permitted, and the children are allowed to work constructively together.

When attention is paid to the physical aspects of the classroom—heat, light, ventilation. Children can become restless and difficult when these things are neglected.

When reasonable standards are set up so that the children know the boundaries and the limits.

When restlessness and disorder are recognized as a sign that the work is not well chosen for the needs of the children or that fatigue or boredom has settled in—that a change of pace or activity is a better answer than scolding and forced attention.

When recognition is given for the good things a child does.

When efforts are appreciated even though the results are not up to standard.

When all children are given a chance to succeed in some area in front of their classmates.

When the cause of behavior is sought even though surface behavior must be treated.

When boredom is avoided and boys and girls are kept busy with things that interest them and have meaning for them.

When children are given an opportunity to work at their own level, without an overemphasis on competition.

When the worth and dignity of every child is remembered and upheld.

When there is mutual respect between teacher and child.

LOOKING FOR REASONS BEHIND

BEHAVIOR PROBLEMS

We are often upset about the lack of discipline in our room because we feel it will reflect on our ability as a teacher if the principal or supervisor should walk in. Sometimes our concern with our own reputation blinds us to the real reasons behind some of our discipline problems. In our absorption with other things, we ignore the signals some of the children are sending out that all is not well with them—signals which, if ignored, can lead to more serious trouble later on. Handling the "surface behavior" is important and does lead to a smoothness of functioning in the classroom, but it loses its value if it covers up the deeper, more underlying problems. When a child hits out at us in anger or destroys property or refuses to hand in an assignment or disturbs the class or is rebellious and aggressive, we may look at this as a discipline problem only: "Jack must be made to behave," and forget what the signal may really mean—the tension, the unhappiness, the feeling of failure, of not being wanted that may lie behind it. This will need our attention, too.

We must always ask ourselves what is behind this behavior? For the way in which we meet the situation should be influenced by the real cause.

We cannot handle all behavior situations in the same way even if they appear the same on the surface. Fred was a happy-go-lucky boy who was always forgetting things. Good-natured and comfortable in the classroom, he was also careless and forgetful. He often forgot his lunch money and would come to his teacher at the last moment and ask for a loan. After helping him several times, his teacher finally said, "Look here, Fred, next time you forget I am afraid you are going to have to miss out on lunch." Fred did forget, and he did miss out on his lunch. But after that he came to school with his lunch money in his pocket. But little Jeremy was a different kind of a child. Timid and afraid, he rarely spoke in the classroom or entered into activities with any spontaneity. One day when the children left the third-grade room for lunch, Jeremy's teacher noticed him at the back of the room with his head on the desk. "Why Jeremy, aren't you coming to lunch with us today?" Jeremy sobbed out that he had left his lunch money at home. His teacher didn't scold but, taking Jeremy's hand in hers, she said, "You will have lunch with me today."

Before we act, we must weigh the behavior in terms of the knowledge we have of the child. "How can what I do best help this child do better next time?" Often the child who has stolen something, the child who has lied to us, the child who has cheated or has been destructive is already a child who has been deprived, or had harsh handling at home, or been exposed to such constant criticism and failure that he cannot trust himself. He is often very afraid of grownups and what they will do or say to him. If we can let him know that we are there to help him as a friend, to listen because we know that behind actions there is always a reason, he will usually talk to us, even if we have to wait a while. This is especially true if he knows that we are fair, because he has watched us with other boys and girls. We should not try to force a child to tell us what he has done or even why he did it. If we

do try to make a child confess, he may do so through fear alone and feel so hostile to us that we cannot help him at all. Or, if he is not sure of us, he may lie to us to protect himself. This is a very natural reaction if we have given a child a feeling that we have jumped at circumstantial evidence, are judging and condemning him rather than trying to get his point of view and help him in a tough situation.

Harsh or threatening ways of confronting a child with what he has done may make a child more conforming out of fear, but they also make him withdraw further from us. They undermine his self-confidence and often increase either his timidity or his rebelliousness and his need to misbehave. However difficult a child has been, it is never helpful to embarrass him or publicly humiliate him. It is best to talk to him in another room or after class. Miss Nesbit did not talk with Ray in front of the other boys and girls in the study hall but saw him later on in the office. It is also a good policy to help a child do something constructive about his wrong actions. Many children feel a considerable amount of guilt over what they have done even if they attempt to "cover up" with bravado. Miss Drew knew this when she said to Ned, "You have taken a lot of my time today and I want you to stay and help me after school."

To understand the reasons behind a child's behavior does not mean to condone it. As children try to develop standards of behavior and values, we as adults should show our understanding of their mistakes and of their confusion as they try to find out what is "right" and what is "wrong." But if we are to help them, we must stay on the side of what is considered "right." Otherwise the confusion of the child is increased. As Ray's teacher said, "I can understand, but I can't let you fight in school."

If we are to be on the side of "what is right," it is necessary for us to weigh carefully our own values. Otherwise, we may confuse "right" with what is comfortable for us as grownups; or we may emphasize as "right" many kinds of superficial behavior that we have come to accept, as a matter of course, as necessary and desirable. It is easy to look at the values of the people among whom we grew up as the "best" values.

KNOWING WHEN AND HOW TO SET

BEHAVIOR LIMITS

In every classroom made up of normal boys and girls, there will be many kinds of behavior problems that have to be dealt with every day. This is what Redl calls "surface behavior." We cannot let an immediate situation get out of hand while we seek for its cause or build for future goals. We must often act—and act now—in order to keep things on an even keel in the classroom. We must handle situations as they arise and later sit down and try to think about the cause and the way in which we met the surface situation.

Children want and need the security of adult control in learning which kinds of behavior are acceptable and which are not. Children of all ages have conflicting desires and find it hard to make choices. They are often puzzled because of ignorance or lack of experience.

An adolescent girl, asked to go to a late party to which she really did not want to go, turned from the phone to her parents and signaled to them "Say no! Say No!" She could not bring herself to say it. She wanted to be able to use them as an alibi to bolster her own inability to hold out against her group. If adults do not help boys and girls gradually to learn acceptable behavior and back them up while they are learning, a child will feel insecure and unable to interpret and handle the situations he must meet as he grows up. Burmeister (10) feels that the more attention we give to our children as individuals, the less discipline they will need. Life is generally more satisfying to such a child. He will be troublesome sometimes, but he will have less need to be diffi-

cult and rebellious. She also feels that although children need to release their feelings verbally and actively, they need, at the same time, to know that there is someone around who will set limits to their own behavior, firmly and consistently.

When a child comes to school, he is old enough to share in setting the limits and making the rules. He is able to understand and discuss the reasons for such rules and limits. When he has taken part in making the rules and is able to understand the reasons and has been permitted to express his feelings about them, he is much more likely to obey them and cooperate with them.

At the same time, we must remember that the experience of children is limited and that we as adults must have the wisdom to know when it is appropriate to share the making of rules with children and when we must say firmly—"This is so" with the reason why. All limits cannot be set by boys and girls. We should not ask the opinion of boys and girls nor give them an opportunity to make rules unless it is a situation in which we feel they are ready and able to help make the decision and we can abide by their choice of the rules. If a group of boys and girls want to drive to a school game with eight other children in a car, we would say *no*. If a younger child wants to cross the street to school at a dangerous intersection, we give no choice; we say cross where the patrol boy is located. If a teacher feels that combinations of numbers must be learned, they are to be learned and the learning must be enforced with practice within the limits of the child's capacity for practice. We need to remember that many normal youngsters, who are neither "hurt children" nor really emotionally disturbed youngsters need to try the teacher out, to test the limits and see how far they will be allowed to go. There is nothing unhealthy about this; it is just a normal expression of trying themselves out. These children simply need to be held firmly and with good humor to the standards that have been set up. Children cannot be expected to like everything they must do in school; some drill will be boring, some subjects will be more interesting and challenging than others, some routines are necessary. It is only natural that growing, active youngsters should want to get out of some of these things, particularly those youngsters who have plenty of drive.

However, if we have to hold them to the line too much of the time, we will need to take a good look at the classroom setup. Are the limits too narrow? Have these boys and girls grown beyond them? Can they take more responsibility and go ahead at a faster, more independent pace? Is there too much drill for children who do not need it? Are these children ready for a greater share of self-discipline? Is there enough free movement and activity in the room? Why do they need to try out the limits?

KEEPING OUR OWN "EMOTIONAL HOUSES" IN ORDER

If we are having trouble with the discipline in our classroom, we sometimes need to look within ourselves. Our own emotional adjustment, our attitude toward our job, our physical health, our efficient organization or our lack of it, our preparation for the day's work, or a temporary personal problem may all walk into the classroom with us. All of us will have off-days when things go wrong, and we are likely then to find the group more difficult and to be more difficult with them.

Grownups often think of how children affect them, and rarely stop to think—how does the youngster feel about this? We may say, "The children in my room are getting on my nerves. They are so noisy and restless and demanding. I am worn out at the end of the day." Rarely do we hear a teacher say, "I've been so tense and irritable the last few days. I've just kept at the children. You can't do this, you mustn't do that. I wonder how they feel about it?"

If a teacher is inconsistent—flies angrily "off the handle" today and is "easy" tomorrow—the children in her room will not know what to expect. They will come to school wondering what the teacher will be like today. Will we have to behave or can we get away with things? Such an emotionally inconsistent climate usually results in a restless behavior pattern in the classroom.

A nagging, quarrelsome, assertive, immature, or uninterested teacher will have difficulty maintaining a wholesome climate for learning in her classroom. She is likely to have confusion, irresponsibility, and lack of cooperation from the children. Often they will respond with moods of their own, flaring up at each other, failing to cooperate with each other or with their teacher. A gloomy teacher who finds life hard will find herself reflected in the children.

Sometimes we have unresolved conflicts or tensions of our own that make us feel resentful against our job and the work we must do, and we take out these feelings on the youngsters. Sometimes we reject a child and are unfair to him because he reminds us of undesirable qualities or unhappy experiences we have had. Sometimes a teacher, remembering his or her own lack of popularity during high school, is particularly hard on the child who is gay and the center of attraction. Or the teacher who has worked hard for his education may have little patience with the child who is obtaining his too easily. The man who wanted to be the athlete or the woman who would like to have been pretty and gay may be much harder on the athlete or the "butterfly" than on the other children. We must know ourselves if we are to understand the way in which we react to the children in our classes.

USING PUNISHMENT SPARINGLY

In any realistic school situation, we realize that sometimes we may have to punish a child as a more forcible reminder that certain behavior is not acceptable and as a way of teaching a better form of action. The important question is—why are you using punishment? Is it out of anger with a child because he has annoyed or embarrassed you, or is it as a means of helping him learn some important lesson in behavior? Josselyn (11) states it this way:

Punishment is at times necessary in order to sharpen the necessity for conformity in regard to important issues. There is no "best" form of punishment. Punishment is most meaningful to the child when it is in proportion to the misdemeanor rather than in proportion to the [adult's] irritation; when, if possible, it has some relationship to the behavior that necessitates it; and when it is carried out consistently once it is imposed.

Punishment is one of the most ancient and universal methods of trying to modify and control human behavior. In the past, punishment and the fear it produced were relied upon almost entirely for producing the "right" kind of behavior in both children and grownups. Both children and adults were punished by the rod, by shame, and by fear. It is in comparatively recent years that punishment has been seen as only one method of trying to teach desirable behavior, and the one which, if it is relied on constantly, is usually least effective. Punishment can sometimes be used effectively to control or redirect the acts of an individual and to prevent the repetition of socially undesirable acts, providing it is used with understanding, discrimination, and the realization that it is only one very small part of the program of guidance toward desirable behavior—the one that is wisely used last. A socialized individual cannot be produced solely by means of punishment or by overdoses of punishment. Punishment means that someone else is putting on the controls. It does not always lead to greater self-control on the part of the person punished,

unless punishment is followed by an understanding of the problems of the individual and he is also helped to work them out. Punishment may be a reminder and a deterrent; it is seldom a cure.

Punishment actually is often given to relieve the tensions in the person who is punishing although he will rarely admit this reason. The boy who is failed has become a source of irritation to his teacher, because she has *failed* with him. The disturber whom she cannot handle is a threat to the apparent discipline in her room. A teacher who has difficulty controlling her class often may be using punishment as a means of covering her feelings of insecurity by being tough.

In the classroom, we must be careful about the kind of punishments we use. It is unwise to use jobs as punishment. A child who is made to stay after school to wash the chalkboard is going to dislike the job. He will not be building a very good feeling about taking pride in his classroom and cooperating with his group to attend to the necessary care of the room. We have destroyed a very important learning by using such a task as a "punishment."

Schoolwork should never be used as a penalty. A child's interest in and love for arithmetic or spelling will certainly not be encouraged if he is given so many spelling words or extra problems to do because he disturbed the class.

It is sometimes necessary to remove a child from a group he is disturbing or ask him to leave the room or even a school social activity. But this should be done with the reason given, so that the boy or girl gradually comes to understand that one cannot disturb the work or play of others.

Sometimes we use a deprivation of privileges, but here we must again be careful or we may deprive a child or children of something important to their well-being. To take recess from a noisy, restive group of children is to deprive them of the very thing they needed to get over their restlessness.

If natural consequences are used, common sense must be used along with them. They are often effective, if not too severe. A group of senior high-school boys got overexcited after a big game in which their school had lost. They took out their excitement by breaking up the windshields of the cars of the opposing team. These boys were old enough to bear the consequences of their lack of control. The damage was assessed and the school helped the boys find jobs so that they could earn the money to pay for the damage. A child who tears up a schoolbook might, in the same way, be asked to earn the money to pay for it or to do a needed job at school in return. A youngster who did not do his homework might be asked to stay after school until it was completed, providing we were sure that the work was suited to him and that it was carelessness or neglect that kept him from completing the assignment, not a legitimate excuse. Sometimes natural consequences are enough reminder without further punishment. The child who climbs in a dangerous spot and is hurt or frightened does not need further punishment for being disobedient.

Most children will resent punishment that is given for failure to comply with a request they consider to be unfair or unreasonable or one which is not understood or is inconsistent with past prohibitions.

Mr. Redding came into the eighth-grade English class in the middle of the year. He insisted that all assignments be completed and returned the following day. This meant taking library books home. The children were confused and upset because the previous teacher had insisted that all library books be kept in their desks at school. Mr. Redding kept after school all those children who had not taken their books home and consequently came to class with incompleted assignments. The children were angry and restless in class and murmurs of "He's not fair. We never had to do this" passed around the room.

If punishment is too frequent, opportunity for learning is lost. The child becomes indifferent and accepts punishment as a natural and disagreeable part of his environment. He may be beaten down and cowed by it, or he may be strong enough to rebel against it. Some strong children accept it as the price they must pay for doing what they want. A group of girls were very anxious to go to an out-of-town game, which the school had said could not be attended. They went anyway, preferring to stay after school for study hall for two weeks to make up for the fun. Some children seek punishment as a way of relieving their feelings of guilt. Others misbehave because through their misdeeds they obtain the "place in the sun" they crave.

There are times when we do not punish a child, even though it appears he may deserve it. If the child recognizes that what he has done was wrong or if he has inadvertently done something very serious, frequently his own deep concern has taught him a grave lesson. In such cases, we would only add to the child's guilt feelings and shame with which he is already overburdened. We do not need to reinforce it from the outside. Such was the situation with Don. In a scuffle on the playground, he tripped his best friend, knocking out a front tooth on some cement curbing. Don knew scuffling was prohibited in that area. But his remorse at having hurt his friend was so great that he needed no further punishment from parents or teacher.

GUIDING CHILDREN TOWARD ASSUMING RESPONSIBILITIES FOR THEIR OWN BEHAVIOR*

The daily management of the classroom should be regarded not as an end in itself, but as a way in which we help boys and girls learn to live together cooperatively in a

*Much of the material in this section is taken from the author's article "Responsibility in Children: The Contribution of the Home," *Child Study,* summer 1956. It is reprinted here with permission of the publishers.

group, to understand what kind of behavior helps people to get along together, and to work together for a common cause. It is also a way in which they can be helped in learning how to respect one another as individuals, how to make personal decisions, and how to achieve ultimate self-guidance.

In our classrooms, we will have many kinds of children. It is not an easy job to help them live and work together in a harmonious way. Neither is it always easy to handle specific problem situations that arise day by day in the classroom. But if we keep the focus on the real goals of guidance, we will be constantly encouraged as we watch the gradual growth of many of our boys and girls as they learn a little better how to use their own judgment, to make wiser decisions, and to begin to choose the kind of values that will make them fine grownups. Miss Lawrence keeps the focus for us when she says:

I have always tried to help each child grow physically, emotionally, socially, and mentally, in order that he might become a happy, useful, and well-adjusted member of society. I have never stopped to think of it in terms of a guidance program but as a matter of good teaching. Guidance and good teaching are synonymous. The competent teacher is concerned with preventing maladjustments and does not look on guidance as a service limited to remedial procedures. I study my children so that I may help them use their capacities better, understand their abilities and interests, develop their abilities as well as possible, and take steps toward self-guidance.

As children learn to think, work, play, and solve problems together in the classroom, they are learning the real meaning of responsibility. Responsibility is an attitude that grows slowly from within a child as he puts his experiences together and weaves a pattern of values into his life. A child may be obedient when he performs the tasks we give him to do in the classroom—he may do his arithmetic assignment, hand his papers in on time, and stop talking when the bell rings. This may be an indication of responsible behavior or it may simply mean that he is afraid of the consequences if he does not do these things. A child may do all of these things, yet when the moment of testing comes—when he must make a difficult choice between doing something he wants to do and something he knows is right to do—he may be unable to make the choice because he has no reliance in himself and has had no real experience in using his judgment. If a child has had an opportunity truly to participate in the cooperative life of a classroom, year after year in school, he will have learned to build reliance in himself for he will have had many experiences in learning to use his judgment and carry responsibility.

Butler (12) writes about some eight-year-olds who are already learning the real meaning of responsibility:

One morning the eight-year-olds were coming into their room by two's and three's shortly before nine o'clock. These were some of their comments as they hurried into the room:

"I get to help clean the cage for the hamsters."

"I'm taking care of the white rats."

"Betty took the raccoon's food to the refrigerator. It is fresh liver."

"The reference book said raccoons eat fish. Is liver like fish?"

"Liver is meat, I know."

"Fish is meat."

"Here is the cabbage for the guinea pigs."

"What must I do with the fresh milk?"

"Give it to the mother rat."

"Let's see if the guinea pigs will drink the milk!"

"Mary is going to help you with the guinea pigs."

It was Mary's first time to help with the cages. She had never had a pet and hadn't liked animals at first. Jim, who was taking part in the chatter, was in charge of listing *the meats and vegetables for the animals for the following day, so he got busy making the chart. He had trouble spelling "vegetable." First he asked Betty how to spell "vegetable." Betty was a good speller. She told him it started with a "v." Willie was watering the plants, but he stopped long enough to help Jim look in the picture dictionary and find the word "vegetable." . . .*

At our ten-thirty playtime all the animals "went out for fresh air and exercise." Harry had read this to us from a book: "All animals must have fresh air and exercise to grow strong and healthy." That was the answer to one of the group's questions. He had proudly found the answer during the reading period.

Responsibility is built upon a child's gradual realization that people need one another, that we cannot go it alone, that sometimes one must share and give as well as take. But at the same time that he is beginning to realize his need for others and their need for him, he is also gradually realizing that he is an individual seeking for the development of himself. He is constantly faced with a choice between doing what he wants to do or putting aside his own immediate wishes for the wishes of other persons or the broader needs of the group. Maturity comes when wise choices can be made and a balance kept between one's responsibilities toward the group and one's own personal needs for growth and fulfillment.

The very concept of responsibility implies the existence of a group, or relationship, to another person. In this fact, however, lies some of the confusion children sometimes feel. What does belonging to a group imply? A school child will be a member of many groups. Some will be groups not completely of his choosing—the neighborhood group, the school group, his church group, his organized club group. There will be many groups of friends that shift and change and to which he must find entry and adapt. There will be shifting groups, which come together for a specific purpose and then disband. All these groups will demand responsibility from him, and sometimes their demands will conflict. How will he know how to choose wisely? A delinquent boy may be a highly responsible member of his gang: he meets his obligations to them and carries them seriously; he may never let his pals down. Responsibility, yes, but what kind? to whom? to the family? to his classmates? to the community? to one's pals? The child is confused and often finds it difficult to know just what choice to make:

"I must be honest, but unless I am dishonest and steal from the dime store, my friends will call me chicken, and then I'll be dropped from the gang."

"I must be honest, but unless I get an A grade my folks will think I'm not doing my best. I can't get an A; therefore I must cheat in this exam—otherwise they'll be mad at me."

"My mother says I must pick up my room tonight. My teacher says I must read 20 pages of social studies before tomorrow. I promised to paint the poster for the school dance. There is not enough time for all. What shall I do? I must be responsible, but to whom?"

If in our classrooms we require of a youngster only conformity through obedience, and do not also encourage him to share in the class plans, to talk things over and express his point of view, to have opinions of his own even if they run counter to our ideas or those of his classmates, he has little chance to develop responsibility through his own achievements and mistakes. At the same time, he needs opportunities to contribute his share toward meeting the needs of his class or his school because his share is really needed and valued. Through such real participation of every member of the class, we can help develop genuine group responsibility plus individual integrity.

148

Because our eyes are on the citizen of to-morrow, we must be careful to remember that the citizen of tomorrow is a child today. There is a danger that we may become so zealous in our quest for ways to develop a sense of responsibility that we may overload boys and girls with platitudes and overburden them with tasks in the name of teaching responsibility. This is the easy way for us as teachers, but it may lead us to a false sense of virtue and accomplishment. We shall really reach children only as we spell responsibility in terms which have meaning in childhood and which allow for the ways of children.

A group of teachers at the Ethical Culture Schools in New York (13) worked out together the following suggestions for the kinds of experiences that are possible for boys and girls as steps toward learning responsible behavior:

... We need ... to consider what specific responsibilities are appropriate for children at different levels of growth and development. A great deal of damage can be done by expecting either too much or too little. Since children spend from twelve to fourteen years in school between nursery and college there is a good deal which can be accomplished and considerable study is needed as to what expectations are appropriate. ...

Whether at home or at school the expectations must be at the child's level of understanding from the four-year-old in the preschool class, learning to share his toys and equipment, to the high school seniors establishing an advisory council to share with the faculty and administrators the responsibilities for the welfare of the entire school. At any age level, active participation in group planning and group living brings a sense of personal value, of belonging, of being needed, which is one of life's deepest satisfactions.

... Even in a nursery where three-year-olds may seem almost like infants newly out of the cradle, you will see evidences that the children are learning to be independent and to assume responsibilities. They can take over many physical routines, unless perfection is expected by the adults. If their clothes are simple and well planned they can do much of their dressing and undressing. They can put away their own belongings if books and shelves are low. Three-year-olds can follow short, simple directions, usually not more than one or two at a time. They can even achieve reasonably peaceful relations with their peers and learn to put some of their feelings into words rather than simply screaming when frustrated by other children, adults, or the materials with which they are working.

Moving on, we notice that the first grader is eager to assume responsibility. It is to him a recognition of growing up and he is right, for it is a very good yardstick of maturity, a term which is frequently difficult to define. He enjoys playing with a larger group and observing the rules of simple games, for he can now follow more complicated directions and his interest span is longer. He can remember general routines and enjoys going on errands throughout the school.

The second grader realizes his responsibility toward an even larger group. He is learning not to interrupt, to wait for his turn in discussions. He can conform to more complicated group regulations, such as those necessary for getting across the street on class excursions. He is able to share in such work projects as painting a mural or building an airplane.

The third grader derives great satisfaction from doing a good job for the group. He is ready also to assume responsibility toward the larger school community. He can arrange and care for aquaria and pets for other classes. He can handle specific academic assignments independently, especially in making up work after an absence. Many eight-year-olds begin to travel alone in the city and are very proud of the fact

*that they are permitted to go back and
forth to school on the public bus.*

*The fourth grader is ready for further
participation with individuals and with
groups outside his own. He understands
the necessity for cooperation in assembly
programs and larger joint activities for the
good of the school, keeping appointments on
time and recalling variations in programs.
Overcoming tardiness is one of the responsibilities that a child often can assume at
this time. He assists in making choices
about his special interests and optional periods and even begins to be concerned
about needs outside his own country. Just
as in his social studies, he is ready for wider
horizons in time and space provided all this
is kept on a child's level. He is interested
in how children live in various countries,
their houses, food, schools and clothing. In
his academic work, he now is given short
assignments and expected to find necessary
information through simple, independent
research. He shows growth in his committee work, he is able to discuss plans, accepting suggestions from other people, dividing
responsibilities, organizing the job to be
done and helping carry it to completion.*

*Fifth graders take on such specific com-
munity obligations as supervision of younger children in the lunchroom; helping them
with their wraps, stories, assemblies, paintings; assisting in the preparation for visiting
groups and for other groups within their
own school. Ten-year-olds are capable of a
real consideration of their own strengths
and weaknesses on the basis of objective
evidence, such as test results, and subjective opinions in conference with their
teachers, parents, and others.*

*Sixth graders take additional responsibil-
ity for the school as a whole and for community projects, also on the children's level.
They are ready to be officers in the elementary student council, to serve in the school
supply room, edit the school newspaper,
work through the Junior Red Cross for
veterans in the hospitals by making place*

*mats, favors, and so forth. Often they con-
struct toys and equipment for younger children in their own school or in day-care
centers, and contribute gifts to children in
Europe or other parts of the world. To a fair
degree, pre-adolescent children have a
sense of community obligation. They must,
however, be allowed to make mistakes—
within limits—because if they feel the adult
is always going to pick up where they forget or fail, they gain less satisfaction from
the experience and learn less from it.*

*Children like to think of their parents as
sharing experiences with them, that parents
and teachers, too, are participating members of their community. One of the serious
joint responsibilities of the three groups—
faculty, parents, and students—especially
at the high school level, is that of social values, the problems of cliques, parties, the
student who feels left out. Adolescents suf-
fer acutely over such situations and these
matters can be dealt with effectively only
when there is a keen sense of consideration
by all and shared responsibility in handling
them.*

*There can be no final rule as to the
amount of responsibility each child, parent
or teacher should take in these various
areas. The important principle is that each
joint undertaking be planned and carried
through by all involved according to their
particular function and qualifications.*

All children are not at the same level of
readiness to carry their share in group discipline. With some groups we may have to
be temporarily the authoritative person
who sets the limits and puts on the controls.
It will depend upon the experiences the
children have had. Some classes are not yet
ready for self-government and it would be
very unwise to impose it upon them. We
must know when a group is ready to share
the group control with us and when we must
temporarily control the situation ourselves. We must ask ourselves, though,
whether the control we are exerting is based

on our belief in a permanent authoritarian control by the teacher, or whether we recognize that we are meeting a temporary situation and are working toward the time when we can help the children in our class be ready to take over gradually more responsibility for themselves.

Sheviakov and Redl (14) give us a nice example of such a situation in their story of Miss Jones.

Miss Jones takes over an eighth grade. This class has built up a bad reputation and includes the worst hoodlums in the school. They and the less-delinquent children in the room are going through a period of vehement body changes and are obviously out of bounds. Things have become so bad that the whole school is in trouble because of them. None of the daily routine, including attendance or any type of work output is functioning any more.

Miss Jones has read a lot about "democratic procedures." So the first thing she does is establish a system of self-government. This has a few positive effects. The attitudes of some of these youngsters are better. They do not show so much obstinacy and spiteful rejection of school or teacher. But it is equally obvious that they cannot handle their affairs. Bullies develop who try to put the regime over on others but keep their own buddies tax-exempt. Rules are made and broken. Beautiful examples of learning take place in the discussions of group affairs, but the children still do not show any change in school attendance and work output, and they still get in everybody's hair.

The mistake is obvious. Miss Jones' idea was right to the extent that an experiment in self-government is the best way for youngsters to learn constructive attitudes toward each other and their community. However, we also know that such an experiment with a group that is not ready will not affect momentary behavior for quite awhile. In a camp her technique might have worked.

With the school demands remaining what they were, though, Miss Jones' technique required a longer waiting time for changes in surface behavior than she could possibly have anticipated. Therefore, the technique was right in terms of basic attitudes, but was harmful because it did not solve even the minimum of actual surface behavior problems that had to be solved.

SELF-GOVERNMENT MUST HAVE SOME LIMITS

We need to be careful not to ask children to ally themselves with adult authority against other children. A class group or a student government council can at times appropriately assign penalties for a limited and selected group of minor offenses. These should be well defined ahead of time so that all the boys and girls realize what these penalties for nonconforming behavior will be. But it is rarely wise to put the burden on one child to report another, unless it can be handled in an impersonal way. Children who are delegated the responsibility of reporting others may be put into severe conflict between their loyalty to their group and their desire to do their assigned job well.

Participation that puts too much disciplinary responsibility on the individual child or on the group, even if the child has been selected by schoolmates, can be harmful to both the child and the group.

Jake was a restless, hyperactive child. He came from a tense and difficult home situation. His father and mother were separated. His mother worked and Jake and his two sisters were cared for by an elderly grandmother. Before the separation took place, the children had been exposed to angry bickerings and open fights between the parents. Jake had always been a tense, hyperactive little boy. There was some question as to whether he might perhaps have had a slight birth injury. He could not sit still. His restlessness in class was very disturbing and difficult to handle. At the end of a day of trying to conform to classroom requirements, he was like a supercharged bomb—he had to let off steam and unfortunately he usually did so on the bus going home. The patrol boy handed in his name many times. He could not control the boy or the situation. There were constant fights, so serious that the driver had to stop the bus. The matter was discussed in patrol, and the patrol leaders decided that Jake was to be deprived of his lunch recess every day for a month as punishment for his behavior.

A decision by the principal and the guidance department of the school would have been more appropriate. Jake was too disturbed a boy to be in the normal classroom and bus situation. The punishment of the patrols was harmful to him. He needed the noon break if he were to stay in the classroom situation at all. He needed, also, the support and understanding of an adult who could bring help to the boy.

Decisions of a disciplinary nature should not be handled by a class or a court of other children. Children cannot know what is behind the behavior of another child and great damage can be done. The punishment of one's peer may be more devastating than that of an adult. The areas should be well defined—those that are suitable for children to participate in and those that must remain in adult hands.

Children can often make the group rules. They can help carry out these rules within a group situation, talking over such questions as "What is bossiness? What does it do to us?" "What happens when our teacher is out of the room? Do we need greater self-control?" But the problem of the individual should be outside the jurisdiction of his classmates.

SOME CHILDREN CANNOT BE HELPED IN THE CLASSROOM

Some children are already so hurt by the time they come to school that it will be difficult and often impossible to teach them values or guide them in establishing desirable behavior within the classroom situation. It is well for us to be able to recognize such youngsters, for, if we do not, we may feel completely defeated as we try to work with them. Such seriously disturbed children do not belong in the normal classroom situation. Whenever possible, they should be referred for clinical help and perhaps placed in a more appropriate school situation if one is available—a school that is able to meet their needs better. Unfortunately, such facilities are not always available and many teachers do find boys and girls in their classrooms who should not be there, and who cannot possibly be taught adequately. Some children can never be "adjusted" to the classroom group by a teacher, however hard she may try. Among these children, we will find those who are seriously disturbed

emotionally and those who are so nearly delinquent that they cannot accept the necessary restrictions and need for cooperation in a classroom group.

This is a problem of very real magnitude, both in terms of the disturbed child who is not receiving the kind of care he needs, and in terms of the other children in the classroom. A disturbed child may upset the learning situation for the entire class. This is particularly true if the emotional disturbance is expressed by lack of cooperation, restlessness, and attacks on the other children.

One really emotionally upset child in a classroom can keep a teacher from having the time, energy, or ability to concentrate on teaching at all, for in such a situation it may be necessary for a teacher constantly to interrupt what she is doing to control the disturbed child.

A sixth-grade boy said to his mother, "I wish Miss Murray could get Bill outside the classroom when he acts up. We all hate it when we have to listen to them talking at each other." And the mother of another child said, "I wish Miss Murray could do something with that boy, for my child comes home either 'up' or 'down' depending upon how Bill has acted that day. His whole school life this year is being upset by Bill and his problems."

We need to be aware that the classroom is not a clinic. *Teachers are not case workers.* A case worker is free to focus her attention on the individual problem of one child at a time. The teacher must keep the focus on teaching thirty or more children at a time. If a child is seriously disturbed and must remain in the classroom, the teacher is asked to carry an impossible burden, which she will rarely be able to meet. We must recognize the limits of what can be done.

A teacher with a disturbed child in her room must have support from her colleagues and from the administration. She cannot be expected to handle the discipline herself; whereas with normal children, this may be the wisest procedure. With Bill, Miss Murray was left to try to control a large, unruly boy with a court record, who really frightened her with his outbursts of anger. She feared for herself and the children in her class. She also felt herself ostracized by other teachers who kept complaining to the principal that she could not control this boy, that he was upsetting and hurting their children on the playground.

A boy as upset as Bill must be regarded as the responsibility of the whole school group. Often a conference between supervisor, principal, visiting teachers, teacher, and the other teachers in the school may result in the pooling of all available resources so that the teacher is not left to bear the brunt of the child's problem alone. These are not easy situations to handle. Often there is little that can be done except to "hold the line" and keep the child under whatever control is possible. If no other course is available sometimes constant periods under supervision in the principal's office or the nurse's room may be advisable. We must do what we can as a stop-gap but must continue to work steadily for more effective ways of meeting the needs of these children for rarely will they respond to guidance in the regular classroom.

If a child's development is obviously retarded, if he steals, if he is a disturber of the class, or if he is far behind in class and his own potential, a teacher usually realizes that such a child needs special help. In such cases, she knows that it is wise to turn to those specialists who can best guide and advise her and cooperate with her in helping the child. There are many other situations in which boys and girls do not realize their potentialities and teachers wonder whether their knowledge and experience are adequate to assist these children, or whether they should seek help from a guidance specialist in the school or community. Sometimes teachers struggle along feeling that they have failed to understand or to help certain children in their classroom, unaware that they really needed the help of a specialist in studying the child and advising the proper procedure.

When children are not able to learn anything constructive from their mistakes or failures or make adjustments to the world in which they live, professional help is needed. This is also true when their mistakes become too serious or when they pull away from life because of the pain their experiences give them.

As teachers, however, we should be able to recognize the symptoms of severely disturbed youngsters. It will be easier, then, for us to cease regarding such a child as simply a "nuisance," a "bad child," a "screwball," or a "queer one." We will be able to approach the handling of the problem with a more sympathetic attitude. This attitude will often be felt by the youngster and will be the first step in getting help for him.

A child's problem is serious when any of the following behavior is noticed: withdrawal from social contact; anxious preoccupation with health or frequent concern with symptoms of illness; other anxious preoccupations that interfere with the child's schoolwork or zest of living; the development, with or without the company of others, of delinquent patterns for securing satisfaction; the inability to make normal progress toward adult identification with one's own sex and toward normal interest in the other sex; chronic unhappiness or anxiety.

Sometimes the recognition of these symptoms may be gradual, perhaps resulting from the cumulative record which the teacher has kept. At other times, the teacher may suddenly realize that the child's difficult behavior is becoming more frequent and more marked—a characteristic pattern of behavior instead of an occasional one. It is well to seek help for a child with any of these forms of behavior as soon as it is recognized, for these are symptoms of emotional tensions that cannot be helped unless fully understood. The total resources of the community are needed in a cooperative effort to bring adequate guidance to such children.

In summary, our goal should be what Clark (15) calls "creative discipline," which he defines in this way:

It is . . . suggested that the goal of creative discipline—parental and social—is to provide for the child and adolescent those social conditions within which he may develop the type of character structure which is consistent with his maximum creativity, a respect for his own humanity, and a functional identity with other human beings— an integrity of self and social empathy. These conditions are obtainable; the product is also obtainable through the most rigorous form of discipline—the discipline of the human ego. . . .

If discipline is directed toward these goals it can be neither punitive, harsh, and rigid, nor chaotically permissive. It necessarily will come with the human sensitivity, flexibility, guidance, and structure which are es-

sential to human creativity and which reflect a self perpetuating respect for the inviolable dignity of all human beings.

REFERENCES

(1) Sheviakov, George V., and Redl, Fritz. *Discipline for Today's Children and Youth.* New Rev. Washington, D.C.: Association for Supervision and Curriculum Development, National Education Association, 1956, p. 64.

(2) Senn, Milton, J. E. "Fads and Facts as the Bases of Child-Care Practices," *Children*, Vol. 4, March-April 1957, p. 46.

(3) Havighurst, Robert J. *Developmental Tasks and Education.* Chicago: The University of Chicago Press, 1948, pp. 25, 35.

(4) Reprinted from *The Arts in the Classroom* by Natalie Robinson Cole by permission of The John Day Company, Inc., publisher. Copyright 1940 by Natalie Robinson.

(5) Laycock, Samuel R. "Toward Better Teaching." *The Saskatchewan Bulletin*, April 1949.

(6) Cole, *op. cit.*, pp. 93-94.

(7) Myrdal, G. *An American Dilemma.* New York: Harper & Brothers, 1944, pp. 1-25.

(8) Witmer, Helen L., and Kotinsky, Ruth. *Personality in the Making.* New York: Harper & Brothers, 1952, p. 135.

(9) Anderson, Harold. "Domination and Socially Integrative Behavior," *Child Behavior and Development*, edited by Roger C. Barker and others. New York: McGraw-Hill Book Co., Inc., 1943, pp. 459-484.

(10) Burmeister, Eva. *Forty-five in the Family.* New York: Columbia University Press, 1949, pp. 194-207.

(11) Josselyn, Irene M. *Psychosocial Development of Children.* New York: Family Service Association of America, 1948, p. 91.

(12) Butler, Elsie. "Living Together in the Third Grade," *Elementary English*, Vol. XXVIII, January 1951, p. 5.

(13) Wagner, Victoria. "Responsibility in Children: The Contribution of the Schools," *Child Study*, Vol. XXXIII, No. 3, Summer 1956, pp. 7-10. By permission of the Child Study Association of America, 9 East 89th St., New York 28, N.Y.

(14) Sheviakov, *op. cit.*, p. 33.

(15) Clark, Kenneth B. "Discipline: Parental and Social," Reference Papers on Children and Youth, prepared for 1960 White House Conference on Children and Youth.

BASIC

UNDERSTANDINGS FOR

TEACHERS

PART TWO

Each child comes to school equipped with a personal endowment of physical, mental, and emotional characteristics that we cannot change. On this basic structure we must develop educational plans that will give each youngster the kind of help in learning he needs to develop to the best of his ability.

Each child brings his family to school with him—his mother and father and his brothers and sisters. His grandparents and great grandparents are present, also, not only through the contribution they have made to his personality through heredity—in his physique, in capacities and limits of his intelligence, and in basic temperament—but also through some of the attitudes, customs, and values that have been passed down from one generation to another.

If we are to use wisely the information we gather about individual children, we will need to be able to evaluate this material against what is known about the growth and development of all children. Does restless six-year-old Larry have a special problem or is he simply showing evidence of normal six-year-old growth? Are the changing moods of thirteen-year-old Stephanie a sign of maladjustment or is this kind of behavior only a sign of the readjustment to be expected of a growing girl who is trying to come to terms with a "different self" as she passes through the physical changes of the adolescent years? Phillip weighs fifteen pounds more than the other children in his room. Is he overweight or is his weight normal for his body build? Is usually reliable EveAnn throwing off the yoke of too much family responsibility by her reckless behavior or is there a more deep-seated problem? What is normal? What should give us concern?

In the previous chapters, we have explored the many ways teachers can help children have satisfying experiences that will lead toward more effective learning. We have considered some wise and some not-so-wise attitudes for working with the youngsters who come into our classrooms. But we have only touched on the physical, mental, and emotional characteristics of children and the family background from which they come. These two aspects—the child and his background—have been mentioned only briefly, as they related to a particular child's experiences or problems.

It is true that there is very little a teacher can do to change a child's physical endowments, his rate of maturation, his supply of preschool knowledge and experiences, his parents, his brothers and sisters, or his general family and cultural background. Yet it is important that we know about all these things for they affect what happens at school. As Plant said, children are not born anew every morning on the doorstep of the school. They bring with them each day all their natural endowments, past experiences, and family and cultural backgrounds.

Certain questions about how children grow and develop and how family backgrounds affect their ability to learn come up regularly. We will attempt to answer these questions in this section. The answers are not complete. They are merely intended to give some insights into the possible reasons why a child is as he is, and why, in some cases, he cannot learn to his capacity.

CHAPTER 6

QUESTIONS ABOUT GROWTH

How much variation in height and
weight is normal among children the same age?

Why are physically mature
children often restless in the classroom?

Is extreme tallness or shortness
in a child a result of some glandular imbalance?

Is there any way of predicting
how tall—or how short—a youngster will be?

Are such qualities as good
coordination and alertness inherited?

Is a physical education program really important?

Just what is "maturation"?

How strongly do children's past experiences
influence their present abilities?

AND DEVELOPMENT

HEIGHT AND WEIGHT

The greatest growth of the body as a whole occurs in two spurts—the initial growth spurt that follows birth and the secondary one at adolescence. In between—and after the adolescent growth spurt—the youngster grows much more slowly.

Height. At birth, most babies are approximately twenty inches long. By the end of a year, they will usually have grown about ten inches—increasing their length by almost 50 per cent. This growth is followed by a period of slow but steady growth in height of approximately two to three inches a year through the elementary-school years. About a year before puberty, a plateau, or resting period, is reached during which gains in height seem to slow up almost to a stopping point. The exact year at which such a plateau can be expected varies with the child, for it depends on the degree of physical maturity of the child rather than his age. Girls usually approach puberty about a year and a half to two years ahead of boys. This means that the plateau of growth in height may be reached by girls as young as nine or ten years old, whereas it is usually not reached by boys until they are eleven or twelve years old. Following the plateau, growth in height takes a rapid spurt that is followed by a gradual slowing down after puberty. Girls usually have attained their full height by the time they are about sixteen. Boys usually have attained their full height by the time they are eighteen or nineteen, but some boys continue to grow until they are twenty or twenty-one. Fast-maturing boys and girls may attain their full height a year or two sooner than the average youngster.

It is now possible to predict with some degree of accuracy what the height of a child will be at full growth. Bayley (1)* states that the average two-year-old girl has usually reached 52.2 per cent of her adult height and boys of the same age, 48.6 per cent. At age eight, most girls have reached about 77.6 per cent of adult height and most boys about 72.4 per cent, and at age twelve, most girls 92.6 per cent, boys 84 per cent.

Growth in size and rate of maturation may be retarded by malnutrition, severe illness, prolonged poor health, or generally unfavorable living conditions. If such handicaps are removed, children are usually able to grow and mature according to their inherited capacities.

Weight. At birth, the average baby weighs about seven pounds. During the first year of life, the baby will put on more weight in proportion to his size than during any other period of his life. During the first five months, he usually doubles his birth weight, and by the end of the first year, he has tripled it. After this, his weight increases at a gradual but slower rate. During the second year, he gains about half a pound a month. By the fifth year, the average youngster will weigh between 38 and 43 pounds, and by twelve years, he will weigh between 80 and 95 pounds.

For the first nine or ten years, the boys are heavier than the girls. Just before puberty, there is a slowing up in weight gain that is followed by a tremendous spurt in weight, particularly among girls, who may gain in one year as much as they have gained in the past three. This is often called the "chubby" period, but it is usually followed by a gradual slimming down during the growth spurt. Thereafter the girl again gains weight in better proportion to her body structure. During early adolescence, girls are often heavier than boys. Boys also gain rapidly at puberty, but usually the gain is not as startling as it may be among many girls. A boy's greatest gain is around fourteen when his bony framework becomes bigger and heavier, his shoulders broaden

*Full references are cited at the end of the chapter.

and his muscles develop. Boys gradually go ahead of girls until in later adolescence they are usually again heavier and remain so in adult life.

In the past, height and weight charts were developed in relation to chronological age. Now we know that such charts are more valid when they take into account body structure. What is normal height and weight for one child may be overweight or underweight for another.

Some experts feel that a child's own progress in height and weight should be recorded without reference to the standard tables. Even when these tables make allowances for body types, there may be many reasons why they are inappropriate for a given child. Furthermore, recent studies have suggested that as a nation we may weigh more than we should for optimum health, so that tables based on present averages show figures higher than are desirable.

BODY STRUCTURE

As teachers, we should be concerned with some practical implications of differences in body structure. If we look at the children in our rooms, we see at once that there are great variations in the body builds of the children. Some are tiny and small-boned; others are large for their age.

If we provide seats of only one size in our classrooms, we may expect to have some wigglers whose feet do not touch the floor comfortably and some slouchers whose bodies are too big for their seats and who must hump over to write or do other seat work. The active, physically strong child may also find sitting still in class much more difficult than his slow-moving, more placid classmate.

The strong, husky child is often steadier and is better able to exercise physical control than other children. He is usually able to take things in his stride. At the same time, his very physical make-up sometimes tempts him to become the bully, for he has the strength to push other children around and to hurt them if they cross him. It also seems true that the slender, sometimes frail child, particularly a boy, may be more likely to withdraw from difficult situations than to tackle them head on. His build will often put him at a disadvantage in sports and in the rough-and-tumble play of growing boys. He may learn from experience not to get involved in fights he cannot handle. Such children may seem tense and anxious in the schoolroom, cry more easily, and need help in meeting physical situations.

SKELETAL AGE

It is possible, through X-ray studies, to estimate the approximate "growth age" of a child. As Bayley (2) reports:

. . . Good records show a close connection between the hardening of the bones at the growing ends of the joints in the hand and the general growth of the whole body. By using X-ray pictures that show typical stages of growth, we can match the X ray of a particular child and assign a "skeletal age." . . .

This procedure will indicate whether a child's pattern of physical growth is rapid or behind schedule and whether he is likely to reach physical maturity ahead of or behind other youngsters.

Such information can also increase the accuracy of predicting adult height. If a youngster is worried because he is too tall, it sometimes helps to be able to tell him that his growth is nearly completed. If he is too short, a doctor may be able to assure him that there is a good chance he will grow taller.

Bayley feels that we should be concerned if a child is more than two years out of line in maturing or if his size and pattern of growth are noticeably different from both his family and other children of his age.

There are studies in process today showing that it is sometimes possible, by the use of hormones under medical direction, to speed up growth in height. These methods of speeding up growth are still experimental and are used only in a few medical centers when a child's growth is so out of proportion with that of his peers that a serious social and emotional problem is beginning to develop.

INHERITED CHARACTERISTICS

Although children everywhere are similar, each child is also different from every other child. Olson (3) writes: "The egg and the sperm unite to produce an individual with a high degree of uniqueness, although the individual will have a substantial similarity to his race, parents, and brothers and sisters."

Each child's particular combination of hereditary characteristics is his alone; differences have been recorded even between identical twins. We do not know all the answers, but we do know that not only physical characteristics—color of eyes, color of hair, blood type, forms of features, structure of body—but also the mental capacity of a child is greatly affected by his hereditary endowment. It seems, too, that special talent for mathematics, music, and possibly art may be inherited.

Just as there are differences in the inherited physiques of newborn babies, individual differences in the behavior of newborns have been observed so soon after birth that experiences in the external environment did not seem able to explain them. In some studies, as reported by Witmer and Kotinsky (4), the traits noticed in the new baby remained consistent in later childhood. The babies studied were all normal babies, and their individual differences in reaction are considered to be normal differences. Some newborn babies from birth are more active and alert than others. Some newborn babies appear more placid and less actively responsive. Later the active youngsters seem to kick and wriggle with excitement when they are played with or offered a toy, while the less active children may do just the opposite, looking at the proffered toy with a still, absorbed attention.

Babies also seem to be different from each other in the way they respond through their senses. Some tiny babies are startled by slight sounds that do not seem to have any disturbing effect on other babies. A light shining in the face of one baby may be very disturbing and he may whimper or cry, whereas another one may just blink. Some babies enjoy being bounced or thrown up in Father's arms; other are easily upset by anything but gentle handling. Some infants seem to notice color and brightness more than others; some react more noticeably than others to familiar and unfamiliar people.

There are also very real differences between babies in the speed with which they respond—some move slowly, others rapidly. The babies who eat and digest rapidly also move rapidly; others always react and perform more slowly.

Medical observation and research have also pointed out that some babies have a high degree of bodily resistance; others seem to have a body system that shows a more severe reaction to any physical disturbance of the organism. An inoculation, a cold, or a sudden change in routine may cause a fever, a digestive disorder, a feeding or sleeping disorder, or a skin eruption in such children.

Basic differences in temperament and constitution persist through life. Even in the same family, children may be very different. Some children always react slowly, others rapidly. Some remain better coordinated all their lives than others, and while coordination improves with practice, no amount of trying will make ballet dancers or tightrope artists or even good carpenters and seamstresses out of all of us. Some youngsters will have a high verbal capacity and will learn easily from books. Some will have good visual perception and will learn through their eyes; others will learn more easily through auditory or kinesthetic perception. One child may have acute perception of color, line, and form and be able to paint or design unusually well. One may have an ear for music, while another may be tone deaf.

In our classrooms, we find boys and girls of many kinds. There are tall and short youngsters, rapid and slow learners, well-coordinated and clumsy children in every group. One interesting thing about the basic differences in youngsters is that they are universal—we find them in children everywhere. We find, too, that the differences in potential are greater between individual children within one racial group than between children of different racial backgrounds.

GLANDS

Although we do not yet know all the functions of all the glands, we do know that the hormones secreted by the endocrine glands seem to maintain a chemical balance within the body and have a powerful effect on development.

The *thyroid,* which is located in the front part of the neck, secretes a hormone that affects basal metabolism. If the thyroid becomes overactive, there may be hyperactivity, loss of weight, and tension. Underactivity of the thyroid results in slowed up, sluggish behavior. Either condition can affect a child's ability to learn.

We do not yet have complete knowledge of all the functions of the *pituitary* gland, but two of its several hormones are of special interest to us here. One is a growth-producing hormone that regulates skeletal growth and shows increased activity both in the early years and during the adolescent growth spurt. If it is overfunctioning, the body grows too much and the individual grows to giant height. If it is underfunctioning, the individual will be a dwarf. The other important hormone of the pituitary regulates the activity of the sex glands, or *gonads.* It is this hormone that stimulates the gonads at the time of puberty. The gonads then secrete hormones that bring about the body changes which result in sexual maturity. If it is overactive, precocious sexual development will occur. If it is underactive, there may be a delay in sexual maturity.

As the sex glands are stimulated at puberty, bodily changes are noticed in both boys and girls. The breasts of the girls develop, hips grow broader, and the menstrual flow begins. In boys, the shoulders grow broader, the beard begins to grow, and the voice changes. Both boys and girls lose the childish contours of the face, and the features become less round and soft. Hair appears in the pubic areas and under the armpits. Although all boys and girls go through these changes at puberty, the time at which the changes occur may be anywhere from nine or ten to seventeen or eighteen years of age. Most girls become pubescent at twelve or thirteen years, most boys at fourteen or fourteen and a half. The changes preceding sexual maturity usually begin to be noticeable a year and a half to two years before puberty.

Because the glandular changes of puberty are also accompanied by increases in height and weight as well as changes in the physical proportions of the body, the young adolescent often seems awkward. He may seem all hands and feet because the parts of his body do not always grow evenly at this time.

These rapidly growing boys and girls often have ravenous, yet finicky appetites. They will demand certain kinds of foods to the exclusion of others. Sometimes they will overeat as an emotional outlet if they are finding their adjustment hard at this period. Overweight is frequently a problem.

There may also be changes in the texture of the skin that temporarily cause acne, an embarrassing condition for the young person. The small glands of the skin secrete more freely, and the top layer of the skin frequently grows more rapidly at adolescence. If the skin grows over the mouth of these glands, the glands become plugged with blackheads. If the plugged gland becomes infected, a pimple results. Sweat glands are also likely to be more active and may give rise to perspiration odor.

As a result of these changes, the adolescent is often self-conscious or concerned—the boy perhaps over a large nose or long legs, the girl over the accentuation of her hips or the rapid development of her breasts.

Jones (5) says that the early maturing girl may experience social growing pains because she is physically, emotionally, and often intellectually farther along than the boys of her age. At the time she is going through the physical and emotional changes that make her interested in boys, she finds that most of the boys are still little fellows who want to be with the gang and not with a girl.

Frequently an early maturing young girl begins to feel that she has already failed socially and that only a dismal future lies ahead of her.

The girl who matures at the time most of the boys are maturing usually has far less trouble fulfilling her emotional and social needs, for now there are enough boys of her size and age who are becoming interested in girls and dates. Her interests and their interests coincide.

Jones goes on to say that the fast-maturing boy who, because of his height, size, and physical development, is in demand by the boys in athletics and by the girls in social situations, usually makes a better adjustment during these years than the boy who is slow in maturing. Boys of the latter type are many times up against real difficulties because they are often not physically large enough nor muscularly well enough developed to want to enter into the sports events that are a major activity during the junior high school years and beyond. If they *do* engage in sports, they do not excel.

Such matters need consideration and understanding from adults, for during preadolescence and early adolescence, there are very real and often difficult adjustments to be made.

As a result of all these adjustments, the focus is on the self, and the young person often tries desperately to "hide" himself in the group. This is often a period of real stress for the young person and for those concerned with his welfare.

PHYSICAL FITNESS

Several recent studies have focused our attention on the fact that although American boys and girls are the best fed in the world and the best cared for in terms of medical care, the physical fitness of our youngsters, as measured by muscular development, is behind that of children of other countries.

A recent study was made by Kraus and reported by Espenschade (6) of 4,458 normal, healthy children between six and nineteen years of age. These children came from suburban and small urban communities in which they had received good health attention. Yet 58 per cent of them failed one or more of the muscular tests given to them. The same study was made on 2,870 European children. Only 9 per cent failed one or more tests. The Italian, Swiss, and Austrian children far surpassed the group of American boys and girls. Three of the tests measured the power of abdominal muscles, two measured the strength of back muscles, one measured the flexibility of back muscles.

Two other American groups have also been tested since. Out of 575 children in Iowa and 1,456 children in Indiana, it was found that 66 per cent of the Iowa children failed one or more tests and 45 per cent of the Indiana children failed. Draft statistics from World War II also gave us cause for thought since they revealed a high percentage of physical deficiency in our young men.

Children need physical activity all through the growing years if their bodies are to develop and function as fully as possible. Little children usually have time to play—their days are filled with spontaneous activity. But as children get older, more and more sedentary occupations tend to fill their time—the hours in school, the TV set at home, the homework that must be done. The long distances youngsters must fre-

quently travel to get to school prevent the child from the good exercise of walking or even of riding a bike because he must ride to school and back on the school bus. Urban living is relieving many children of the active outdoor chores that are necessary in a rural community. The increasing interest in professional sports makes many children spectators rather than participants.

If the body is to develop well, we must pay attention to the physical climate of the classroom, and we must see that there is time and opportunity for vigorous active play in the daily program of each child. If possible, such play should be out of doors where it can be accompanied with the noise and the release of pent-up energy that have necessarily been under control in the classroom. When outdoor play is not possible, children should have regular periods of exercise in the gym or the chairs and desks should be pushed back in the classroom so that there is room for bodily exercise. La Salle (7) puts it well when she says:

Activity is a basic need of all human beings. For children it ranks in importance with food and sleep. It is essential to their normal growth. They need to run, jump, climb, bat, catch, and throw. . . . Through movement they grow. They are so constituted as to need an enormous amount of vigorous movement of the torso and limbs. Strong, energetic use of the large muscles is necessary for the development of the organic systems of the body. . . .

Children must have from four and a half to six hours daily of vigorous muscular exercise for desirable growth. . . . Through this daily play time . . . a reserve of energy and endurance is built. Such reserve will not come with normal maturation if adequate activity has not been present in childhood.

Although there will always be wide variations in the physical abilities of boys and girls, it is important for the school to see to it that every boy and girl has an opportunity to be a participant in some form of muscle-building, body-developing physical activity. This does not mean that every child will be able to respond to the same program of physical education, for all children are different in physical structure and in energy drive. Some children will be able to carry their physical activity far beyond that of others. A well-planned program of physical activity will take into account the needs of varying kinds of children.

However, a word of caution in the matter of competitive sports is necessary. The rapid growth of the long bones and of the body organs during the later childhood and early adolescent years is one of the reasons for the statement by the American Academy of Pediatrics (8) that although active sports are desirable for growing boys and girls, overly competitive sports may put too much strain on them. A boy in the excitement of competition may push himself beyond the point of normal fatigue unless the coach is well aware of the wisdom of pulling a boy or girl out of a game before this point has been reached. Fatigue is often evident in adolescents—partly as a result of the drain from their rapid growth—but elementary-school boys and girls rarely seem tired. If they are in good health, they have abundant energy and need to release some of the surplus in strenuous physical activity. They should not, however, be allowed to overdo.

Espenschade (9) puts physical education into focus when she says:

When we stop to realize how different each child is from each other one, it is easy to see that what is good for one may not be good for another. This is certainly true of exercise. The amount and kind needed and enjoyed by one may be entirely inappropriate—even harmful—to another. Some children are quite literally "built" for exercise and enjoy large amounts of vigorous activity. The needs of others are more moderate. A unique pattern of endocrine factors, determined in large part by heredity, shapes the body and controls the rate of growth of each child. Almost certainly these same factors regulate the characteristic energy level also. Energy level in any individual is related to a basal metabolic rate. It may be momentarily influenced by time of day, state of health, amount of sleep, kind of breakfast, and a host of other things, but the overall pattern is a part of the individual and an essential part of personality. There is a sex difference in energy level in the direction of greater energy in boys than in girls, but the difference between sexes is less than that between individuals of the same sex.

MATURATION

Growth involves the readiness or maturity to pass from one stage of development to another. As we know, the baby is equipped with all of his organs at birth, but they are immature in their development. Although the brain and the nerves to the various organs and muscles are present at birth, they cannot function as they will later. At birth, the baby can respond only automatically; he is still too immature in his bodily functions to respond with voluntary movements. Although his bones and muscles are present, they are not mature enough to function in the process of standing.

In the same way, we know that the child cannot be successfully toilet trained until his muscles are ready for the process of conscious control and release at a given time; neither can he be taught to throw a ball in a straight line until the muscles of his arm are well developed and he has achieved a certain level of eye-hand coordination. Nowhere in the world can a child be taught to speak the language of his group until the physical mechanism for speech is ready. In the classroom, we see that same limitation: the child cannot write well until he is capable of the steady control and the acute perception necessary for holding a pencil and forming letters. Reading is possible only when he is ready not only to focus with his eyes on the written page but also to differentiate between different symbols. A two-year-old cannot understand the meaning of *safety* or of the abstract concepts of *cooperation, generosity, kindliness,* or *honesty* that a twelve-year-old can.

Physical maturation or "readiness" to pass from one stage of growth to another comes from within. We have very little to do with it except in the ways we provide or fail to provide an environment in which the physical growth of children can take place.

We can, however, encourage growth in other areas of the personality. We can be ready to offer opportunities for a particular learning when a child shows that he is ready to take the next step—whether it is feeding himself, learning to read, going downtown alone, or deciding what he wants to do when he has finished school. But in the area of learned behavior, it is sometimes difficult to know just when a child is ready for the next step. Readiness is complex. It involves the total personality of the child. Nevill and Markham both had the mental capacity to learn, but because of the experiences they had had as they were growing up, they were not emotionally ready to settle down to the task of learning to read.

With special effort, one can sometimes teach ahead of the real readiness or mat-uration point, but the advantages gained are doubtful. We can, with effort, teach a normally intelligent child to read and do numbers before he is really ready emotionally and in his language development, but he may perform by rote without real understanding and the difficult learning may make him very tense. A girl may be taught to sew before she has good eye-hand coordination, but the stitches will be crooked and the sewing will take much effort and may result in dislike of the task. When too much is expected too soon or when too much pressure is put on a child to achieve what we think he should be able to achieve, the strain tends to produce tensions and even battles between us. Such tensions slow up growth.

When we approach learning from a developmental point of view, we are better able to understand whether or not a child is ready for the next step, for we look at what he is able to do rather than at what is average for his age. We begin where he is and go on from there. This means that in the same classroom we may have one or more youngsters who are ready to go beyond the point at which their classmates are, as well as others who are far behind.

The principle of readiness does not mean waiting and doing nothing until a child decides he is ready to learn. It means cooperating with the growth of the child by offering the appropriate experiences that will lead to the next step ahead for him. The majority of boys and girls are "ready" for certain learning experiences at approximately the same time. That is why we are able to develop a basic curriculum from which to work. But there will always be children who will need special opportunities to go ahead or to go more slowly than others of approximately the same age. If a child is having difficulty keeping up with the group, or if he seems bored or ahead of the group, we may need to study him to find out at what point he is too mature or not mature enough for the learning opportunities we are offering in our class. For instance, a child who does not read in the sixth grade should have been spotted and helped at his own developmental level long before he reached the sixth grade. Sometimes the classroom teacher is not able to do the necessary study of such a child alone; she will need the help of the school psychologist or of clinical facilities in the community.

Sometimes, we confuse the point of readiness because we are apt to judge a child by one outstanding characteristic and to overlook the other sides of his personality. We may hold him back because he is not ready in one area and fail to realize that he is fully ready to go ahead in another. Growth will not always be in balance in all areas.

Sydney was a brilliant boy who was capable of entering a class of rapid learners in his high school. He needed the stimulation of working with other boys of high intelligence. In junior high, in spite of his ability, he had not shown the achievement that might have been expected for his I.Q. of 153. He had been restless, a disturber, a boy who took little responsibility. He was very popular and had been a leader among the boys who had caused a good deal of trouble in the school by vandalism and rowdiness. For this reason, his junior high principal would not recommend him for the rapid learning group. He said, "He is irresponsible and has never grown up. He is not ready or mature enough for the rapid learning group." The high-school counselor, after talking with Sydney, decided that intellectually, he was well ready for the work of the rapid learning class and decided to give him a try at it. Within the first six months, Sydney began to produce—caught up in his interest in the work he was offered and the stimulation of working with other boys and girls whose minds were as keen as his own.

We also sometimes overestimate the readiness of a child by focusing on one aspect of his personality. The child who is physically large and well developed may find himself under pressure to carry responsibility and act the way he looks. We say, "He looks like a man. He is a big fellow. Why does he act like a child?"

Sometimes, when a child has difficulty with his schoolwork, we think of him as "slow and dull" and miss his point of readiness to go ahead in other ways—such as taking responsibility in practical affairs. Such a child may be able to handle practical situations well or be quite far along in his relationships with other people. We may tend to underestimate and overlook some of his real strengths and capacities.

Paul was a slow little boy who was plodding his way through his schoolwork. He had an I.Q. of 80. He would never do too well in reading, writing, or arithmetic. In the classroom, he never made any trouble. As one teacher said, "Paul is a good boy. He never disturbs us." And because he was a "good boy" he sat through five grades doing what he could but never really being part of the class. His fifth-grade teacher made a visit to Paul's home. He shyly showed her his garden, which was a thing of beauty. Not only were the vegetables planted in orderly, well-weeded rows, but he had planted a gay border of flowers. His mother liked flowers for the table, he said. Next day, his teacher asked if he would take over the care of the plants in the classroom and if he would like to bring some of his flowers to school to make the schoolroom pretty. Paul's face lit up. He took his responsibility well. As his teacher said, "Paul has a green thumb—you should see the plants in our room. They thrive." Paul had a strength that had been overlooked. When his teacher became aware of it, she was able to find steps ahead for Paul, which he was well ready to take—steps that might ultimately lead into a very satisfying vocation for Paul when his school days were over. It also helped the other children in the class appreciate Paul a bit more, and it drew him into real participation with the other children in the classroom. He taught them many things about growing plants that year and they in turn began to notice him and include him in their games. By the end of the year, Paul's silence was broken; he was laughing with the other children and entering into many of the classroom activities. There were steps ahead for Paul.

The best conditions for the realization of any child's potentialities for growth during the hours he is in school are found in a classroom in which security is given to him through friendliness, acceptance, guidance, and an understanding of his developmental needs and of his personal feelings. In such a classroom, he is emotionally free to grow because opportunities are provided for him to learn as he is ready to do so. Sometimes a child with fewer potentialities but excellent nurture at home and at school will pass more smoothly through the developmental stages of growing up and will achieve more in proportion to his abilities than a child with higher potentialities and poor nurture.

Finally, we must recognize the fact that youngsters do not reach maturity—for all time—at one specific time in life. We accept as normal both the physical growth spurts and the plateau periods; we do not expect physical growth to be always at the same pace. We know and expect that one part of the body may grow more rapidly than another, that not until the body ceases to grow will body proportion be achieved. Yet it seems more difficult for us to understand and accept irregular social and emotional growth or periods when a child does not seem to achieve the potentialities of which he is capable. We may be disturbed, as Marian's parents were, if a youngster who has shown she can take responsibility, seems to regress and behaves less responsibly than in the past.

Marian's parents had always been very proud of her neatness. Ever since she was a little girl, she had picked up her toys and put them carefully away. Her coat was always on its hanger, her rubbers in the rubber box. When she entered junior high, her mother helped her redecorate her bedroom in a more grown-up fashion. Marian was very proud of it and followed her pattern of putting things away. But in the eighth grade, she grew up all of a sudden. She discovered the fun of doing things with a group of boys and girls, school activities filled her thoughts, her homework kept her very busy, and she began to hang on the telephone, carrying on long conversations with her special girl friends. Her mother was dismayed—the beautiful room was a shambles—shoes in the middle of the floor, the bed hastily made and the attractive cover thrown on top, the closet door open, and the desk covered with papers. Her mother began alternately to scold and to despair—"What had happened to Marian?" Her father entered into the picture when Marian's grades came home— where were the A's of elementary-school days? When her mother asked for an accounting of the messy room, Marian burst out, "But Mother, I haven't time to pick up my room! I have so much to do this year."

Marian had a temporarily bad case of "adolescence." Her development had not come to a dead stop; she would grow through this stage and come out a normal, healthy young person on the other side, provided her parents and her teachers could take this stage in their stride and continue to give the steady guidance and support that a developing youngster needs. This, too, is part of the developmental pattern.

PAST EXPERIENCES

Although differences in heredity and constitution set the basic potentialities of children and result in a wide divergence in what they are able to accomplish, there is an even wider range of differences resulting from variations in their education and other experiences and in the circumstances in which they grow up. Although all children follow the same pattern of physical development, their social, emotional, and even in some degree their mental development will be influenced by the habits, attitudes, and values of the group among whom they grow up and by the particular experiences they have.

The ability to do schoolwork well, for example, will depend on the child's innate ability to comprehend the work, plus his readiness to learn the particular task at the specified time, plus the skill of the teacher. Reading, writing, and arithmetic do not come naturally in the same sense as sleeping, swallowing, and walking. There are highly intelligent boys and girls in many parts of the world and even in our own country who do not know how to read and write. Whether they will have an opportunity to learn these skills will depend on the kind of family and community in which they are growing up and the value the adults in the community put on this kind of learning.

Ned had grown up in a community in which the schools were of low caliber. He had quit school when he was eleven. Nobody in his small community had much use for "book larnin'," and his father needed him to help scratch a living out of a small plot of land that provided food for the family. But at eighteen, Ned, a tall, uncouth boy, was called into the army by Uncle Sam. When he was exposed to new experiences, his fine mental ability began to be evident. He became interested in improving his reading and took advantage of all the schoolwork that was offered to the boys in the army. In a matter of months, Ned could read well and began to bury himself in books. When he left the army, he went to night school and caught up with his high-school education. He then used his G.I. bill and went to college. Now in his thirties, he is a successful research man in agriculture. The capacity had always been there, but he had been denied the necessary learning experiences.

Nathan, too, had his problems, but he was helped over the points of strain that might have blocked satisfactory growth. Nathan was fortunate enough to experience a family life that continued to provide affection, interest, and support in spite of the many difficult experiences through which both Nathan and his family had to pass.

Nathan was an "army child." Because of the nature of his father's work, his family moved constantly from one part of the country to another. As his mother said, "Although there would be many hardships, we felt keeping the family together was all-important." Their longest stay in any one home had been for two years. Nathan attended twelve schools in eleven years. Nathan had other problems, too. When he started to talk, he spoke with a lisp, and his speech was unintelligible until he was almost six. This perhaps made him even more dependent on his twin brother who, somehow or other, seemed able to understand him. He became so very dependent on his twin that he would burst into tears if he was separated from him. Some good speech therapy was procured and gradually his speech became understandable. He did have a hard time learning to read but by third grade, with some remedial help, he had caught up, his lisp had almost completely disappeared, and Nathan seemed to be finding himself.

One summer, his twin brother contracted polio and died within a few days. Nathan's constant companion and pal was gone. Nathan had always been a quiet, shy child but now, he temporarily withdrew into himself. Just at this time, the family was faced with another move. Fortunately for Nathan his teacher in the new school was a warm and kindly person who drew the troubled youngster gradually back into the world of children. Nathan is still a quiet, seemingly shy boy; he does well in school but worries sometimes because he is not "as smart" as his older brother who is a top student. He has many hobbies and interests, which his parents encourage. His home is open to the neighborhood boys and girls, and his mother encourages him to bring friends. But Nathan's family stood by the boy with such understanding and encouragement that at sixteen, he is developing into a fine young man. His growth has not been steady. He still has his problems. As his mother says, "Nathan still needs more confidence in himself. Criticism still makes him draw into himself." But his teachers feel he is already a leader in his own steady, quiet way.

The loss of a brother, the changing of schools, the need to make friends over and over again, and the competition with a brilliant older brother, are not easy situations for a boy to meet. But Nathan's family retained a close bond that helped Nathan grow into a fine, capable young man.

If we are to teach a child well, we must understand the significance of the things he has learned through his previous experiences and the way these past experiences have shaped, and continue to shape, his personality. For what a child "learns," in or out of school, through discovery or through being taught, will influence the way in which he will be able to use and develop the potentialities with which he is endowed. We cannot effectively separate learning and development in this area. It is the differences in the past experiences of which we must be aware if we are to know what each child needs from the learning experiences in our classroom.

Anderson (10) puts growth and development into focus for us when he says:

The most obvious fact of growth and development is progress from infancy to adult life. All of us have known infants and adults. So common and universal are growth and development that we take them for granted without realizing how complex and wonderful they are. . . .

Growth and development are not merely changes in physical size or bodily proportions. Changes occur in almost every relation within and without the human being. For our present purposes, we may call attention to the increased range of objects and experiences to which the growing person responds; to his increased strength, speed and motor skill; to his growing intellectual and problem solving capacity; to his greater ease in using language and
communicating with others; to his enriched social life with its web of interrelations; and to his changing interests, activities, and values. From the dependence of infancy the person moves to the maturity and responsibility of adult life. . . .

. . . [The child has] to be understood in terms of the developmental level he has reached rather than as a miniature adult. A common error in the popular and scientific literature on children involves projecting adult processes or states backward and assuming that children possess the characteristics of the mature person.

REFERENCES

(1) Bayley, Nancy. "How Children Grow," *The Encyclopedia of Child Care and Guidance,* edited by Sidonie M. Gruenberg. Garden City, New York: Doubleday and Company, 1954, p. 762.

(2) *Ibid.,* p. 761.

(3) Olson, Willard C. *Child Development.* 2nd ed. Boston: D.C. Heath and Company, 1959, p. 19.

(4) Witmer, Helen L., and Kotinsky, Ruth. *Personality in the Making.* New York: Harper & Brothers, 1952, pp. 29-51.

(5) Jones, Harold E. "Adolescence in Our Society," *The Adolescent, A Book of Readings,* edited by Jerome M. Seidman. New York: Henry Holt and Company, 1953, pp. 50-60.

(6) Espenschade, Anna. "The Many Meanings of Exercise," *Child Study,* Vol. XXXIII, No. 2, Spring 1956, pp. 15-17. By permission of the Child Study Association of America, 9 East 89th St., New York 28, N.Y.

(7) La Salle, Dorothy. *Guidance of Children Through Physical Education.* Second Edition. New York: The Ronald Press Company, 1957, p. 5.

(8) Committee on School Health, American Academy of Pediatrics. "Competitive Athletics," *Pediatrics,* Vol. 49, No. 4, October 1956, pp. 672-676.

(9) Espenschade, *op. cit.,* pp. 17-18.

(10) Anderson, John E. "The Development of Behavior and Personality," *The Nation's Children 2: Development and Education,* 1960 White House Conference on Children and Youth, pp. 43-44, 53-54.

CHAPTER 7

QUESTIONS ABOUT

How important is personal contact
between home and school?

Why don't parents look at
their children's faults as objectively
as they should?

Judging from the inadequate
homes some children come from, wouldn't
these children be better off in
a less personal but steady environment?

What is a "good" home anyway?

Is it enough for parents just to
love their children—or is something else
needed in order for children
to grow and develop well?

Are there any problems peculiar to a
child's position in the family—as the oldest,
middle, youngest, or only child?

Is it possible for parent and
child to have irreconcilable personalities?

Are families really less close
than they used to be?

HOME AND FAMILY

HOME AND SCHOOL

Neither home nor school can succeed alone. Sometimes the school develops a good learning experience for a youngster only to have it destroyed by lack of interest or support in the home. Sometimes the home has developed attitudes of curiosity and eagerness only to see these qualities lost in the boredom of a poor classroom. Home and school must work together if a healthy climate for learning is to be provided for children.

Many parents have a deep interest in the school: they want to be close to the school problems and to be of real help with the education of their children. Others come only under pressure and show little real concern for the progress of their children.

It is wise for a teacher to try to get to know as many parents as possible early in the year, so that she may know what kind of people they seem to be, before situations arise that need their attention. One teacher tried to establish a friendly feeling with the parents of her children by giving a tea early in the year. At this tea, she described the goals for the year, helped parents meet one another, and gave them an opportunity to see her as a person to whom they could come freely if and when they felt the need.

We can draw parents into sharing the responsibility of helping their child be able to learn by arranging class meetings and individual conferences willingly when parents seek them, by making telephone calls or writing little notes to tell a mother about something fine or interesting her child has done, by phoning to find out why a child is absent, and by expressing sympathy for sickness or trouble. If a teacher gains the reputation of being really interested, parents are more likely to feel free to come to her with questions about their child.

We will not be able to reach all the parents, but it is possible through parent-teacher conferences to meet many of them. In many schools, the importance of such conferences is recognized and time is given for them. Unfortunately, there are still some schools in which time is not allowed for talks with parents and in which parents and their ideas are not particularly welcomed by the school.

In talking with parents, it is important to give them the feeling that what they tell us will help us understand their child—that their contribution is valuable and welcome. After all, parents have lived with their children for many more years than we have known them. As we talk with parents, we must listen between the words for the real meanings of what they are communicating to us in order to glean invaluable information about experiences children have had at home as well as some of the attitudes and feelings the parents have toward their children. The pride, the irritation, the disappointment, the genuine concern that parents evidence as they talk to us can add much to our picture of the child and his family. However, we must be careful not to pigeonhole our impressions or to put labels on them; we must, instead, store them away, test them, and think about them as we constantly try to evaluate and discover the real learning needs of a child.

The relationship between the school and the parents may affect the work of the school as a whole as well as the learning opportunities of the individual child. When the school and the parents are not in sympathy with one another and are not working together, the program of the school may be seriously damaged.

Many parents come to talk to the teacher with genuine trepidation. They still carry over from their own school days the feeling that an interview with a teacher always means something "bad" has happened. One highly intelligent and successful father confessed that when he had to go to his first parent-teacher conference (a requirement in his son's school), he still felt the old butterflies in his stomach that had always plagued him as a boy when he was called to his teacher's desk. We need to remember this feeling that many parents have, however unreasonable it may seem, and try to put them at their ease.

Sometimes it is even a good idea to abandon the security of our desks and sit side by side with a parent, where we can talk less formally. At the same time, parents usually do not respond well if we become so "chummy" that we lose our role as teacher and counselor. The parent looks to us for knowledge about his child and sometimes for guidance in helping his child adjust better to the school requirements. Many parents feel insecure and uncertain when the relationship becomes too close and the roles each should play become blurred.

Each one of us has his own approach to people, and our approach should be our own—not that of a colleague whom we admire. Parents respond to the teacher who is comfortable and natural—whose genuine interest in their child makes them feel that "Here is someone with whom I can talk about my child—about my pleasure in him or about my worries about him."

Parents are quick to sense our feelings toward their child. If they feel that we do not like him, if they sense that we find him a problem or a nuisance, a barrier may go up very quickly. It goes up quickly, too, if our interest in the well-being of the child is construed as a rejection of the parents, particularly of the mother. She will be especially resentful if we indicate that she has failed to give the child the care and understanding he needs.

Parents thrive on praise and encouragement, as we all do. We will find that interviews go better if we start with a child's strengths rather than with his weaknesses, for each youngster does have his good points.

Sometimes we plunge into an interview too rapidly. Bill is a problem; we are not going to tolerate his behavior any longer, and we want his mother and father to know about it. But we must try to size up the parent as well as the child. Some parents respond well when we come right to the point. With others, we must move more slowly. Sometimes we can draw the parent out through sympathetic listening and a well-placed question: "How do you feel Bill is doing in school?" In this way, we can sometimes maneuver the interview so that the parent will be the first to bring up the problem, or some point related to it, and will ask our point of view about it. Sometimes this is not possible for as we talk together we find that the parent does not recognize the problem or even know that one exists.

It may take several meetings before some parents can take a frank and honest discussion of their child. With some parents, it will never be possible. In case of any difficult situation with parents, it is wise to ask the principal either to see them himself or to be present at the interview.

PARENTS' DEFENSIVENESS

Many parents today are highly sensitive about their roles, especially the more intelligent ones who are well-read and are anxious to do a good job with their children. Such parents are often oversensitive about the failure of a youngster and feel that it is they who are being criticized. Emotions all too often enter in and the parent is quickly on the defensive.

Too often we become irritated with parents because we expect them to be as objective as we are and to discuss their children with the calmness and insight we can show. It is the rare parent who can do this. The mother—for it is usually the mother who is free to come to school in the daytime—is emotionally involved in her youngster. Although she may try and should be helped to attain perspective about her youngster, she can never be completely objective. If she were she would have lost some of the peculiar strengths of that close bond that makes the parent-child relationship valuable. "My child is the dearest child in the world—even with all his faults." Children need that strong feeling of acceptance behind them, and good parents give it. A good teacher, on the other hand, should have a warm and even affectionate feeling for the children in her room, but she should be able to leave them at school. Her emotional bond to an individual child should not be so close that she has difficulty allowing him to pass on to another teacher next year. In this difference between mother and teacher in emotional attachment and capacity for objectivity lies one of the most significant reasons why our conferences do not always succeed. Too frequently we grow impatient with the mother.

Fathers, while close to their children, are often able to be more objective about them than mothers. The father is often better able to see the child through the eyes of the world and may be a very valuable ally in helping a mother who is too involved

with her feelings for the youngster to see his real needs.

A mother may also become hostile and resentful if she feels that we have taken over the role of mother to her child. This is particularly so if the child is difficult to handle at home but enjoys coming to school and shows much affection for his teacher. In the child's relationship to us, the mother may sense a rejection and hostility to herself. This is too hard for most mothers to take. We must always keep our role clear—we are the teacher; she is the mother.

If a parent is too disturbed by a situation or is too involved in a sense of guilt or failure to be able to talk things through, he or she may make a scapegoat of the teacher or the school system with the old and oft-repeated accusation, "Well, if she were a good teacher, my child would pay attention!" or "If she were a good teacher, my child would know how to read. There is nothing the matter with him!" It is all too easy to respond in kind with, "After all, parents are to blame if their children don't behave and won't learn. If they gave them good breakfasts and disciplined them properly, I wouldn't have these problems!"

At present, there is much criticism of both parents and teachers, so perhaps we are both a bit oversensitive. But when an interview produces mutual antagonism, it might as well be ended because no help for the child will come out of it. Being critical of one another builds up subtle barriers, which make it more difficult for us to meet each other and talk about our common interest—the child. A mutual recognition that life with Junior is highly rewarding but does have its difficulties would do wonders.

IMPORTANCE OF FAMILY

All over the world, children grow up in some sort of family group. These groups may differ in size and composition. In some

countries, the family group is large and spreads out to include many relatives, all living together in one community or even under one roof. Sometimes the family group is made up of three generations with grandparents living in the home or the young family living in the home of the grandparents. Or it may be the small two-generation group that is most typical in the United States.

It is in their homes that boys and girls can feel valued and loved because they are themselves—"our Tom," "our Betty," "our Mary"—instead of because of what they achieve. This feeling of acceptance is essential for the development of the personality. It is through this experience of being loved and wanted in the home that children learn how to love and how to be loved by others. Children who do not have this close bond of affection with their families rarely learn to care deeply for other people.

No satisfactory substitute has been found for the home in supplying this basic security we all must have. If we do not have it in our childhood experiences, we continue to seek for it throughout our lives. As a child gets older, he may turn away from the family group toward those of his age—his friends or his "gang"—for the loyalty, warmth, and support his family has never provided. The child who is not wanted, the child who feels he is not really liked may withdraw into himself or hit out in anger and rebellion at the world.

Experiments have been tried through the years to bring children up in child groups rather than in family units, but such experiments have failed unless they have also included close ties with the parents and continuing contacts with them.

Bowlby (1)*, in his report to the World Health Organization, has reviewed the studies that deal with what happens to children who do not have parental care:

Among the most significant developments of psychiatry during the past quarter of a

*Full references are cited at the end of the chapter.

century has been the steady growth of evidence that the quality of the parental care which a child receives in his earliest years is of vital importance for his future mental health. . . . What is believed to be essential for mental health is that the infant and young child should experience a warm, intimate, and continuous relationship with his mother (or permanent mother-substitute —one person who steadily 'mothers' him) in which both find satisfaction and enjoyment. It is this complex, rich, and rewarding relationship with the mother in the early years, varied in countless ways by relations with the father and with the brothers and sisters, that child psychiatrists and many others now believe to underlie the development of character and of mental health.

. . . The services which mothers and fathers habitually render their children are so taken for granted that their greatness is forgotten. In no other relationship do human beings place themselves so unreservedly and so continuously at the disposal of others. This holds true even of bad parents—a fact far too easily forgotten by their critics, especially critics who have never had the care of children of their own. It must never be forgotten that even the bad parent who neglects her child is nonetheless providing much for him. Except in the worst cases, she is giving him food and shelter, comforting him in distress, teaching him simple skills, and above all is providing him with that continuity of human care on which his sense of security rests. He may be ill-fed and ill-sheltered, he may be very dirty and suffering from disease, he may be ill-treated, but unless his parents have wholly rejected him, he is secure in the knowledge that there is someone to whom he is of value and who will strive, even though inadequately, to provide for him until such time as he can fend for himself.

Those who work in family welfare agencies also recognize the importance of belonging to a family group and try to keep families together—even if they are not very adequate. They find that children do better when they are with their own parents, even if those parents fail them in many ways. When the home cannot care for its children or when the children come from families that are the "worst cases" or when children have been fully rejected by their parents, child placement agencies try to find good foster homes and substitute parents.

"GOOD" VS. "POOR" HOMES

In the United States, we usually identify the middle-class family as the typical American family and tend to judge family standards by this yardstick. We often forget that there are many families with different ways of life and different values who are also American—Greek families, Italian families, Mexican families, Japanese and Chinese families, English families, families with the close-knit pattern of the deep South, migrant families. All these families have children who come to our schools and may be found in our classrooms. Many of them will have taken on the pattern of the middle-class family and will be indistinguishable in their ways, customs, and values, one from the other. But many youngsters, particularly those whose families have tended to remain clustered together in a racial or occupational group, have values and customs that are different from those we may have come to look on as desirable family standards.

Because of the occupational necessities of the father of the family, many families are being uprooted and there is an unprecedented mixing up of people from everywhere. With increasing frequency, we are likely to find children with varied family backgrounds in the same classroom. These children will not all have the same standards of behavior, the same attitudes, or even the same values we have grown to accept as desirable.

A report of the American Psychiatric Association (2) brings this problem into focus for us:

. . . It is possible to speak of The American Family *only if we realize that we mean the ideal or typical family of the dominant middle class. Actually there is no such thing as a single family type which can be said to be representative of all America. We have the kind of variation in families which results from our having within one nation large groups of people with quite different cultural backgrounds—groups which still have recent memories of other countries. There are also all the families which are midway between those of rather clear-cut ethnic background and those dominantly American. Differences of another kind can be distinguished in the families of the several economic class levels. Furthermore, aside from all such differences as these, there is much more diversity in individual families—even those of the middle class— than is commonly the case in most societies.*

It is this very diversity which leads to the stressing of the dominant or "typical" family pattern. We could not long hold together all our differences if there were not at the same time a strong sense of conformity and oneness. Thus there exists a kind of consensus regarding the relationships and roles that should exist in the "Good Family." There is, in other words, a kind of model family according to which all others tend to be judged and like which many others are striving to become. It is this model which is the typical family of the middle class.

Because we have this model in our minds, it is very easy for us to misinterpret some of our impressions about the home life of our children and the personalities and ways of their parents. It is only human for us to project our own backgrounds, our own sense of values, into our appraisal of a home situation. Yet this is something we must carefully watch and take into account in our evaluation. Too often, we automatically judge a pleasantly appointed home to be a good home. The physical surroundings may be good for the physical health of the child, but physical surroundings do not make a home.

The story of the St. Johns children is the story of a family in which there are real potentialities for fine growth. The three little sisters could, and quite possibly still will, develop into fine adults. But during the years of growing up, the way has been confused by the neglect and lack of understanding of their parents. The teacher who tells their story—particularly the story of Janice—puts it this way:

Janice was an attractive eight-year-old. When she was happy, her light-blue eyes sparkled, her face was rosy, and her smile was a wonder to behold. She had a good sense of humor—when she was in the mood. She wore well-chosen clothing. Her little dresses indicated expensive design and materials, but they were not kept in good condition. Rips and tears were not mended, buttons were not replaced, and shoulder straps were not secure. She often had to get pins from me to keep her clothing in place for the day. Her shoes, Mary Janes or sneakers, were always run down and in poor condition, holes in her socks were unmended.

Day after day, week after week, Janice had no supplies. She had to borrow—more accurately to beg—from classmates and from me. Even the matter of getting lunch was a major problem for Janice. Sometimes she came with a home-prepared lunch and had to buy milk. This meant she had to carry money to buy it. Often the money was lost during the morning. On some days she arrived with no money, no lunch, and no instructions for either herself or her little first-grade sister, Priscilla.

In class Janice daydreamed, was moody, doodled, wandered around the room, and copied the work of other children. Occasionally she read well and with expression. But usually she paid little attention to her work. She often seemed tired and unhappy. Her work was far below her potential.

When I decided to make a home visit I took Janice with me in my car from school. She enjoyed being my guide. She pointed out the apartment houses in which her friends lived. The St. Johns' apartment was a large, modern one facing the park. It was attractively furnished with many beautiful pictures and brass pieces Mrs. St. Johns had collected in Europe.

Janice showed me their playroom. This room was well-furnished, with only adult articles in sight. A fancy bar stood on one side of the room and on the other a very large television set. The room was too neat and clean for three active children to use it.

Janice's room was attractively furnished with white and pink furniture and ruffled curtains at the windows. There was not a single toy in sight, nor did Janice offer to show me any of her treasures. Priscilla shared the room with her. The beds were the day couch variety placed along opposite walls. There were plenty of cushions on them and two very large dolls. The unchildlike lack of clutter was much in evidence here, too.

Mrs. St. Johns told me that she was a journalist busy with an important piece of contract work for a public relations firm. She employed a fulltime daily maid in the home. She described her husband as a business executive with a "top" job. She said, "He is a very stern and exacting man. He believes in carrying out the very letter of the law. That's why he is so exacting with us. He is much wedded to his job and is always having conferences and conferences. I just don't know what they could find to talk about so much. We quarrel a good deal."

She told me that last year Mr. St. Johns had decided to do something with Janice. He took her several times to his club to teach her to swim. He wanted her to do well because he is an excellent swimmer himself. Her father lost interest when Janice was reluctant to get her face wet, which meant that he could not teach her the proper system of breathing. That ended the swimming, for his patience with her was strictly limited.

Mrs. St. Johns spoke of her own disappointment over Janice's ballet lessons. Janice had begged for lessons and her mother had hoped that she might become a ballerina and maybe a stage success someday. She had been very angry and expressed bitter disappointment in Janice when she did not do as well as she had hoped.

There was no demonstration of warmth and affection between mother and children during the time I was there. There was just a sort of tired interest. After the girls had come in several times, she remarked, "I just don't know how I could have done so poorly with my children. They are such a disappointment." In reminiscing about Janice as a baby, there was warmth and feeling but not towards the child herself nor her sisters. She called Janice "their thousand-dollar baby"—special suite, a high-priced obstetrician, and all the other trimmings.

When asked about eating and sleeping habits, there was a tone in Mrs. St. Johns' voice that indicated she just didn't pay too much attention to such details. She was not concerned that Janice was a finicky and light eater, for she "drank loads of milk." She did make much of the fact that Janice was a sloppy eater. In reply to my concern that Janice was often tired in school she said that since they had gotten the television set the children's bedtime had been most erratic. Both Mr. and Mrs. St. Johns would become engrossed in a program and getting the children to bed became a matter of who would go and do it.

As is apparent, neglected children are found not only in the homes of the poor; they may also be found in the homes of the well-to-do. When parents focus on their own needs only, the children are often unable to focus on their work in the classroom. On the surface, the St. Johns' home would have seemed to be a good home for the children, but there is something more that we must look for if we are not to overlook some "good homes" which do not on the surface appear to fit the model. The feeling that exists in the family group is the most important factor.

It is very easy for us to misjudge a seemingly less desirable home. Carla's father drank heavily and deserted the family, but there were qualities in the home that enabled Carla to develop into a fine young adolescent in spite of the handicap of her background. Her story is told by a teacher who first met Carla in the settlement house in which she was working during the summer months.

This is the story of one of the nicest children I have known. Carla Garner is an enthusiastic, attractive, friendly girl of thirteen. She is well liked by her peers and the adults in the community as well.

Carla lives in one of the congested slum neighborhoods of a large seacoast city. The houses in this area are in very poor condition, some with outside toilet facilities and many without hot water. A highly transient population is mostly responsible for the shabby appearance of the dwellings, although the homes are also quite old. The majority of people staying here are from southern small towns and farms. The educational level averages about seven grades. These people come to the city for good jobs (wharfmen, laborers, etc.). This neighborhood seems attractive to them because of the low rental, and during their stay, they usually move around in the area, to another section for awhile and then back again. Over half of the children have attended at least four schools by the time they have reached the sixth grade.

In Carla's neighborhood also live the "pillars," those people whose families have always lived in the area. They seem to be third-generation Italian, Polish, French, and English people. These people are also in a low group financially but tend to keep their homes clean and in good repair. This, I would say, comes both from old traditional habits and pride of ownership. These families center their activities around the Catholic church in the neighborhood and the majority of the children attend parochial school, as do many other children in this community. Carla attends the public school and is an active participant in all school activities. She lives with her mother and grandmother in a house that has been owned by the grandmother for over forty years.

Angelina, Carla's mother, had quit school in the eighth grade to help supplement the family's income by working in a neighborhood store. She soon met Peter Garner, her future husband. He was a big, muscular blond who worked on a street labor crew. After three years, they were married in the nearby Catholic church and moved into a small house near her old home.

They were both deeply religious. Mr. Garner worked steadily and his wife was active in the neighborhood lodge. They were well liked and highly respected by the area people. Carla was the only child.

About three years ago, Mr. Garner began drinking heavily and causing public disturbances. He abused his wife and told her that he was tired of marriage and for her to get out or be put out. Angelina went to her mother's home until her husband pleaded for her return. This happened about three times more. She then began drinking in private to calm herself. Ten-year-old Carla was taken to the hospital four times during this period for "acute nervous indigestion." She had been calm and peaceful earlier but had become restless, nervous, and thin. One day, Mr. Garner disappeared. He has not contacted his wife once, nor made any effort to offer any support for the child.

Angelina and Carla moved in with the grandmother, who lived on a small pension.

Angelina obtained a job at the settlement house. She had a way with little children that was inspiring. Immediately, she began to learn crafts, games, and stories to try with the young children. Angelina was rapidly regaining her self-respect and through her own efforts. She has been working full time for a year now and is quite pleased.

Carla is a popular member of the "crowd" at the settlement house. She is mascot of the twelve-to-fifteen-year-old boys baseball team. She gained her place because she played so well with the girls. The boys wish that she could be catcher in their regular games. Three or four other girls in her gang play softball at the playground and it has become a co-ed activity at times. Last week, a little boy on the "midget" team confided to me that he would either like to be able to pitch like Frankie or to catch like Carla.

Carla is looking forward to learning how to play basketball this fall so that she may play with the settlement house's team. She attends the house dance once a week with her girl friends and seems adept at dancing. She is fond of ping-pong and likes to swim, although she confesses that she really does not know how, "just what I taught myself, kind of a dog paddle."

Carla is in excellent health now. All traces of her nail biting and digestive disturbance of a few years ago have disappeared.

Carla has regular tasks to perform at home. Drying dishes, making the beds, and sweeping the front stairs and walk are her jobs. Most of these can be done in the morning, before the neighborhood activities begin. Almost all of the girls have similar duties. Carla is quite faithful with her work and sometimes helps with heavy cleaning.

She does baby-sitting once or twice a month for the people next door. This is done with her best friend for company. She is saving the money for the carnival to be given by the church in late August.

It is hard to know just what Carla thinks about the desertion by her father. Angelina says that she wants Carla to respect him because he is her father and that she, Angelina, never speaks ill of him when Carla is near. She wants to stay with her mother and wants Daddy to come back so that things could be as they were when she was little. Angelina probably feels this way also, "I'd like him back if he could do right by us and lead the kind of life that all decent folks do. He used to be a good man, honest he was. I have my job now and I can take care of us, but it's hard on Carla and Mama. Honest, it makes me so mad when I think of what he is doing to that child, I don't know what to do. Not one cent, not one blessed cent has he sent me for that child."

In this neighborhood, at least six out of ten children are living in broken homes, either with one parent or with step-parents. This type of thing is accepted, which makes it easier for both mother and daughter. This trouble has apparently made no difference in Carla's social status.

The relationships in the home seem to be excellent. There is a fine rapport in the group. All admire and respect each other. The strong religious life of the family seems to be quite helpful now, for they believe that God will do what is best. Next, Carla has an average intelligence, which makes it possible for her to adjust with reasonable success to the present conditions. Her health has come back to its former state. The removal of the constant conflict in the home is most likely responsible for the improvement. Also, the restoration of security in the home. Carla improved as her mother's condition improved. Having someone whom she respects, like the director of the settlement house, to talk to also helps. Carla is doing well in her efforts to meet life and to be a worth-while citizen.

Although both mothers and fathers are needed by children, we must not overlook the fact that children from disturbed and broken homes can be helped to maturity, as Carla was, if they receive love and care, either from one parent in the family, from relatives, or from a mother substitute. Sometimes quarrels, dissent, and tensions between the parents in the home are more damaging to the children than divorce.

When a home has been broken, we need to understand the hurt and confusion the child has experienced, but we must also recognize the positive factors that may remain in the home in spite of the parents' separation or divorce. By a matter-of-fact acceptance of the situation, it is possible to convey to the child our conviction that just because he does not have a normal home life does not mean that he cannot grow up into a mature and capable person.

PARENTAL LACK OF "KNOW-HOW"

Escalona (3) learned from her studies that most parents would like to rear their children well but that many of them do not know how. She believes that although the parents' attitudes and feelings toward their children are the most important factors, a certain amount of "know-how"—understanding what can be expected of children, being aware of the fact that behavior is caused—would be helpful.

Parents sometimes make mistakes because they expect too much of their children too soon. They do not know what children should be able to do or to understand at given ages. Some parents put pressures on their boys and girls to succeed, for instance in their schoolwork, at a level beyond their capacity of attainment. Many parents expect their young children to behave in ways suitable for much older children. Sometimes they do not know

enough about individual differences and expect a younger child to behave just as an older child does. Most parents know little about developmental sequences or about the relationship of physical growth and development to a child's readiness for and ability to perform a certain task or skill they may require of him.

Parents are usually anxious to have a youngster be successful. In their very eagerness to do the right thing for their children and in their concern lest they fail, many parents bring their youngsters up with criticism rather than encouragement. When blame, criticism, and pressure are constant, a child may feel that he is not loved.

We often tend to blame parents when their children come to school without the feeling of security and confidence in themselves that we would like to see and would expect the family to provide. But simply blaming parents will not help the child. A more fruitful course is to try to give the parents encouragement and emotional support and help them, if possible, to carry out their parental responsibility. Sometimes such a course requires the help of professional people and community leaders. It is not easy to bring boys and girls up today; there are many pressures on families that are not of their creating. Parents are not always equipped to do what has to be done in a complex family situation.

BROTHERS AND SISTERS

It is not the parents alone who influence a child's relationship to the family group; there are usually brothers and sisters, too. The only child and the oldest child (for a time) have their parents to themselves, but most of the children in our classroom will have at least one brother or sister, and many will have several.

A child's sense of belonging to the family group may be greatly influenced by his feelings about his brothers and sisters and their feelings and attitudes toward him. In every family, a drama is being played out as each child seeks his place in the sun— his parents' affections. All brothers and sisters will have some little core of jealousy and rivalry toward the others in their family. It is only as a little child grows up in a home that makes him feel he is loved and valued that he is able to begin to share his parents' love with brothers and sisters. In most homes, after the initial struggle when a competitor appears, a child finds that there is enough love for all and that it is safe to share. Yet he will probably never completely get over his feelings of jealousy or rivalry toward his brothers and sisters, but his more positive feelings will make his rivalry less intense and his jealousy quite bearable. Children who quarrel within the family group will often rise to the defense of one another with great loyalty outside the home.

There may be wide differences between children in a family group. All may not have the same degree of basic intelligence, the same talents, or even the same degree of physical energy or drive. If children in a family are compared with one another or are expected to achieve the same degree of excellence in the same fields, tensions are bound to arise between them. This is particularly true if the price of their parents' love appears to be success. Charles was doing poorly in school in spite of a superior I.Q. His teachers kept reminding him of his brother's reputation as a student. They prodded him with, "You're smart, too. You can do as well if you try." At home his parents constantly compared him unfavorably with his brother and urged him to apply himself better. Finally, Charles began truanting from school. When his counselor talked to him, he found that the boy could not face the continual comparison with his brother. He felt that he was neither liked nor wanted at home. He longed to get away and "be myself," as he put it. He felt that nobody, not even his parents, thought of him as "Charles" but only as a shadow and inadequate duplicate of his valued older brother. When he was transferred to a school where no one knew him and his parents were helped to understand his feelings, the boy developed in his own pattern and found himself in his own way.

A child sometimes feels trapped because of his position in his family group. Perhaps he is the oldest child and has had many responsibilities put on him to be an example to younger brothers and sisters; or perhaps he has had to carry too much responsibility of helping with the care of younger brothers and sisters so that he has come to resent the demands his parents put upon him. Or he may be the middle child, caught between an older brother or sister who has certain privileges (denied to him) and a younger child who is babied and shown much physical affection (which he has outgrown). This youngster may feel he is not loved as much as the other two—the privileged and the cuddled—and may withdraw into himself or hit out at the others in an attempt to assert himself. Or he may be the baby who is kept from growing up because there are so many others to do things for him and to protect him from making his own mistakes.

Some children come from large families in which there has been little time for attention to the individual youngster. Often these children are sturdy, for they have learned the necessity of meeting many of their own needs and also of taking care of one or more younger brothers or sisters. But sometimes, in a large family, a sensitive child or a timid child may fail to get the individual support and understanding he really needs. Problems that need attention may be overlooked.

An only child or a child in a small family may get much individual warmth, affection, and attention. On the other hand, he may have fewer opportunities to develop a sturdy independence. As Gruenberg (4) says:

The most important consequence of the shrinking family is perhaps the new attitude mothers and fathers have toward their children. Where there are only one or two children, the individual child is naturally more precious to the parents. Within the small family, the parents not only shower the child with all the "advantages" they can afford, but they also focus upon him all their anxieties. And they are likely to seek in the child's achievements the fulfillments of their own aspirations. Thus they often find it difficult to let the child be himself.

Young fathers and mothers generally are aware that they had more advantages than their own parents, and also that they did not fully use these advantages. They therefore not only want to do all they can for their children, but are likely to demand everything possible from them. With so few children, parents have no margin for error as had parents of larger broods. In the larger home of the past, with its many closets, an occasional skeleton might be overlooked. Today's cozy family finds it hard to welcome the odd child, or the child who is different, who does not conform. Mothers and fathers hover protectively over the child, but at the same time they may push him to do his utmost according to their notions of what a child should do, without considering his own particular capacities, limitations, and needs. They are disappointed when he fails to come up to their expectations or does not equal the performance of a brother or sister. They resent a child's apparent lack of "appreciation" for the opportunities they have worked so hard to provide. The resulting pressures upon the child may lead to misunderstandings between the generations and unhappiness for both parents and children.

We need to be aware that the child's position in the family group or the size of the family in which he grows up may present certain types of problems in some cases. But we cannot say that any one size of family group or any special position in the family is more desirable than another. Each child has his own place, his own personality, and his own combination of experiences within the family group. But these are not determined alone by size of family or position in relation to his brothers and sisters. Much more important are the interactions between the child and the different members of the family and of the family group as a whole. And these interactions include many factors and combinations of factors that are unique with each child. Whenever a child, for whatever cause, feels less loved, wanted, or valued than a brother or sister, he will respond by sending out signals through his behavior. He may tease or be quarrelsome; he may whine, cling, or cry easily; he may withdraw into himself; he may respond with frequent outbursts of anger or temper tantrums. These are some of the ways he may try to make known his great need for an equal place with the others in the family group.

PARENTS "AT ODDS" WITH THEIR CHILDREN

Although most parents want to love their children equally, many of them have preferences for certain kinds of youngsters and let these preferences show all too plainly to their children. By the tone of voice, the thoughtless remarks, the extra praise, the obvious feeling of pride with which they speak of one child, or the detrimental remarks they make about another, parents communicate to their youngsters their real feelings about one child or another.

One point that is often overlooked is that there may be very real constitutional differences in temperament between a parent and a child. Witmer and Kotinsky (5) feel that organic factors often affect the way parents and children influence each other. A constitutionally passive child may be a constant source of irritation and concern to a very energetic parent. In order to avoid continual conflict and frustration, there must be mutual understanding and accommodation between such a parent and child. Actually, even under the best of circumstances, parents and children must *learn* to get along together if there is to be happiness for all.

Sometimes we find that a parent feels more strongly drawn to one child in a family than another, with good results for the one child and unhappy consequences for the other.

In the Norris family, both Mr. and Mrs. Norris felt a sense of pride and satisfaction in their gentle, attractive, older daughter. She did so well in school. She was a leader in her church group. She played the piano well. She always looked so pretty with her well-brushed hair and her well-chosen clothes. But Judith, the younger daughter, did not get on so well with her mother and father. As her mother said in exasperation, "She just isn't my kind of a child!" Judith was a tomboy. She preferred blue jeans to the pretty dresses her mother chose so carefully for her. There were constant battles over muddy shoes on the kitchen floor, the raiding of the refrigerator by Judith and her hungry young friends, and homework that wasn't finished. Judith got along better with her father, but even he would grow irritated with her carelessness. Judith was full of life and energy. She did not fit the picture her mother had of what a little girl should be like. The older sister felt secure and happy in the family group, but as Judith grew up she began to feel less loved, less a part of the family circle. Little problems grew into big ones until her family felt they could not put up with her angry outbursts and sullen moods and sought the help of a guidance clinic. Judith just did not "click" with her family; they loved her, but they did not understand her temperament and her needs—so different from their own.

Differences in temperament or in speed of reaction may start a cycle of exasperation and frustration that carries over into many relationships between parents and children. A father with a quick and brilliant mind may try to help a child who is having trouble in school, but the difference in the speed of comprehension and ability between the two may be so great that the child is troubled rather than helped. He may become tense and difficult because he feels that his father is irritated and angry with him for not learning faster; and the father may feel frustration because he finds he cannot teach his child. As a result, a battle of wills may develop between them. Or sometimes a slow and easy-going mother may find herself bringing up an active, energetic small boy who exhausts her as she tries to keep up with his demands and his needs. She may scold and nag as she attempts to keep him under control. The child, in turn, may feel that her scolding means that he is not loved or wanted, and he may, in turn, react with rebellion and defiance. These situations in families can often cause tensions that result in learning problems in the classrooms. It is hard to know which provoked the reaction at the beginning—the parents' feelings about the youngster's behavior or the behavior of the youngster, but whichever came first, it is necessary for the cycle of unhappy interaction to be broken and a new cycle started with better understanding between parent and child.

Sometimes a father or mother has a preference for boys. When a daughter is born, a name has not even been chosen and such remarks are made as "Oh well, we'll love her just the same," or "You can't win every time. Perhaps the next one will be a boy." As the little girl grows up, Father may make comments about how nice it would be to have a boy to take fishing. Or it may be a girl who is preferred, and a mother or father makes slurring remarks about how messy and noisy boys are or "I always wanted a little girl. They stay so much closer to a mother." Sometimes a little girl tries to please her boy-loving father and turns herself into a tomboy trying to win his favor, or a son becomes over-effeminate as he tries to be gentle and neat like the little girl Mother wanted.

Parents who value book learning and find their own success in life and greatest satisfactions in a world oriented and encircled with academic achievements may find themselves drawn to the child who is an avid learner. They may show obvious irritation with and disappointment in the child whose interests run toward physical activity or work with his hands. Such parents may show such obvious disappointment and distress over a report card that bears C's instead of A's that they may give their child a warped picture of himself as a failure instead of a child who has values and talents of his own.

Sometimes a parent really overvalues a child who shows a special gift or talent that draws him into the limelight and brings prestige and praise and reflected glory to the parent. Such a child may receive a great deal of his parents' attention and love and more than his share of the material benefits the family can afford. The other children may feel like "stepchildren" in their own family group.

There are parents, too, who have an aversion to the active, the boisterous, or the aggressive child. They may look on this child's superabundance of energy as something "bad"—a "will to be broken"—and they may strive to turn such a youngster into their picture of what an acceptable child should be. They are unable to see values in the child's drive and wage a continual battle to thwart it instead of helping the child direct his energy into productive channels.

And there are the parents who are so biased in favor of the quiet, conforming, polite, and well-behaved youngster, they are unable to see that this child whom people compliment them on as behaving "like a little grown-up" is in reality in danger of growing up to be a person so submissive to authority and inhibited as to prevent him from living a full and rich adult life.

Then there are the parents who try to live their own lives again through their children. A father who had wanted to be a varsity football player pushes his son into playing football; if his son is a child whose physique or interest does not take him in this direction, the father shows only too plainly not only his disappointment but even his disgust that his child should turn out to be a "sissy who wants to read books." Or a mother who did not have a gay social life may anxiously hover over her daughter, pushing her into social situations at an early age, so that "she may have the kind of life I never had." When what a parent wanted in his own life colors his reactions toward his children, the youngsters in the family will have little chance to grow according to their own pattern, unless that pattern fits their parents' eager desires and plans.

The tragedy is that most parents are not aware of their biases or of the pressures they are putting on their boys and girls to be the children mother and father want. It is inevitable that many of these children should become the troublemakers or the hard-to-teach youngsters who cause us concern at school.

CHANGING FAMILY LIFE

In the history of our country, the pictures of father and mother were pretty clearly defined in middle-class families. Father was the head of the house. In him lay all authority. If he wished, he could even punish his wife. He was not expected to help in the home, except with heavy work such as cutting the wood or hauling the water. The housework belonged to the women of the family. In many families, the women were even expected to see that father's boots were shined, his slippers warmed, and his pipe filled. In return, the man of the house was expected to provide an adequate living for his family and to uphold his place in the councils of the community. He handled all financial and property matters. He often had his shop or office in his own house. He was there for three meals a day and knew well what was happening in his own household. He saw to it that his sons received a proper education or training for a trade and that his daughters had a suitable dowry. The discipline was usually reserved for him. Often such a father was kindly, loving, and benevolent, but sometimes he was harsh and severe with little realization of the real needs of the members of his family. In such a case, there was no recourse; the family had to put up with it. The father knew that he was the head of the house—his role was unquestioned.

The modern father, on the other hand, is often away from his home for many hours of the day. He does not always have many opportunities to get to know his children. He may see them only at the table at night. Some fathers become discouraged and pull away from the family group, bury themselves in their work, and then in the evening paper, feeling unwanted and unnecessary. We are all too familiar with the many cartoons of the American father trying to keep up with the bills or the TV father acting the inadequate buffoon. This is not the total picture. Most American fathers are doing a wonderful job with their family life, but many others are discouraged about their relationship with their children and their own poorly defined role in their home. If there are to be good interpersonal relationships within the family circle, the father must have a real and vital part in the family group. Many thoughtful people today are questioning the confusion of roles that seems to be occurring between father and mother. An editorial by The Staff of the Child Study Association of America

(6), which is necessarily concerned with the role of the father in the family, points up this concern:

Attention has long been focused on the mother of the family. Detailed knowledge of how mother and child interact has added greatly to our understanding of what goes into the making of personality.

Yet we also know that a home needs two effective parents and that the clarity and assurance with which the father perceives and carries out his role, equally vital yet in many respects different from the mother's will profoundly affect his children's true coming of age. By giving scant consideration to the father of the family we may have lost half of the picture, getting an incomplete view of how the boy becomes a man, the girl a woman.

This is a time when women do not see themselves as wives and mothers only, but as human beings with ever widening scope. This trend has had inevitable consequences for men, profoundly affecting a man's image of himself and his relation to others. For many reasons, the father today is living with his children in ways that are new and often confusing.

The role of the mother has also changed over the years. In modern urban life and even in many sections of rural life, many functions of the home are now handled by other agencies. The education of the children, the family's different forms of recreation tend to draw the family members away from the home instead of encouraging them to remain in it. Because the work of the woman in the home of the past was more obvious, we tend to overlook and minimize the importance and time-consuming elements of her present work in the home. Her work is not only that of cook, housekeeper, laundress, carer for children, and economic expert, it is also that of chauffeur. She must often spend many hours driving members of her family back and forth and cover long distances in order to fulfill family needs. Shopping is tiring and complex; she cannot just run down to the corner store for a few items but must think and plan her menus for the trip to the supermarket. She must buy wisely and well in order to stay within her budget, which is rarely augmented by food from the garden or milk from the family cow. In addition, she must be an understanding counselor who is expected to be aware of the psychological implications of her family's problems. This offers a challenge to the modern mother. It is very rewarding to be the mother in a home held together by affection and an understanding of the needs of the individual members, but it also involves more emotional strains and often increases her anxiety. It is much less tangible than the work of the home used to be.

Modern woman also feels called upon to develop her own interests, for no longer is she considered working against the welfare of her family if she is interested in activities outside her home. In fact, she is under considerable pressure to be "a person in her own right"—so much so that this has often become an end in itself. The home no longer stops at the front door. It is considered essential for a mother to follow her home responsibilities into the community and use her abilities to see that the job of the community, as an extended home for her children, is done well. The modern mother is under pressure from all sides to contribute, to serve, to take part with both time and money.

The pressure of obtaining financial security is sometimes another threat to family unity. The modern woman must often face the conflict of deciding whether to stay within her own home or enter the labor market. Many mothers feel they must work in order to add to the financial support of their families. This is not an easy decision for a mother to make because far too often she is aware that she is leaving her children to inadequate care or to no supervision at all. She must often also carry the double load of her outside job and the household responsibilities. The tensions and strains resulting from such a double load all too often are reflected in the tensions of the children we see in the classroom. There are working mothers who are able to carry the double load with success, but far too many others are overburdened and unable to meet the real needs of their boys and girls.

The patterns of the past have been broken and the patterns of the future have not yet been made. Yet, as Gomberg (7) says, we cannot move backward; we must move forward with our times:

In viewing the influence of society on personality we may look back nostalgically to past historical periods which we have not yet fully outgrown, where the roles of man, woman, and child were more clearly defined. Even though we look forward, we cannot be sure of living to see the full magnificence of that democratic future where true equality of self-fulfillment will finally be achieved, and the battle of the sexes will cease to be the primary struggle. Yet we know that there is no trading with the past nor borrowing from the future, and that painful as it may be to evolve our own standards, we must do so if our values are to be attuned to our present world.

Actually, in the daily experience of people who work with families, one finds vignettes of every kind of family. For instance, there is yesterday's family, where the autocratic father still reigns and the passive mother still is the household drudge. . . .

Quite often, on the other hand, we find the reverse: the aggressive, possessive, controlling he-woman, and the passive, dependent she-man. Then there are the families where uncertainty reigns, and usually when that occurs the child is impelled to dominate and exploit the uncertainties. Finally we find, in hopeful numbers, the first glimpses of tomorrow's family, where the

woman's maturity, development and self-fulfillment are not a threat to the man, but mean simply that a richer human being brings more to the marriage, to family life, and to parenthood. Where the man is not struggling so hard to establish his masculinity by the outer vestments of authority, there is an inner fulfillment of his native qualities. This, obviously, is a happier soil for the children to grow in, and a more meaningful atmosphere for the fulfillment of family life.

REFERENCES

(1) Bowlby, John. *Child Care and the Growth of Love.* Penguin Books Ltd., 1951, pp. 11, 76.

(2) Committee on the Family, Group for the Advancement of Psychiatry, American Psychiatric Association. *Integration and Conflict in Family Behavior,* Report No. 27, August 1954, p. 15.

(3) Escalona, Sibylle. "Emotional Development in the First Year of Life," *Problems of Infancy and Childhood,* edited by Milton J. E. Senn. New York: Josiah Macy, Jr. Foundation, 1951, pp. 11-19.

(4) Gruenberg, Sidonie M. "Changing Patterns of Family Living." From *Our Children Today,* edited by Sidonie M. Gruenberg and The Child Study Association of America. Copyright 1952 by the Viking Press, Inc., and reprinted by their permission.

(5) Witmer, Helen L., and Kotinsky, Ruth. *Personality in the Making.* New York: Harper & Brothers, 1952, p. 90.

(6) Child Study Association. "The Man in the Family," Program Statement of Annual Conference, *Child Study,* Vol. XXXIV, No. 3, Summer 1957, p. 2.

(7) Gomberg, Robert M. "Tomorrow's Family," *Child Study,* Vol. XXXIV, No. 3, Summer 1957, p. 8. By permission of The Child Study Association of America, 9 East 89th St., New York 28, N.Y.

A FINAL WORD

KNOWLEDGE VS. WISDOM

A book or course on child development is not necessarily a blueprint for being a good teacher. We need to go beyond the information in this or any other book if we are really to understand children. The capacity to become aware of the feelings and needs of children is acquired slowly—through day-by-day experiences. This is one of the challenges of the schoolroom.

In the pursuit of information about children, we must be careful not to neglect the cultivation and development of the age-old quality of wisdom. The dictionary tells us that wisdom is the ability to judge soundly and use facts with understanding as they relate to life and conduct. Its development depends on interested attention to people and the gradual development of the capacity to recognize what they are feeling and what they may do next. Necessary facts can be gained from books, but wisdom is gained largely from the experiences of life. Knowledge of facts and theories may contribute new lights and methods, but wisdom makes the methods valuable.

As we read books about child growth and development, we may sometimes feel bewildered as one theory after another is presented in the study of the growth and development of children. Sometimes these theories conflict with one another.

By its very nature, the study of child growth and development must cut across many fields of study. We no longer argue about which is more important—the nature of the child or the environment in which he grows up—for we know that it is the interweaving of the two that produces the personality of the child as we see him in our classroom. We need the facts that come from the *biological sciences* concerning the growth of the human organism and the ways in which the failure to meet growth needs adequately may react unfavorably upon the total development of a boy or girl in school. We need the information the *psychologist* can give us about the learning process, and the norms and tests and measurements that have been developed to help us assess the learning ability and progress of our students. The *clinical psychologist* and *psychiatrist* can give us insight into the basic emotional needs of children, while the *anthropologist* can help us understand the demands of our culture on the children who are growing up in it and can tell us how other cultural patterns shape children in other parts of the world. We need the slant of the *sociologist* to help us understand the effect on the child of the community and the kind of home in which he grows up. No one approach is enough to give full and complete understanding of the dynamic growth of a child.

It is natural that those who are absorbed in a particular area of study may tend to overemphasize the place of their findings in the total picture. This sometimes confuses us.

The research worker who is concentrating on what has happened to the child since birth may seem to underemphasize the potentialities and drives that a child brings with him when he is born.

Those who are studying heredity may seem to overlook the powerful effect of environment on the growth of the child. They may minimize the fact that normal development can be blocked for emotional reasons and that a child who has inherited a high intellectual capacity may be unable to learn to read if he is disturbed by tensions in the family group.

Those who are focusing on the tremendous formative influence of the first few years of life sometimes ignore the impact of later years. Some go so far as to insist that the pattern cannot be changed as life develops, even putting the fifth year as the time when the pattern is rigidly set. Yet other studies and the results of therapy indicate that one's personality and reactions to life can be changed and modified in some measure all through the life span until the final changes of senility begin to take place. Certainly the behavior pattern of a youngster who has spent his early years in an unhappy environment can be modified when his parents are helped to fill his needs better or when he is moved to a warm and kindly foster home. And the modifying effects of therapy can be striking even when the strains of early life are severe.

There is much knowledge and understanding to be gained from each of these points of view. None should be disregarded if we are to avoid over-weighing the importance of one area and over-looking that of another or being swept along by a currently popular point of view that is unsound.

Thirty years ago, the child-study movement was thrown off center by the dynamic personality of John B. Watson who contributed considerable factual knowledge but very little wisdom concerning the needs of children. Having demonstrated the conditioned reflex in children, he proceeded to organize "child training" in terms of "conditioning." With this limited concept, he totally neglected the broad, human, emotional needs of the child who was expected to grow up in what was essentially an emotional vacuum.

Since that time, psychiatrists and clinical psychologists have been adding to our knowledge of the child's need for love, security, and freedom to grow. They have emphasized that the emotional environment in which a child is reared determines whether or not he is able to fulfill his potential maximum growth. Many professional people at first interpreted the new findings to mean that children grow best without restraints—that frustration in early childhood must be avoided and that love is the one essential to growth. They followed the pendulum as it swung over toward extreme "permissive" behavior. More recently, the pendulum has swung again. As studies show us, love, though essential, is not enough. Boys and girls must also have the kind of steady guidance that helps them develop a growing sense of responsibility for their own actions and goals. There is danger that the pendulum may once again swing too far and that children may be subjected to pressures to conform and obey adult authority—pressures that ignore what has been learned about the emotional growth needs of boys and girls and the ways in which they learn best. As Polier (1)* has indicated, our recognition of the need for increased responsibility upon the part of youngsters for their own behavior may be overdone to the point that it takes us "back to the woodshed," where punishment and pressure, without understanding, governs adult relationships to wayward children.

As teachers, we must remain students—listening, reading, and evaluating the information that comes to us through studies and research. We must learn to read thoughtfully and train ourselves to question theories before we accept them. We must try to put together the ideas from each school of thought whose validity can be supported. We must constantly try to find out what can add a significant understanding to child growth and development, what can be used in the practical life of the classroom.

*Full references are cited at the end of the chapter.

We must also still be prepared to leave some areas open with a question mark, using what seems the most valid at the moment, but always ready to permit change in our approach as new and proven information reaches us. We sometimes may have to try what appears to be a good lead —or even a good hunch. We cannot always wait to act until all knowledge is in.

If we have wisdom as well as facts, we will be able to mellow what we learn with common sense and a flexibility of approach. What works in a laboratory or in a controlled situation may have to be adapted for practical application in class. Long ago, Davis' (2) classic study showed that over a given period of time a child who is allowed a choice among wholesome foods will select the balanced diet his body needs. These findings contain important truths that can be used at home or in the school cafeteria and raise the question as to whether it is wise or necessary to battle with a child over foods that are distasteful to him— that perhaps he should be allowed some selection. Yet obviously it would be neither practical nor desirable for a mother or a school to offer children a tray on which there were thirty different varieties of basic foods from which a selection was to be made.

Studies of learning have shown us that children may learn more when they help choose and plan the learning activities. We can use the concept that interest is a basic motivation of learning, even though it is not always possible to simulate the conditions of a small laboratory school group in which the children can be successfully permitted a wide area of choice. We must take the point that "interest and need for information motivate learning" and use it to the best of our ability even though we may need to structure the learning situation carefully in order to be able to function with a large and diverse class of children.

Perhaps it all adds up to this. For real understanding of children, we must use the facts we have gained from our studies to try to see how children really feel about the things that happen to them and what is behind the things they do. This is the reason for studying individual children and trying to find ways of really knowing each child in our classroom.

Children know their friends. They know the people who are sincerely trying to understand them. They do not demand perfection from those who teach them. They will respond to us even when we make mistakes, for children have a great capacity to recognize someone who is trying to understand—and they will meet us more than halfway.

Teaching is not an easy job. It can be baffling, tiring, and frustrating at times. But if we bring to the classroom a basic interest in people, especially children—an interest that draws us ever deeper into the process of trying to understand the dynamics of human growth and behavior— teaching can be one of the most satisfying and rewarding experiences of our lives.

REFERENCES

(1) Polier, Justine Wise. *Back to What Woodshed?* Public Affairs Pamphlet, No. 232, 1956.

(2) Davis, Clara. "Self-Selection of Diet by Newly Weaned Infants," *American Journal of Diseases of Children*, 36: 651-679, 1928.

BIBLIOGRAPHY

BIBLIOGRAPHY

GENERAL EDUCATION

Adler, Mortimer J., and Mayer, Milton. *The Revolution in Education.* Chicago: The University of Chicago Press, 1958. A stimulating discussion of the basic issues confronting education in the modern age of science technology and in a democracy.

Jersild, Arthur T. *When Teachers Face Themselves.* New York: Teachers College, Columbia University, 1955. Points out that education should help children and adults know themselves and develop healthy attitudes of self-acceptance.

Keliher, Alice V. *Talks to Teachers.* Darien, Conn.: Educational Publishing Corp., 1958. A wise and thoughtful presentation of philosophy of education and an approach to teaching that will be stimulating and helpful to all teachers. Introduction by Eleanor Roosevelt.

Mitchell, Lucy Sprague, and others, eds. Bank Street College of Education. *Know Your Children in School.* New York: The Macmillan Company, 1954. A description of children and their teachers in actual school situations.

Mitchell, Lucy Sprague. *Our Children and Our Schools.* New York: Simon & Schuster, Inc., 1950. A report on meeting the educational needs of children from two to twelve.

Prescott, Daniel A. *Factors That Influence Learning.* Pittsburgh: University of Pittsburgh Press, 1958. Emphasizes the human factors involved in learning.

Tillich, Paul. *The Courage to Be.* New Haven, Conn.: Yale University Press, 1952. A thoughtful, challenging, and inspirational book for those who would think through their roles both as teachers and as individuals. Also available in paperback.

Warner, W. Lloyd, and others. *Who Shall Be Educated?* New York: Harper & Brothers, 1944. A thoughtful book that is as pertinent today as it was when it was written.

CHILD DEVELOPMENT

Almy, Millie. *Child Development.* New York: Henry Holt and Company, 1955. Uses case histories to show clearly and simply how development embraces both continuity and change. Built around the histories of six boys and girls whose family background, personality, and progress toward adulthood have evolved from Dr. Almy's study of data, gathered at Harvard University, School of Public Health. From birth to 18.

Bayer, Leona M., and Bayley, Nancy. *Growth Diagnosis.* Chicago: The University of Chicago Press, 1959. A scientific presentation of the longitudinal study of physical growth and development.

Blair, Arthur Witt, and Burton, William H. *Growth and Development of the Preadolescent.* New York: Appleton-Century-Crofts, Inc., 1951. A helpful discussion concerning the growth and behavior, social attitudes, and adjustment problems of children during the preadolescent period.

Breckenridge, Marian E., and Vincent, E. Lee *Child Development: Physical and Psychological Growth Through the School Years.* 3rd ed. Philadelphia: W. B. Saunders Co., 1955. A good overall review of child development that pulls together current research in the field.

Crawford, John E., and Woodward, Luther E. *Better Ways of Growing Up.* Philadelphia: Muhlenberg Press, 1948. Among the very best books that help boys and girls understand their own problems of development. The chapter "Ties That Bind" is especially helpful in guiding youngsters toward understanding better their feelings about parents.

Gesell, Arnold, and Ilg, Frances L. *Infant and Child in the Culture of Today*. New York: Harper & Brothers, 1943. The classic presentation of the developmental stages of the early childhood years.

Gesell, Arnold, and Ilg, Frances L. *The Child from Five to Ten*. New York: Harper & Brothers, 1946. A continuation of the early studies of each stage of the child's developmental progress through the elementary school years.

Ginzberg, Eli, editor. *The Nation's Children, 2: Development and Education*. Golden Anniversary White House Conference on Children and Youth. New York: Columbia University Press, 1960. A compilation of articles on child development and education written especially for the White House Conference.

Gordon, Ira J. *Children's Views of Themselves*. Washington, D.C.: Association for Childhood Education International, 1959. Gives insight into the feelings of children in the classroom. Pamphlet.

Gruenberg, Sidonie M., and the Staff of the Child Study Association, eds. *Our Children Today: A Guide to Their Needs from Infancy Through Adolescence*. New York: Viking Press, Inc., 1952. An excellent symposium that will help teachers achieve a better understanding of children's needs in a changing society.

Havighurst, Robert J. *Human Development and Education*. New York: Longmans, Green & Co., Inc., 1953. An analysis of the interrelationship of biological, emotional, and developmental factors in learning at different stages of growth.

Hymes, James L., Jr. *The Child Development Point of View*. New York: Prentice-Hall, Inc., 1955. A book for parents and teachers that discusses what children are like, how they feel, and how they learn and grow.

Jenkins, Gladys G., Shacter, Helen, and Bauer, W. W. *These Are Your Children: A Text and Guide on Child Development*. Expanded edition. Chicago: Scott, Foresman and Company, 1953. How children grow and develop from birth through adolescence; what they are like and how they may be guided. Includes case stories of children with special problems.

Josselyn, Irene M. *Psychosocial Development of Children*. New York: Family Service Association of America, 1948. Outlines ways in which children can be helped to overcome the problems inherent in different stages of the growth

process. Approached from the psychoanalytic viewpoint.

Martin, William E., and Stendler, Celia B. *Child Behavior and Development*. Rev. Ed. New York: Harcourt, Brace & Co., 1959. Stresses the influence of our present-day culture on learning and growth.

Menninger, William C., and Leaf, Munro. *You and Psychiatry*. New York: Charles Scribner's Sons, 1948. A simple description of the structure and growth of the personality covering the years from infancy to psychological maturity.

Murphy, Gardner. *Human Potentialities*. New York: Basic Books, Inc., 1958. A stimulating discussion of the potentials in each human being and better ways of developing them.

Pratt, Caroline. *I Learn from Children*. New York: Simon & Schuster, Inc., 1956. A story of a pioneer school, telling of the development of children's powers as they are given the opportunity to learn and create.

Sheehy, Emma Dickson. *The Fives and Sixes Go to School*. New York: Henry Holt & Co., Inc., 1954. Discusses curriculum planning and classroom management. Shows a fine understanding of the teacher's role and its difficulties.

Witmer, Helen, and Kotinsky, Ruth. *Personality in the Making*. New York: Harper & Brothers, 1952. Expanded presentation of findings of the White House Conference on Children and Youth. Gives important insights into the development of the personality.

CHILD GUIDANCE

Almy, Millie. *Ways of Studying Children, A Manual for Teachers*. New York: Bureau of Publications, Teachers College, Columbia University, 1959. Emphasizes the importance of good school records and discusses sources of information and how this information can be used to obtain greater insight into the ways children feel, think, and behave.

American Council on Education, Staff of the Division on Child Development and Teacher Personnel for the Commission on Teacher Education. *Helping Teachers Understand Children*. Washington, D.C.: American Council on Education, 1945. A report on a project that helped teachers in one school system gain a greater insight into children's emotional needs.

Association for Supervision and Curriculum Development. *Fostering Mental Health in Our Schools*. 1950 Yearbook. Washington, D.C.: National Education Association, 1950. A recognition of the importance of mental health in the learning process as it is revealed in both teachers and students.

Association for Supervision and Curriculum Development. *Growing Up in an Anxious Age.* 1952 Yearbook. Washington, D.C.: National Education Association, 1952. A practical analysis and discussion of the problems that children and young people face in a period of rapid change.

Association for Supervision and Curriculum Development. *Guidance in the Curriculum.* 1955 Yearbook. Washington, D.C.: National Education Association, 1955. Points up those aspects of guidance that can be handled by teachers at all school levels, with a thorough discussion of how teachers can be assisted by specialists in and outside the school.

Bowlby, John. *Child Care and the Growth of Love.* Baltimore: Penguin Books, Inc., 1954. Summary of the report presented at the World Health Organization. Deals with the effect on children of too early and ill-advised separation from their mothers.

Buhler, Charlotte, and others. *Childhood Problems and the Teacher.* New York: Henry Holt and Company, 1952. An interesting collection of helpful articles giving insight into the problems of children that should be of concern to the teacher.

Detjen, Ervin W. and Mary F. *Elementary School Guidance.* New York: McGraw-Hill Book Co., 1952. Discusses the problems of disturbed children with practical suggestions for activities for working with them.

D'Evelyn, Katherine E. *Meeting Children's Emotional Needs.* Englewood Cliffs, N.J.: Prentice-Hall, Inc., 1957. A recognition of the fact that we cannot teach children unless we are also able to recognize and at least partially meet their emotional needs in the classroom.

Driscoll, Gertrude P. *How to Study the Behavior of Children.* (Practical Suggestions for Teaching, No. 2.) New York: Teachers College, Columbia University, 1941. Material to help the teacher learn to detect a child's behavior problems, with direct help on the practical problems of behavior.

Frank, Lawrence. *Feelings and Emotions.* New York: Random House, 1954. A basis for understanding the role feelings and emotions play in the individual life and how they can be effectively integrated for more adequate social participation. Paperback.

Frank, Mary and Lawrence K. *How to Help Your Child in School.* New York: Viking Press, Inc., 1950. Covering the years from pre-school to junior high school age, on the stages of growth and learning of children at home and at school. Also available in paperback.

Gillham, Helen L. *Helping Children Accept Themselves and Others.* New York: Bureau of Publications, Teachers College, Columbia University, 1959. Shows how those who work with children can help them change the picture of themselves that has resulted from being a minority group member, coming from a poor home, or having a physical handicap.

Gruenberg, Sidonie M., ed. *The Encyclopedia of Child Care and Guidance.* New York: Doubleday & Co., Inc., 1954. An excellent reference for all those who are involved and concerned with children.

Hymes, James L., Jr. *Behavior and Misbehavior: A Teacher's Guide to Action.* New York: Prentice-Hall, Inc., 1955. A simple, straightforward discussion of the ways in which acceptable behavior can be taught to stable children and emotionally handicapped children.

Kough, Jack, and De Haan, Robert. Teacher's Guidance Handbooks, Vol. I, Identifying Children with Special Needs; Vol. II, *Helping Children with Special Needs.* Chicago: Science Research Associates, 1956. Practical suggestions that help the classroom teacher identify children who are in need of help with possible ways of meeting their needs.

Krugman, Morris, ed. *Orthopsychiatry and the School.* New York: American Orthopsychiatric Association, 1958. Describes a wide variety of mental health services in different school situations.

Lane, Howard, and Beauchamp, Mary. *Human Relations in Teaching.* Englewood Cliffs, N.J.: Prentice-Hall, Inc., 1955. A valuable consideration of the emotional, social, and intellectual needs of children in their school life, with some excellent guides for helping meet these needs.

La Salle, Dorothy. *Guidance of Children Through Physical Education.* Second Edition. New York: The Ronald Press Company, 1957. A broad overview of physical education with specific suggestions as to how we may better meet the needs of children in our classrooms through play and physical activity.

Nichols, Hildred, and Williams, Lois. *Learning About Role-Playing for Children and Teachers.* Washington, D.C.: Association for Childhood Education International, 1960. Explains and gives examples of how role-playing can be used in the classroom. Pamphlet.

Overstreet, Harry A. *The Mature Mind.* New York: W. W. Norton & Company, Inc., 1949. Points out the development of personality in the individual as it relates to his need for maturity in meeting the tensions of our time.

Prescott, Daniel A. *The Child in the Educative Process*. New York: McGraw-Hill Book Co., 1957. A lively and stimulating presentation of how scientific methods can be used by classroom teachers to deepen their understanding of each pupil. Includes a few detailed case histories to show how this understanding of a child's physical, intellectual, social and emotional being can be used to help him learn most effectively.

Preston, George H. *The Substance of Mental Health*. New York: Rinehart & Company, Inc., 1943. A simple presentation of the basic principles of mental health and emotional adjustment.

Redl, Fritz, and Wattenburg, W. *Mental Hygiene in Teaching*. 2nd ed. New York: Harcourt, Brace & Co., 1959. A wealth of material that will help teachers use the principles of mental health in building good relationships with their pupils and in understanding emotional development.

Ross, Helen. *Fears of Children*. Better Living Booklet. Chicago: Science Research Associates, 1951. A helpful pamphlet on the beginning of fears in young children.

Russell, D. H. *Children's Thinking*. Boston: Ginn & Company, 1956. Results of more than 1000 research studies of how children think. Covers foreign as well as American studies. Outstanding chapter summary of mental development in children. Good bibliography.

Shayon, Robert Lewis. *Television and Our Children*. New York: Longmans, Green & Co., Inc., 1951. Presents the problems of television in relation to children and suggests solutions.

Sheviakov, George V., and Redl, Fritz. *Discipline for Today's Children*. New revision by Sybil K. Richardson. Washington, D.C.: Association for Supervision and Curriculum Development, National Education Association, 1956. A stimulating discussion of discipline in the classroom. Contains insights into the behavior of both teacher and child in the classroom and their interrelationship as it affects the group. Pamphlet.

Stewart, Robert S., and Workman, Arthur D. *Children and Other People: Achieving Maturity Through Learning*. New York: The Dryden Press, Inc., order from Holt, 1956. A book for teachers that emphasizes the importance of understanding oneself in order to help children. Includes helpful suggestions concerning the difficult child in the classroom and ways in which he can be helped to become a member of the group.

Strang, Ruth. *Helping Children Solve Problems*. Chicago: Science Research Associates, 1953. Stresses the fact that the right kind of help is important for a child. Building of confidence, a positive approach to learning, and a knowledge of the individual child are fundamental if the teacher is to help the child solve his problems. Pamphlet.

Thurstone, Thelma, and Byrne, Katherine. *Mental Abilities of Children*. Chicago: Science Research Associates, 1951. An informal presentation that helps put mental testing into focus. Pamphlet.

Wall, E. D. *Education and Mental Health: A Report Based on the Work of a UNESCO-Sponsored European Conference*. New York: International Documents Service, Columbia University Press, 1956. Deals with mental health as it affects education and the child's emotional and social learning and his intellectual capacities. Includes sections on handicapped children, teacher training, and the relation between home, school, and community.

Warner, Ruby H. *The Child and His Elementary School World*. Englewood Cliffs, N.J.: Prentice-Hall, Inc., 1957. Emphasizes the new experiences the child faces as he leaves the world of the home for the world of the school.

Washburn, Ruth Wendell. *Children Know Their Friends*. New York: William Morrow & Company, 1949. A pleasant approach to children's learning and growing and the parents and teachers who work with them. Based on the author's wide experience.

Witty, Paul A., ed. *Mental Health in Modern Education*, NSSE, 54th Yearbook, Pt. 2. Chicago: The University of Chicago Press, 1955. An account of modern trends in mental health with the emphasis on normal child development and the prevention of behavior difficulties.

GIFTED CHILDREN

Birch, Jack W., and McWilliams, E.M. *Challenging Gifted Children*. Bloomington, Ill.: Public School Publishing Co., 1955. Useable and practical suggestions, particularly in the section on high school language arts. Pamphlet.

Cutts, Norma E., and Moseley, Nicholas. *Teaching the Bright and Gifted*. Englewood Cliffs, N.J.: Prentice-Hall, Inc., 1957. A practical book, particularly in locating and dealing with those children who are under-achievers.

De Haan, Robert F., and Havighurst, Robert J. *Educating Gifted Children*. Chicago: The University of Chicago Press, 1957. A discussion of the education of gifted children with detailed suggestions of how the general principles can be applied in the community school and classroom.

French, Joseph L., ed. *Educating the Gifted.* New York: Henry Holt & Co., Inc., 1959. A comprehensive survey of literature in the field of the gifted. Brings together reports of interesting studies and of actual programs designed for gifted boys and girls.

Hall, Theodore. *Gifted Children: The Cleveland Story.* Cleveland: The World Publishing Co., 1956. A concrete and challenging account of the 25-year-old program of the Cleveland Major Work Class Program.

Havighurst, Robert J., and others. *A Community Youth Development Program.* Chicago: The University of Chicago Press, 1952. A community program for fostering gifted children and helping potentially maladjusted children.

Hildreth, Gertrude H., and others. *Educating Gifted Children at Hunter College Elementary School.* New York: Harper & Brothers, 1952. A description of the current experiment at Hunter College Elementary School of educating gifted children in a separate school.

National Education Association, Educational Policies Commission. *Education of the Gifted.* Washington, D.C.: National Education Association, 1950. An analysis of special teaching methods, motivation, work habits, and identification of the gifted.

National Society for the Study of Education. *Education for the Gifted in School and College.* 57th Yearbook, Part II. Chicago: The University of Chicago Press, 1958. A broad discussion of the problems involved in the education of the gifted, presented by outstanding people in the field.

National Society for the Study of Education. *Education of Exceptional Children.* 49th Yearbook, Part II. Chicago: The University of Chicago Press, 1950. A helpful presentation of the objectives in teaching the gifted with helpful suggestions of ways to meet their needs in the classroom.

Strang, Ruth. *Helping Your Gifted Child.* New York: E. P. Dutton & Co., Inc., 1960. A practical book on how to help a gifted child realize his potential.

Witty, Paul A., ed. *The Gifted Child.* Boston: D. C. Heath & Company for the American Association for Gifted Children, 1951. An outstanding collection of nontechnical papers by leading authorities on the problems of gifted children and how to help them find their places in the home, the school, and the community.

CREATIVE WORK AND PLAY

Alschuler, Rose H.; Hattwick, La Berta W.; and others. *Painting and Personality: A Study of Young Children.* Chicago: The University of Chicago Press, 1947. A pioneering work that shows how young children may reveal their emotional experiences, their adjustments and maladjustments, through their paintings.

Anderson, Harold H., editor. *Creativity and Its Cultivation.* New York: Harper & Brothers, 1959. Fifteen well-known writers discuss creative power in their own fields and suggest how creativity can be fostered and encouraged in everyday life.

Andrews, Gladys. *Creative Rhythmic Movement for Children.* Englewood Cliffs, N.J.: Prentice-Hall, Inc., 1954. Includes art, language, and dance material and presents in a creative way the teaching and understanding of children's spontaneous actions.

Burger, Isabel B. *Creative Play Acting: Learning Through Drama.* New York: The Ronald Press Company, 1950. A practical guide to play-acting, stressing the use of the child's natural abilities and initiative.

Cole, Natalie R. *The Arts in the Classroom.* New York: The John Day Co., 1940. A vivid description of the author's experiences in the arts with a racially mixed group of children in a California school.

Hartley, Ruth E., and Goldenson, Robert M. *The Complete Book of Children's Play.* New York: Thomas Y. Crowell Co., 1957. Shows how the development of children can affect their interest and skills, and how play can stimulate this development.

Landeck, Beatrice. *Children and Music.* New York: William Sloane Associates, 1952. A guide to the various ways music can be used to enrich a child's life.

Lease, Ruth G., and Siks, Geraldine B. *Creative Dramatics: In Home, School, and Community.* New York: Harper & Brothers, 1952. A stimulating discussion of ways in which to work with children in home, school, and community dramatics in order to develop their creative abilities.

Lindstrom, Miriam. *Children's Art: A Study of Normal Development in Children's Modes of Visualization.* Berkeley: University of California Press, 1957. A discussion of the artistic development of children from their earliest years to maturity. Contains useful suggestions, particularly for the nine- to twelve-year-olds.

Lowenfeld, Viktor. *Creative and Mental Growth.* 3rd ed. New York: The Macmillan Co., 1957.

A basic book on the teaching of art. Relates art to life and suggests ways in which a child may grow through art.

Robertson, Seonaid M. *Creative Crafts in Education.* Cambridge: Robert Bentley, Inc., 1953. Discusses many kinds of craft activities and the ways to develop creativity. Written by a craftsman and teacher with a good understanding of children.

Sheehy, Emma Dickson. *There's Music in Children.* Rev. ed. New York: Henry Holt & Co., 1952. Suggestions for helping children to learn and to love music.

Walker, Pamela Prince. *Seven Steps to Creative Children's Dramatics.* New York: Hill and Wang, Inc., 1957. A "how-to" book on stimulating children in creative dramatics. Included are three children's plays as well as a recommended list of others.

Ward, Winifred. *Playmaking with Children, From Kindergarten Through Junior High School.* 2nd ed. New York: Appleton-Century-Crofts, Inc., 1957. Creative dramatics for children from kindergarten through junior high school.

Wilt, Miriam E. *Creativity in the Elementary School.* New York: Appleton-Century-Crofts, Inc., 1959. Stresses creativity as a basic ingredient in any elementary-school program.

FAMILY

Anshen, Ruth Nanda, ed. *The Family: Its Function and Destiny.* Rev. ed. New York: Harper & Brothers, 1959. Experts in various fields of family living have contributed to this stimulating picture of family life and its inner structure in different cultures.

Bossard, James H. S., and Boll, Eleanor Stoker. *The Large Family System: An Original Study in the Sociology of Family Behavior.* Philadelphia: University of Pennsylvania Press, 1956. Interesting insights into the behavior and interactions of members of the large family group.

Despert, J. Louis, M.D. *Children of Divorce.* New York: Doubleday & Co., Inc., 1953. Gives insight into the problems of divorce as it concerns children.

English, O. Spurgeon, and Foster, Constance J. *Fathers Are Parents, Too: A Constructive Guide to Successful Fatherhood.* New York: G. P. Putnam's Sons, 1951. A discussion of the father's contribution to the emotional health of the family.

Ginzberg, Eli, editor. *The Nation's Children, 1: The Family and Social Change.* Golden Anniversary White House Conference on Children and Youth. New York: Columbia University Press, 1960. A compilation of articles on family problems written especially for the White House Conference.

Komarovsky, Mirra. *Women in the Modern World: Their Education and Their Dilemmas.* Boston: Little, Brown & Co., 1953. A discussion of the problems of women today and of the goals of their education.

Levy, John, and Munroe, Ruth. *The Happy Family.* New York: Alfred A. Knopf, Inc., 1938. A classic on marriage and family life. One of the best in the field.

Neisser, Edith G. *Brothers and Sisters.* New York: Harper & Brothers, 1951. Discussion of the friction and jealousy found in normal children, with ways of handling the problem. Includes a chapter on twins.

Neisser, Edith G. *The Eldest Child.* New York: Harper & Brothers, 1957. The special position of the eldest child—how it affects his relationships at home, at school, and in later life, and especially how it colors his attitude toward others and toward himself and, thus, how it affects his behavior.

Ogburn, W. F., and Nimkoff, M. F. *Technology and the Changing Family.* Boston: Houghton Mifflin Co., 1955. Emphasizes that many of the changes in the modern family can be traced directly to the inventions and improvements in our technology. Discusses the trend toward romance, the lowering age at marriage, the decreasing size of the modern family, and the loss of functions of the family.

Smith, William Carlson. *The Stepchild.* Chicago: The University of Chicago Press, 1953. An important contribution to a much neglected area of our knowledge.

HOME-SCHOOL RELATIONS

Hymes, James L., Jr. *Effective Home-School Relations.* Englewood Cliffs, N.J.; Prentice-Hall, Inc., 1953. A guide to principles and practices that will help parents and teachers work together more effectively.

Langdon, Grace, and Stout, Irving. *Teacher-Parent Interviews.* Englewood Cliffs, N.J.: Prentice-Hall, Inc., 1954. A useful guide for making parent-teacher conferences more profitable.

Strang, Ruth. *Reporting to Parents.* New York: Teachers College, Columbia University, 1959. Suggestions for improving reporting practices. Paperback.

ADOLESCENCE

Bernard, Harold W. *Adolescent Development in American Culture.* Yonkers, N.Y.: World Book Co., 1957. A comprehensive and well-balanced discussion that emphasizes the importance of the American culture in helping to determine the direction of adolescent development. Stress is on the force of the culture as it creates adolescent problems and shapes adolescent behavior.

Farnham, Marynia F. *The Adolescent.* New York: Harper & Brothers, 1951. Presents the social, emotional, and physiological factors that characterize this period of growing up.

Fleming, Charlotte Mary. *Adolescence, Its Social Psychology.* New York: International Universities Press, 1949. A scholarly English summary of recent research in the various human sciences that contribute to a more complete understanding of the nature and needs of adolescents.

Frank, Lawrence K. and Mary. *Your Adolescent at Home and School.* New York: The Viking Press, Inc., 1956. A positive approach to the problems of the adolescent. Also available in paperback.

Gesell, Arnold, and others. *Youth: The Years from Ten to Sixteen.* New York: Harper & Brothers, 1956. The third volume of the study of developmental stages from the tenth to the sixteenth year.

Havighurst, Robert J., and Taba, Hilda. *Adolescent Character and Personality.* New York: John Wiley & Sons, Inc., 1949. A challenging study of adolescent youth in a typical midwestern town, which describes and evaluates the relation of character, personality, and the social environment.

Hollingshead, August B. *Elmtown's Youth: The Impact of Social Classes on Adolescents.* New York: John Wiley & Sons, Inc., 1949. A picture of American small-town youth in school and at home, emphasizing the part the class system plays in their behavior.

Jersild, Arthur T. *The Psychology of Adolescence.* New York: The Macmillan Co., 1957. Contributes to a better understanding of what growing up really involves. Stresses the point that since there is a great deal of the adolescent in all of us, we can use our own lives as laboratories for studying the adolescent.

Johnson, Eric W. *How to Live Through Junior High School.* Philadelphia: J. B. Lippincott Co., 1959. Contains helpful suggestions based on answers to questionnaires sent to several hundred seventh- to eleventh-graders. Includes excellent chapter on cheating.

Josselyn, Irene M. *The Adolescent and His World.* New York: Family Service Association of America, 1952. An explanation of adolescent behavior based on psychoanalytic theory. Well-written and helpful for those with psychological background.

Landis, Paul H. *Adolescence and Youth.* 2nd ed. New York: McGraw-Hill Book Co., 1952. Presentation of the major problems facing young people in America.

Landis, Paul H. *Understanding Teen-Agers.* 2nd ed. New York: Appleton-Century-Crofts, Inc., 1955. Contains material obtained through public opinion polls concerning the personal standards of values of normal youths.

Meek, Lois Hayden, and others. *The Personal-Social Development of Boys and Girls with Implications for Secondary Education.* New York: Progressive Education Association, 1940. Program and practice in the secondary school examined in the light of the personal-social needs of adolescents.

Remmers, H. H., and Radler, D. H. *The American Teen-Ager.* Indianapolis: The Bobbs-Merrill Company, Inc., 1957. The results of a poll by Purdue University scientists on a representative cross section of our population.

Stone, L. Joseph, and Church, Joseph. *Childhood and Adolescence, A Psychology of the Growing Person.* New York: Random House, 1957. An excellent study of children with a fine chapter on the meaning of maturity.

Wittenberg, Rudolph M. *Adolescence and Discipline.* New York: Association Press, 1959. Discusses the ways we can help adolescents develop an inner control that will gradually lead to self-discipline.

SEX EDUCATION

Bibby, Cyril. *Sex Education: A Guide for Parents, Teachers, and Youth Leaders.* 2nd ed. New York: The Macmillan Co., 1948. A thoughtful, analytic presentation of the subject by a British health educator. Offers a number of practical approaches to the problem.

Child Study Association of America. *What to Tell Your Children about Sex.* New York: Pocket Books, Inc., 1959. Discusses children's questions and possible parental answers.

Gruenberg, Sidonie M. *The Wonderful Story of How You Were Born.* New York: Doubleday & Co., Inc. (Hanover House), 1952. A well-told story for reading aloud for elementary school age children with a helpful guide for parents inside the jacket.

Lerrigo, Marion O., and Southard, Helen, in consultation with Senn, Milton. *The Dutton Series on Sex Education*. New York: E. P. Dutton & Co., Inc., 1956. A series on sex education, approved by the joint committee on Health Problems in Education of the NEA and the AMA.

Levine, Milton I., and Seligmann, Jean H. *A Baby Is Born*. New York: Simon & Schuster, Inc., 1949. An explanation of birth for children from six to ten.

Levine, Milton I., and Seligmann, Jean H. *The Wonder of Life*. New York: Simon & Schuster, Inc., 1952. Factual sex information for the elementary school child.

Museum of Science and Industry (Chicago) and the University of Illinois Professional Colleges (Chicago). *The Miracle of Growth*. New York: Pyramid Books, 1956. The human story from the time of conception until the child matures and conceives another. Presentation of biological facts plus the miraculous quality of life and growth.

Scheinfeld, Amram. *The Human Heredity Handbook*. Philadelphia: J. B. Lippincott Co., 1956. Summarizes briefly what we know and do not know about human heredity. Discusses the problem of inheritance of physical, mental, and behavioral characteristics as well as diseases and defects.

GROUPS

Cunningham, Ruth, and others. *Understanding Group Behavior of Boys and Girls*. New York: Teachers College, Columbia University, 1951. Of special help to those who are interested in using the techniques of sociograms and sociodrama in the classroom.

Thelen, Herbert A. *Dynamics of Groups at Work*. Chicago: The University of Chicago Press, 1954. A unique and highly readable combination of theory and practical experience in the functioning of six different types of working and learning groups.

SOCIO-CULTURAL

Benedict, Ruth. *Patterns of Culture*. Boston: Houghton Mifflin Company, 1934. Describes effects of culture on the life of young people, with detailed descriptions of the customs of a number of different cultural groups. Also available in paperback.

Bossard, James H. S. *The Sociology of Child Development*. Rev. ed. New York: Harper & Brothers, 1954. Normal social development of children in a group setting.

Childs, John L. *Education and Morals: An Experimentalist Philosophy of Education*. New York: Appleton-Century-Crofts, Inc., 1950. A discussion of the role of moral values in enriching and stabilizing our way of life and a re-evaluation of our educational philosophy.

Davis, W. Allison, and Havighurst, Robert J. *Father of the Man*. Boston: Houghton Mifflin Company, 1947. Emphasizes the importance of differing social backgrounds and cultural attitudes in shaping an individual's personality.

Eells, Kenneth W., and others; under the chairmanship of Allison Davis. *Intelligence and Cultural Differences*. Chicago: The University of Chicago Press, 1951. A discussion of the effect of cultural differences among children as they influence the results of the tests customarily used in the school situation.

Havighurst, Robert J., and Neugarten, Bernice L. *Society and Education*. Boston: Allyn and Bacon, 1957. A textbook that uses material from social anthropology and sociology to help teachers understand how the individual becomes a cooperating member of society.

Mead, Margaret. *Male and Female*. White Plains, N.Y.: William Morrow & Co., Inc., 1949. An anthropologist's analysis of cultural pressures and their different impacts on sex roles and the family. Drawn from the author's wide experiences in studying many cultures—primitive and civilized.

Mead, Margaret, and Wolfenstein, Martha. *Childhood in Contemporary Cultures*. Chicago: The University of Chicago Press, 1955. A discussion of child rearing in other cultures, a help in understanding children's growth, and the differences that develop in various cultures.

PREJUDICE

Allport, Gordon W. *The Nature of Prejudice*. New York: Doubleday & Company, Inc., 1958. A comprehensive, penetrating, and readable study of the origin and nature of prejudice. Paperback.

Baruch, Dorothy W. *The Glass House of Prejudice*. New York: William Morrow & Company, 1946. Discusses causes and cures of prejudices among many groups. Includes factual material concerning social customs of the groups discussed.

Benedict, Ruth, and Weltfish, Gene. *The Races of Mankind*. New York: Public Affairs Committee, 1943. Summarizes the scientific facts that refute current misconceptions concerning racial differences and racial superiority.

Clark, Kenneth B. *Prejudice and Your Child*. Boston: Beacon Press, 1955. An objective discussion of prejudice with suggestions for the school, community agencies, and parents in dealing with feelings of prejudice in children.

Goodman, Mary E. *Race Awareness in Young Children*. Reading, Mass.: Addison-Wesley Press, Inc., 1952. A study based on testing, intensive interview, and long observation of both parents and children.

Trager, Helen G., and Yarrow, Marian R. *They Learn What They Live: Prejudice in Young Children*. New York: Harper & Brothers, 1952. A pioneer study of intercultural education in the early school years.

RELIGION AND MORALITY

Fahs, Sophia L. *Today's Children and Yesterday's Heritage: A Philosophy of Creative Religious Development*. Boston: Beacon Press, 1952. A nonsectarian book presenting a philosophy of religious teaching.

Fitch, Florence Mary. *One God: The Ways We Worship Him*. New York: Lothrop, Lee & Shepard Co., Inc., 1944. A presentation of the beliefs and ceremonials of the three major faiths in America—Jewish, Catholic, and Protestant.

Meyer, Agnes E. *Education for a New Morality*. New York: The Macmillan Co., 1957. A recognition of the needs to seek more deeply for a sense of values in this changing world.

SPECIAL PROBLEMS

Cutts, Norma E., and Moseley, Nicholas. *Teaching the Disorderly Pupil in Elementary and Secondary School*. New York: Longmans, Green & Co., Inc., 1957. An unusual book in its emphasis on the disorderly pupil in the classroom with practical suggestions on how to help him adjust to the group.

Dolch, Edward W. *Helping Handicapped Children in School*. Champaign, Ill.: Garrard Press, 1948. Useful material on working with the handicapped child in the classroom.

Featherstone, William B. *Teaching the Slow Learner*. Rev. and enlarged ed. (Practical Suggestions for Teaching, No. 1). New York: Teachers College, Columbia University, 1951. Concise and usable suggestions for teaching the slow learner.

Glueck, Sheldon, and Glueck, Eleanor. *Delinquents in the Making: Paths to Prevention*. New York: Harper & Brothers, 1952. A readable report of the author's extensive research in the contributing causes of delinquency.

Goodenough, Florence L. *Exceptional Children*. New York: Appleton-Century-Crofts, Inc., 1956. An excellent text on the understanding of exceptional children with special emphasis on the child's general adjustment and happiness.

Heiser, Karl F. *Our Backward Children*. New York: W. W. Norton & Company, Inc., 1955. A helpful book discussing mental retardation with emphasis on the difference between emotional disturbance and retardation.

Ingram, Christine P. *Education of the Slow Learning Child*. 2nd ed. New York: The Ronald Press Company, 1953. Discusses the education of the slow learning child with specific suggestions for classroom activities and learning units for each age level.

Magnifico, L. X. *Education for the Exceptional Child*. New York: Longmans, Green & Co., Inc., 1958. A readable text on the education of the exceptional child.